DATE DUE

NOV 15 2006			
FE 1 5 '09			

Demco, Inc. 38-293

The music of Haydn, Mozart and Beethoven forms a cornerstone of the modern repertoire, but very little is known about the context in which these composers worked. This volume of twelve essays by leading international scholars covers some of the musical traditions and practices of this little-understood period of music history. Beginning with the early decades of the eighteenth century, the volume documents selected aspects of musical life and style from the late Baroque period through to the early years of the nineteenth century. Among the prominent musicians of the time who are discussed at length are Georg Reutter (Haydn's teacher), Antonio Salieri (Mozart's colleague) and Joseph Wölfl (a rival of Beethoven).

Music in eighteenth-century Austria

Music in eighteenth-century Austria

edited by
DAVID WYN JONES

Published by the Press Syndicate of the University of Cambridge
The Pitt Building, Trumpington Street, Cambridge CB2 1RP
40 West 20th Street, New York, NY 10011–4211, USA
10 Stamford Road, Oakleigh, Melbourne 3166, Australia

© Cambridge University Press 1996

First published 1996

Printed in Great Britain at the University Press, Cambridge

A catalogue record for this book is available from the British Library

Library of Congress cataloguing in publication data applied for

ISBN 0 521 45349 6 hardback

Contents

		page	
List of plates		page	ix
Preface			xi

1 Introduction: new challenges, new perspectives   1
DAVID WYN JONES

PART I   OVERTURE, SYMPHONY AND CONCERTO

2 The trumpet overture and sinfonia in Vienna (1715–1822):   13
rise, decline and reformulation
A. PETER BROWN

3 The early Classical violin concerto in Austria   70
CHAPPELL WHITE

PART II   TRADITIONS IN SACRED MUSIC

4 Haydn's *Missa sunt bona mixta malis* and the *a cappella* tradition   89
DAVID WYN JONES

5 Johann Baptist Vanhal and the pastoral mass tradition   112
BRUCE MACINTYRE

6 The Austrian pastorella and the *stylus rusticanus*: comic   133
and pastoral elements in Austrian music, 1750–1800
GEOFFREY CHEW

PART III   OPERA AND DRAMA

7 The applausus musicus, or Singgedicht: a neglected genre of   197
eighteenth-century musical theatre
ROBERT N. FREEMAN

8 The operas of Antonio Salieri as a reflection of Viennese opera,   210
1770–1800
JOHN A. RICE

9 Lorenzo da Ponte's Viennese librettos   221
KONRAD KÜSTER

| 10 | Viennese amateur or London professional? A reconsideration of Haydn's tragic cantata *Arianna a Naxos*
JULIAN RUSHTON | 232 |

PART IV PIANOS AND PIANISM

| 11 | The Viennese fortepiano in the eighteenth century
EVA BADURA-SKODA | 249 |
| 12 | The Beethoven–Wölfl piano duel
TIA DENORA | 259 |

Index — 283

Plates

4.1	Portion of title-page of Haydn's *Missa sunt bona mixta malis*	104
7.1	Title-page of the textbook to Albrechtsberger's *Singgedicht*	200
7.2	'Spes Josephe', finale to K. Kohaut's *Securitas Germaniae Josepho II.*	204

Preface

The eleven principal essays in this volume were originally presented as papers at an international conference organized by the Centre for Eighteenth-Century Musical Studies, University of Wales, Cardiff, and held at Dyffryn House, near Cardiff, in July 1991. That year, of course, was the Mozart year. Rather than adding to the many conferences devoted to the composer, the organizers of the Cardiff conference, led by Professor Michael F. Robinson, decided to devote the occasion to exploring music and musical life in eighteenth-century Austria, seeking a context for the well-documented careers of Haydn and Beethoven, as well as Mozart. For there is a striking imbalance between the amount of literature available on these major figures and that devoted to musical practice in general in the period: we know everything about Mozart – sometimes too much – but very little about the traditions and conventions that helped fashion his individuality. It is in this spirit of trying to broaden the perspective on musical life in Austria in the eighteenth century that these essays are presented. The combined results of eleven individual essays cannot pretend to be a comprehensive survey of the topic, and all the contributors would probably join the editor in maintaining that much more research and evaluation are needed before such an account could even be contemplated, but it is hoped that this modest contribution will stimulate wider interest in one of the most fascinating and under-explored areas of musical history.

I wish to record my thanks to the contributors for their willingness to revise their original papers, and for their patience during what turned out to be a long gestation period. I am grateful also to the Department of Music, University of Wales, Cardiff for underwriting the cost of the music examples. Dexter Edge read all the essays and provided much valuable advice and criticism. Malcolm Boyd was the hospitable and efficient organizer of the original conference and has maintained an enthusiastic interest in the progress of this volume; I am particularly grateful for his assistance with proof-reading. Finally, Penny Souster of Cambridge University Press deserves the thanks of all the contributors and especially those of the editor for seeing the book through to production.

David Wyn Jones

1

Introduction: new challenges, new perspectives

DAVID WYN JONES

In 1969 Jens Peter Larsen published an article entitled 'The Viennese Classical School: A Challenge to Musicology'.[1] With an initial flourish worthy of Mozart's 'Jupiter' symphony he declared that 'It seems unlikely that there is any other important period of Western music for which a common basis of real knowledge is still lacking so much as in the case of the Viennese Classical School of the second half of the 18th century.' While recognizing the permanence and vitality of a century of scholarship devoted to the main figures of the period, Haydn, Mozart and Beethoven, Larsen pointed out the shaming fact that in comparison with scholarship in the Medieval and Renaissance – to which the Baroque can now be legitimately added – there was no 'research tradition' in the later period, by which the author meant three or four generations of scholars working in the period as a whole and not solely on the great figures. Larsen's implicit view was that 'real knowledge' meant investigating the context in which the great figures worked. He went on to elaborate three areas in which systematic and fundamental research was required. First, the problem of the source material should be tackled. The provision of accurate catalogues and inventories was needed, a central repository for microfilmed sources established and, of particular importance to instrumental music (Larsen himself was especially interested in the symphony), the material should be scored up and readily distributed. Second, knowledge of the historical background needed to be improved. By this Larsen did not mean the political, social or economic background, but an accurate chronology of composers and their works, both in manuscript and in printed form. Third, Larsen made a heartfelt plea for stylistic

---

[1] J. P. Larsen, 'The Viennese Classical School: A Challenge to Musicology', *Current Musicology*, ix (1969), pp. 105–12. Similar views appear in several other articles by the author; see 'Some Observations on the Development and Characteristics of Viennese Classical Instrumental Music', 'Towards an Understanding of the Development of the Viennese Classical Style', 'Traditional Prejudices in Connection with Viennese Classical Music' and 'The Style Change in Austrian Music between the Baroque and Viennese Classicism', all contained in Larsen, *Handel, Haydn, and the Viennese Classical Style* (Ann Arbor, 1988), pp. 227–49, 251–61, 281–91 and 301–13.

analysis that was sympathetic to the period, especially to the transitional years between the Baroque and Classical eras.

Nearly thirty years later it would be easy to pick holes in Larsen's manifesto. Some of his proposals are impractical and, certainly, his very positivist approach is unfashionable in the scholarly world of narrativity, semiotics, reception theory and gender studies. Yet Larsen's central plea for the study of all musical life and all music from this epoch retains its vibrancy. The essays in this book were born out of a conference that was specifically, if not provocatively, designed to reaffirm the value of such scholarship in a year, 1991, that was largely devoted to celebrating the achievement of one figure; the contributors are all in that general sense willing disciples of Larsen. He, of course, was not alone in uttering such views but it is appropriate to ponder to what extent recent modern scholarship, as reflected in this volume and elsewhere, has responded to them.

Significant strides have been made in the control of source material from the period. Thematic catalogues covering all or most of the output of leading composers such as Joseph Eybler (1765–1846), Michael Haydn (1737–1806), Ordonez (1734–86), Vanhal (1739–1813) and Wagenseil (1715–77) have appeared;[2] for composers of symphonies the thematic catalogues contained in the volumes devoted to Austrian composers in the Garland series *The Symphony* are invaluable,[3] as is the information in Jan LaRue's *Catalogue of 18th-Century Symphonies*.[4] For sources of printed editions the ten volumes (plus further volumes of addenda and corrigenda) of RISM Series A1, *Einzeldrucke vor 1800*, provide a quick access to the holdings of libraries,[5] and an equivalent service for librettos is provided by Claudio Sartori's catalogue of printed opera librettos in Italian.[6] These fundamental bibliographical tools, of which the foregoing are only representative, have enabled scholars at least to map out the territory and to begin to traverse it; many of the essays in the present volume make ready use of such material. But it is only a beginning, and the output of many composers still remains either fully or partially uncatalogued. For instance, while bibliographical information on the operas of Salieri (1750–1825) is readily

---

[2] H. Herrmann, *Joseph Eybler: thematisches Werkverzeichnis* (Munich, 1976). C. H. Sherman and T. D. Thomas, *Johann Michael Haydn (1737–1806): A Chronological Thematic Catalogue of his Works* (Stuyvesant, New York, 1993). A. P. Brown, *Carlo d'Ordonez 1734–1786: A Thematic Catalog* (Detroit, 1978). A. Weinmann, *Themen-Verzeichnis der Kompositionen von Johann Baptiste Wanhal* (Vienna, [1987?]). H. Michelitsch, *Das Klavierwerk von Georg Christoph Wagenseil. Thematischer Katalog* (Vienna, 1966). H. Scholz-Michelitsch, *Das Orchester- und Kammermusikwerk von Georg Christoph Wagenseil. Thematischer Katalog* (Vienna, 1972).

[3] B. S. Brook, general editor, *The Symphony 1720–1840: A Comprehensive Collection of Full Scores in Sixty Volumes* (New York, 1979–86).

[4] J. LaRue, *A Catalogue of 18th-Century Symphonies: Volume I: Thematic Identifier* (Bloomington, 1988). For a comprehensive list of thematic catalogues see B. S. Brook and R. J. Viano, *Thematic Catalogues in Music: An Annotated Bibliography*, 2nd edn (Stuyvesant, New York, 1995).

[5] *Répertoire International des Sources Musicales. Series A1. Einzeldrucke vor 1800* (Kassel, 1971–).

[6] C. Sartori, *I Libretti Italiani a Stampa dalle Origini al 1800* (6 vols., Cuneo, 1990–3).

accessible[7] there is little modern information on the composer's church music, which dominated his output from the early 1790s to his death. Existing bibliographical work on many other composers, such as the two Reutters (father and son, who between them served the *Hofkapelle* in Vienna for over seventy years), Gregor Werner (1693–1766, Haydn's predecessor at the Esterházy court) and Dittersdorf (1739–99) needs to be updated and synthesized. Basic work on the RISM series for manuscript sources of the period has been carried out for many years but often the project has seemed in danger of collapsing under the sheer weight of material; a CD-ROM version is promised for 1995. Yet control of this material is a fundamental prerequisite for understanding the development of music in eighteenth-century Austria, since music publishing arrived comparatively late. Artaria started publishing music in 1778, Torricella in 1781 and Hoffmeister in 1784; even then publishing practice played only a limited part in the musical life of Vienna and beyond compared with that of Amsterdam, Berlin, London and Paris, which had long-established traditions of music publication. Manuscript sources for such staple parts of the modern repertoire as Mozart's operas and Beethoven's concertos and symphonies have been undervalued.[8] Part of the reason for this particular and general neglect is that the provenance and chronology of manuscript material are more difficult to deal with than those of published music. Thanks primarily to the stimulating work of scholars such as Wolfgang Plath[9] and Alan Tyson,[10] studies of handwriting and paper types are now much more sophisticated than they were a generation ago, and the next few years ought to see an increasingly sure control of the vast manuscript copying industry in eighteenth-century Austria.[11]

Unfortunately, the stalling of the manuscript volumes in the RISM project is symptomatic. The organization could do much more to facilitate the collection of basic raw material, including catalogues of individual libraries, of composers, of genres, of watermarks, of the handwriting of copyists, and of newspaper and journal advertisements; and computer technology could easily accelerate both the accumulation and distribution of such material.

---

[7] R. Angermüller, *Antonio Salieri: sein Leben und seine weltlichen Werke unter besonderer Berücksichtigung seiner 'großen' Opern* (3 vols., Munich, 1971–4).

[8] For instance, Barry Cooper has drawn attention to some remarkable changes that Beethoven made in the text of the Fourth Piano Concerto after it had been published. B. Cooper, 'Beethoven's Revisions to His Fourth Piano Concerto', in R. Stowell, ed., *Performing Beethoven's Music* (Cambridge, 1994), pp. 23–48.

[9] W. Plath, 'Beiträge zur Mozart-Autographie I: Die Handschrift Leopold Mozarts', *Mozart Jahrbuch 1960/61*, pp. 82–117; and 'Beiträge zur Mozart-Autographie II: Schriftchronologie 1770–1780', *Mozart Jahrbuch 1976/7*, pp. 131–73.

[10] A. Tyson, *Mozart: Studies of the Autograph Scores* (Cambridge, Mass., 1987).

[11] The following is an indication of the rich evidence that is to be uncovered: C. Eisen, 'Mozart's Salzburg Copyists: Aspects of Attribution, Chronology, Text, Style and Performance Practice', in C. Eisen, ed., *Mozart Studies* (Oxford, 1991), pp. 253–307.

A similar picture of a jig-saw slowly being filled in, with available single pieces drawing as much attention to the surrounding void as to themselves, is apparent when it comes to the availability of the music itself. For the first time ever, nearly all of Joseph Haydn's music is now published in a sound editorial format – something that no doubt would have particularly pleased Larsen, the founding father of modern Haydn scholarship – and is prompting the kind of attention on single works hitherto accorded only to the output of Mozart and Beethoven. Julian Rushton's essay on the cantata *Arianna a Naxos*, a work which Haydn himself placed at the centre of his efforts to impress musical London in 1791 but which was not published in a modern edition until 1965, is representative of this type, encouraging a reassessment of the composer's image as well as uncovering the dynamism of his style. The steady progress of the Fux *Gesamtausgabe* is allowing scholars to reassess this major composer too, like Haydn respected but not always understood.[12] The series of volumes devoted to the national history of music in Austria, the *Denkmäler der Tonkunst in Österreich* is now over a hundred years old but the number of volumes devoted to music of the eighteenth century in the recent past is disappointingly small, three volumes in the last twenty years.[13] In compensation the *Diletto Musicale* series (Munich and Vienna), the *Denkmäler der Musik in Salzburg* (Bad Reichenhall), the *Musica Antiqua Bohemica* (Prague), the *Recent Researches in the Music of the Classical Era* (Madison), and the three Garland series, *Italian Opera 1640–1770*, *Italian Oratorio 1650–1800* and *The Symphony 1720–1840* (New York), have offered much interesting music from eighteenth-century Austria.

Finance and individual perseverance have always determined the speed of progress in providing the basic raw material of catalogues and scores. Recently, these have been joined by a third controlling force. It is becoming increasingly unfashionable in academia, especially but not exclusively in the United States, to undertake this basic kind of work, cataloguing and scoring. Musicology has become very receptive to influences from other disciplines such as linguistics, literature, economic history and sociology, but the very interpretations and thought-provoking constructions that this cross-fertilization encourages are sometimes undermined by the shakiness of the historical data on which they are based. Those concerned with music in eighteenth-century Austria will have to continue to assert the importance and integrity of primary work in the field.

Intellectual curiosity of the individual has always meant that exploration of new musical territory cannot be controlled by a masterplan. A Marshall Plan for the study of music in eighteenth-century Austria might act as an energizer

---

[12] The essays in the following volume contribute vitally to the rehabilitation of Fux and his music: H. White, ed., *Johann Joseph Fux and the Music of the Austro-Italian Baroque* (Aldershot, 1992).

[13] The three volumes are *DTÖ* cxxxi, containing symphonies by Adlgasser (Graz, 1980); *DTÖ* cxxxvii, containing instrumental music by Stepan von Ehrenstein (Graz, 1984); and *DTÖ* cxlvi, containing a mass (1809) by Salieri (Graz, 1988).

but would soon collapse; a more *ad hoc*, even uncoordinated, approach, that simultaneously deals with sources, chronology, style and synthesis in diverse parts of the repertoire and at different times in the century, is inevitable. Volumes such as this one clearly reflect this situation, one that is likely to continue for many years. Perhaps, however, it is not premature to draw attention to some of the changes that have occurred in the modern image of the era in the last generation or so.

Larsen was perfectly content to use the expression 'Viennese Classical School'. A translation of 'Wiener klassische Schule', it and the associated term 'Viennese Classical Style' derive from the writing of Guido Adler and Wilhelm Fischer at the beginning of the twentieth century.[14] Prompted by the fact that four major composers, Haydn, Mozart, Beethoven and Schubert (five if one adds Gluck), were associated to a greater or lesser extent with the capital city, it was a simple formulation, conveniently fortified by the appearance of the very historically minded Second Viennese School at the same time. But the 'greater or lesser' associations of the composers with Vienna need to be remembered. Only Beethoven and Schubert lived and worked in the city for most of their creative lives and can therefore be said to be Viennese. Haydn lived in the city in his youth and its musical practices, from those of the *Hofkapelle* to those of Kurz-Bernardon's German opera troupe, certainly helped fashion his development. But from 1759, when he joined the Morzin court, and especially 1761, when he joined the Esterházy court, the composer usually lived and worked elsewhere, Lukavec, Eisenstadt, Eszterháza and London. It is easy to exaggerate Haydn's self-proclaimed isolation at the Esterházy court and there is ample evidence that he visited Vienna often, kept in touch with its musical life and was dependent on its commercial vitality for anything from violin strings to opera singers, but his own career from 1761 to 1795 was not governed by the city and its resources; only in the last fourteen years of his life, the period of *The Creation* and *The Seasons*, did his musical life interact consistently with that of the capital. Similarly in the case of Mozart. He lived in Vienna for the last ten years of his life. Before that he was based in Salzburg and spent much of his time travelling throughout Europe, so that his stylistic development up to the age of twenty-five was as much influenced by Salzburg, Milan, Mannheim, London and Paris as it was by Vienna. The coining of the term 'Viennese Classical School' reflects a time when only the later works of Haydn and Mozart were known and performed, a fact that in turn encouraged the inevitable interpretation that the 'mature' Classical style 'arrived' c. 1780. 'Viennese' is clearly unsatisfactory for the careers of Haydn and Mozart, and its broader application to cover composers such as Dittersdorf (who worked in

---

[14] G. Adler, *Handbuch der Musikgeschichte*, 2nd edn (2 vols., Berlin, 1929–30); W. Fischer, 'Zur Entwicklungsgeschichte des Wiener klassichen Stils', *Studien zur Musikwissenschaft*, iii (1915), pp. 24–84.

Grosswardein and Johannisberg), Michael Haydn (who after a few years at Grosswardein lived all his adult life in Salzburg) and Pichl (1741–1805, who spent most of his working life in the employ of Joseph II's brother, Archduke Leopold, in Milan) needs to be challenged too. Indeed, broad accounts of musical history in the period still sometimes have the absurd sub-text that Sammartini (1700/01–75), Johann Christian Bach (1735–82) and Schobert (c. 1720–67) were contributing to the Viennese Classical Style rather than to the vitality of musical life in Milan, London and Paris.

Of the eleven essays in this volume only five deal with a Viennese dimension: A. Peter Brown on the tradition of orchestral music in C major with trumpets and timpani; John A. Rice's essay on the operas of Salieri which, as he suggests, are a better reflection of the broad history of opera in the city than the combined output of Gluck and Mozart; Konrad Küster's study of the librettos that Da Ponte wrote during his stay in Vienna between 1781 and 1791; Eva Badura-Skoda's observations on the history of the Viennese pianoforte; and Tia DeNora's study of salon culture at the turn of the century and the effect it had on the reputations of two composers, Beethoven and Wölfl (1773–1812). In addition, my own essay deals with a Fuxian tradition that was particularly strong in Vienna, even though the work, Haydn's *Missa sunt bona mixta malis*, was composed in Eisenstadt. All the other essays deal essentially with material that is not Viennese; indeed two essays, those by Geoffrey Chew and Robert Freeman, deal with genres that were essentially unknown in the capital, the pastorella and the applausus musicus respectively. Keeping Vienna as a focal point for the study of music in this era risks undervaluing the often distinctive traditions of music and music-making outside the city: in other cities such as Salzburg, Linz, Prague and Pressburg (Bratislava); as found in many monasteries throughout the Austrian lands up to the reforms of Joseph II, and in a few cases beyond; and at the aristocratic courts, typically divided between the countryside and the capital. This broadening view of musical life with its several layers of interacting traditions is certainly complex, but the one that it replaces is misleadingly narrow and not untinged by sentimentality.

In recognizing the limitations of the epithet 'Viennese' – the German 'Wiener klassische Schule' would be accurately if more cumbrously translated as the 'The Classical School of Vienna' – it must be admitted that it is impossible to find an entirely suitable alternative. This volume has opted for the word Austria. But which Austria is meant? To limit the coverage to present-day Austria would be anachronistic and would mean the exclusion of Haydn's Eszterháza and Mozart's Prague, for instance. The Habsburg dynasty ruled as an 'Imperial and Royal' family ('Kaiserlich und Königlich'), denoting two overlapping geographical areas. Successive generations of the family had been emperors of the Holy Roman Empire, nominally elected to this position but in practice unopposed; the Empire consisted essentially of all German-speaking areas throughout Europe except Switzerland, plus the Belgium and Luxembourg of today and the mixed-language areas of Bohemia and Moravia. In terms of direct government rather than arm's-length influence, the dynasty exercised most control over the lands it had skilfully inherited over the centuries, constituting the Monarchy: most of present-day Austria, the Czech Republic (then Moravia and the Kingdom of Bohemia), Slovakia, Hungary (another kingdom), Slovenia, Croatia, much of Romania and parts of Poland. Although there were many linguistic and ethnic divisions in the Monarchy that were never to be bridged, these territories were subject to increasing centralized Habsburg control in the eighteenth century, making them more focused on Vienna. There was a certain internal coherence to the musical life of the Monarchy too: its sacred music was largely determined by the liturgy of the Catholic church, the dominant faith, but it featured German-language material too; its concert life was predominantly private rather than public; and it was largely self-sufficient in composers and works, unlike the increasingly cosmopolitan musical lives of Britain and France.

Apart from being comparatively unfamiliar to the modern reader, the term Austrian Monarchy has the disadvantage that it does not include the Salzburg of Adlgasser (1729–77), Eberlin (1702–62), Hafeneder (1746–84), Michael Haydn, Leopold Mozart (1719–87) and Wolfgang Amadeus Mozart. The ecclesiastical principality of Salzburg, ruled over by a prince-archbishop, was part of the Empire and not of the Monarchy. In practice, however, the Habsburg family exercised considerable influence over the territory and it naturally looked east to Vienna for political direction; the Colloredo family, it will be remembered, had a palace in the city from which Mozart was famously booted. While retaining local characteristics, its musical life had more in common with the Monarchy than with other cities, such as Mannheim to the west or Milan to the south. It would be pedantic, if not absurd, to exclude Salzburg.

There is one more telling drawback to the word Austria. For most of the eighteenth century few people would have called themselves 'Austrian'; Mozart, like many individuals from Joseph II downwards, would have used the term 'German'.[15] Towards the end of the century as the Napoleonic wars forced the Habsburg dynasty to defend its hereditary lands, that is the Monarchy, a more palpable sense of an Austrian identity emerges, consolidated when the Austrian Empire was formally created in 1804 and the Holy Roman Empire dissolved in 1806; three years later, in 1809, Beethoven sketched a song on a text by Collin, 'Östreich über Alles'.[16] Perhaps the earlier more neutral associations of the word Austria are an advantage, encouraging a view of

---

[15] See Mozart's letter of 5 February 1783: 'I prefer German opera, even though it means more trouble for me. Every nation has its own opera and why not Germany?' E. Anderson, ed., *The Letters of Mozart and his Family*, 2nd edn (London, 1966), vol. ii, p. 839.

[16] See D. Johnson, A. Tyson and R. Winter, *The Beethoven Sketchbooks: History: Reconstruction: Inventory* (Oxford, 1985), pp. 187–8, 192.

musical development that is not unnecessarily encumbered by nationalist concerns; geographical and political complexities notwithstanding, its use as a 'catch-all' is surely a pardonable convenience.

An even more neutral term appears in the title of this volume, 'eighteenth-century' rather than 'classical'. This is not only in deference to those authors, notably A. Peter Brown and Robert Freeman, who consider music from the early part of the century, music that would conventionally be labelled Baroque, but as a recognition that the labels Baroque and Classical tend to declare two fixed points of stylistic development at the beginning and end of the century. This has had two unfortunate consequences.[17] It implies that there was a sudden switch of direction, even a revolution in musical language in the middle of the century; such a dramatic view has some plausibility in musical development in other parts of Europe, notably in the musical taste of London and Paris in the 1760s, but stylistic development in Austria throughout the century is strongly evolutionary with conservative and progressive elements continually intermingling, a characteristic particularly evident in the repertoire discussed by A. Peter Brown, Chappell White, David Wyn Jones and Geoffrey Chew. The second unfortunate consequence is that 'transitional' works are undervalued because they do not exhibit the full characteristics of the *a priori* definition of Baroque and Classical; these labels have their value but they need to be used with circumspection.

Post-war scholarship in this period has focused to a significant extent on the symphony, with other instrumental genres such as the concerto and, especially, the quartet receiving less attention. The implicit aim – made explicit in another article by Jens Peter Larsen[18] – was to study the origins of the central Teutonic tradition of the symphony. The true contribution of the so-called 'father' of the symphony was unveiled in Robbins Landon's book, *The Symphonies of Joseph Haydn*, published in 1955, a monumental work of scholarship that stimulated further research into the Austrian symphony;[19] and the already mentioned Garland project is eloquent testimony to over thirty years of work in the genre. A rough and conservative estimate of the number of symphonies produced by Austrian composers in the period would run to 2,000[20] and scholarship has barely covered a quarter of this repertoire in any detail. While work on the

---

[17] For a comprehensive discussion of the historiography of the term 'classical style' see J. Webster, *Haydn's 'Farewell' Symphony and the Idea of Classical Style: Through-Composition and Cyclic Integration in his Instrumental Music* (Cambridge, 1991), pp. 335–57.

[18] 'Concerning the Development of the Austrian Symphonic Tradition (*circa* 1750–1775)', in Larsen, *Handel, Haydn, and the Viennese Classical Style*, pp. 315–25.

[19] Appendix II of the book contains a list of 134 doubtful and spurious symphonies attributed to Haydn; Robbins Landon indicated the likely author for a substantial proportion of these. Austrian composers mentioned include Dittersdorf, Franz Dussek (1736–99), Gassmann (1729–74), Gyrowetz (1763–1850), Michael Haydn, Hofmann (1738–93), Hoffmeister (1754–1812), Holzbauer (1711–83), Kimmerling (1737–99), L. Kozeluch (1752–1818), Ordonez, Pichl, Pleyel (1757–1831), Schneider (1737–1812), Sonnleithner (1734–86), Vanhal and Zimmermann (1741–81).

[20] This number is deduced from LaRue, *A Catalogue of 18th-Century Symphonies*.

symphony will surely continue, a fundamental question needs to be asked. Was the genre as central to musical life in eighteenth-century Austria as the modern perception of its importance, nurtured in the nineteenth and twentieth centuries, would have us believe? Mozart scholars have often pointed out that in the composer's last decade the composition of new symphonies was much less of a priority than piano concertos and operas. He was not alone. Albrechtsberger (1736–1809), Bonno (1710–88), Eybler, Gluck (1714–87), Salieri, Süssmayr (1766–1803) and Tuma (1704–74) were all composers who did not contribute significantly to the genre. If musicians did think about the relative importance of genres then they would have placed opera at the top of their ambitions (as Haydn did in his autobiographical sketch of 1776),[21] and then, because of its central place in a deeply Catholic society, church music. Most of the symphonic repertoire was written as entertainment music for private concerts and was not intended to be as ambitious as opera or as elevating as church music; when symphonies were played in church services, theatres and public concerts they were of secondary importance to respectively the mass, the play, and concertos and vocal numbers.[22]

Clearly modern scholarship is not yet ready to offer a comprehensive view of musical life at any stage in the history of music in Austria in the eighteenth century. Not surprisingly, the most promising period for a synthesis would seem to be Mozart's last ten years in Vienna. Good control of the operatic repertoire of this period exists and there is an increasing understanding of how Mozart's Italian and German operas fitted into the repertory; concert life is well documented, though the instrumental and oratorio output of composers active in Vienna has not been as well studied as that of Mozart's operatic colleagues; the output of music publishers is chronicled; documentation on performance practices across the genres is accessible; and the importance of music in salon culture and Freemasonry has been extensively written upon. Entirely on the debit side there is little information about dance music, the consequences of Joseph's reforms as they affected church music, and understanding of the manuscript copying industry is in its infancy. Finally, the English-speaking reader, at least, will feel insecure in the broader history of the decade until the second volume of Derek Beales's revisionist biography of Joseph II becomes available.[23] But

---

[21] See H. C. Robbins Landon, *Haydn: Chronicle and Works. Haydn at Eszterháza 1766–1790* (London, 1978), pp. 397–9.

[22] On the status of the symphony in the eighteenth century see N. Zaslaw, *Mozart's Symphonies: Context, Performance Practice, Reception* (Oxford, 1989), pp. 510–44. For performances of symphonies in church and in the theatre see respectively Zaslaw, *Mozart's Symphonies*, pp. 70–91; and E. R. Sisman, 'Haydn's Theater Symphonies', *Journal of the American Musicological Society*, xliii (1990), pp. 292–352.

[23] The first volume of Beales's biography appeared in 1987: D. Beales, *Joseph II: I: In the shadow of Maria Theresa 1741–1780* (Cambridge, 1987).

A preliminary bibliography for this period would include the following. O. Biba, 'Die Wiener Kirchenmusik um 1783', *Beiträge zur Musikgeschichte des 18. Jahrhunderts. Jahrbuch für österreichische Kulturgeschichte*, i (1971), pp. 7–67. V. Braunbehrens, *Mozart in Vienna 1781–1791*, trans. T. Bell (London,

even this near-comprehensiveness cannot be extended to the immediately surrounding decades, the 1770s and 1790s. Indeed, it cannot be claimed for any other significant period in the century, a salutary if not numbing thought for the music historian. Larsen's 'Challenge to Musicology' remains.

1990). D. Edge, 'Mozart's Viennese Orchestras', *Early Music*, xx (1992), pp. 64–88. J. Hurwitz, 'Haydn and the Freemasons', *Haydn Yearbook*, xvi (1985), pp. 5–98. M. S. Morrow, *Concert Life in Haydn's Vienna: Aspects of a Developing Musical and Social Institution* (Stuyvesant, New York, 1989). O. Michtner, *Das alte Burgtheater als Opernbühne von der Einführung des Deutschen Singspiels (1778) bis zum Tod Kaiser Leopolds II* (Vienna, 1970). E. West, 'Masonic Song and the Development of the *Kunstlied* in Enlightenment Vienna', *Austrian Studies*, ii (1991), pp. 71–87. A. Weinmann, *Die Anzeigen des Kopiaturbetriebes Johann Traeg in der Wiener Zeitung zwischen 1782 und 1805* (Vienna, 1981). Weinmann, *Die Wiener Verlagswerke von Franz Anton Hoffmeister* (Vienna, 1964). Weinmann, *Vollständiges Verlagverzeichnis Artaria & Comp.* (Vienna, 1952). N. Zaslaw, ed., *Mozart's Concertos: Text, Context, Intepretation* (Ann Arbor, 1995). Zaslaw, *Mozart's Symphonies. Zaubertöne. Mozart in Wien 1781–1791*, exhibition catalogue (Vienna, [1990]).

PART I

Overture, symphony and concerto

2

The trumpet overture and sinfonia in Vienna (1715–1822): rise, decline and reformulation

A. PETER BROWN

In 1955 H. C. Robbins Landon was the first writer to recognize the subgenre of the C major trumpet symphony which, according to his reckoning, included some fifteen works by Haydn spanning from the 1750s to the London symphonies of the 1790s.[1] Two years later at the Isham Library Conference on Instrumental Music, Landon called attention to another C major symphony by Carlo d'Ordonez (1734–86) scored for two choirs of trumpets and timpani in addition to the usual orchestra of strings, two oboes and two horns.[2] While no symphony by Haydn duplicates Ordonez's scoring, these compositions, together with works such as Mozart's 'Linz' (K425) and 'Jupiter' (K551) symphonies, and Beethoven's First Symphony, can be regarded as belonging to a broadly based Viennese symphonic tradition that begins at the end of the seventeenth century, peaks during the reign of Charles VI, declines with Maria Theresia's rule, and becomes reformulated during the last quarter of the century.

In the broadest sense, the beginnings of the subgenre extend back to Monteverdi's *Orfeo* Toccata, which first sounded in 1607 at Mantua. While Italian outgrowths of the toccata were to flourish as opera sinfonias during the seventeenth and eighteenth centuries,[3] in Vienna such pieces first emerged during the time of Leopold I, where they introduced dramatic vocal works for celebratory occasions: birthdays and namedays of the Emperor and Empress as well as the marriage of the Archduchess Maria Antonia to Maximilian Emanuel. Though two of these sinfonias are in D major, the Viennese tradition distinguishes itself from its Italian counterpart by its almost strict adherence to the key of C major. Caldara's D major overture to *Il nome più glorioso*, an opera performed

---

[1] H. C. Robbins Landon, *The Symphonies of Joseph Haydn* (London, 1955), p. 227. Symphonies Nos. 20, 32, 33, 37, 38, 41, 48, 50, 56, 60, 63, 69, 82, 90 and 97.
[2] H. C. Robbins Landon, 'Problems of Authenticity in Eighteenth-Century Music', in D. G. Hughes, ed., *Instrumental Music: A Conference at Isham Memorial Library, May 4, 1957* (Cambridge, Massachusetts, 1959), pp. 34–5.
[3] See H. Hell, *Die neapolitanische Opernsinfonie in der ersten Hälfte des 18. Jahrhunderts* (Tutzing, 1971), pp. 16–35 and *passim*.

Table 2.1 *Trumpeters ('Musikalische Trompeter') at the imperial court 1680–1775*

		Leopold I	Joseph I
	Name	1680 1681 1682 1683 1684 1685 1686 1687 1688 1689 1690 1691 1692 1693 1694 1695 1696 1697 1698 1699 1700 1701 1702 1703 1704	1705 1706 1707 1708 1709 1710 1711 1712
Musikalische Trompeter	Wolf Khlepauer	———	
	Georg Sigmund Hammer	————————	
	Andrea Wagenhuber	———————————	
	Marx Khämpfl	———————————	
	Tobias Andrea Pernebmer		————————
	Johann Reinhardt Engl		————————
	Thomas Bonn		————————
	Johann Grünauer		————
	Sebastian Nassoto		————————
	Georg Gortschek		———————
	Nicolas Jesorka		———————
	Franz Joseph Hollandt		————————
	Franz Turnovsky		————————
	Franz Küffel		
	Thomas Augustin Wlach		
	Johann Florian Zischek		
	Andreas Zechart		
	Matthias Schmidt		
	Rudolph Hein		
	Matthias Koch		
	Johann Michael Rebhindl		
	Franz Bonn		
	Franz Schön		
	Rudoph Koberer		
	Johann Christian Grienauer		
	Ernst Sessler		
	Johann Hanisch		
	Johann Ernst Peyer		
	Ferdinand Holtzl		
	Franz Kreybich		
	Ferdinand Weidlich		
	Andreas Häbler		

THE TRUMPET OVERTURE AND SINFONIA IN VIENNA

Charles VI   Maria Theresia

1713–1740   1741–1775

pension?

pension?

in Barcelona on the nameday of Charles III of Spain, later Emperor Charles VI, was composed in 1709.[4] After Caldara moved to Vienna, every trumpet work he composed was in C. In Austria trumpets in C are found in symphonies, overtures and the like, as well as in the most celebratory of solemn masses.[5]

Though the brief reign of Joseph I (1705–11) was both politically and artistically a hiatus, one of Fux's operas, *Gli ossequi della notte* (1709), for the nameday of the Empress Amalia Wilhelmina, adumbrates what was to become a standard scoring for the overtures to operas that marked the namedays and birthdays of the Emperor and Empress: either an orchestra in two choirs (as in this case) or, more usually, an orchestra with two choirs of trumpets and timpani. Additionally, in the last years of Joseph's reign, trumpeting became integrated into the more formalized setting of the overture/sinfonia.

When, after his coronation in Frankfurt, the erstwhile Charles III of Spain entered Vienna on 28 January 1712 as Emperor Charles VI, he brought with his entourage from Barcelona no fewer than ten court trumpeters to add to the established band of his late brother Joseph I (Table 2.1).[6] Within the protocols of the *Hofstaat* (the Imperial and Royal Household) the number of trumpet and timpani choirs signalled the ranking of an event within the liturgical as well as the imperial yearly cycle.[7] In both the *Hoffeste* (Court Festivals) and *Festtage der Heiligen* (Feast Days of the Saints), the participation of trumpeters and timpanists was appropriate for all ranks of celebrations except for the *Gewöhnliche Andachten und Solemnitäten* (Customary Prayers and Devotions) and *Gehwöhnliche Gottesdienste* (Customary Mass services) (Table 2.2). The highest-ranking events required two choirs of trumpets and timpani.

Charles's personal motto was 'Fortitudine & Constantia'. The Habsburg Emperor's own territorial pretensions to the throne of Spain were likened to the Pillars of Hercules. In 1723 Heraeus, friend of the architect Fischer von Erlach, established the association of the Herculean pillars with the Emperor's motto. Its manifestation are the two pillars of the Karlskirche in Vienna.[8] Since the operas performed on *Galatage* (Gala Days) were paeans to the Emperor and were usually scored for two choirs of trumpets and timpani, they became

---

[4] Österreichische Nationalbibliothek, hereinafter A-Wn, Cod. 18868.
[5] Only four studies of trumpet music in the Austrian lands have appeared. Three, dealing with trumpeters and music in Moravia during the eighteenth century, are by J. Sehnal, published in Czech with German summaries in *Acta Musici Moraviae*, lxxiii (1988), pp. 175–207; lxxiv (1989), pp. 255–68; and lxxv (1990), pp. 173–203. See also A. P. Brown, 'Caldara's Trumpet Music for the Imperial Celebrations of Charles VI and Elisabeth Christine' in B. W. Pritchard, ed., *Antonio Caldara: Essays on his Life and Times* (London, 1987), pp. 3–48. The best survey of Baroque trumpet music is P. L. Ciurczak, 'The Trumpet in Baroque Opera: Its Use as a Solo, Obbligato, and Ensemble Instrument' (Ph.D. diss., North Texas State University, 1974). A more diffuse study is D. L. Smithers, *The Music & History of the Baroque Trumpet before 1721* (Syracuse, 1973), which is reviewed by M. Rasmussen in *Journal of the American Musicological Society*, xxix (1976), pp. 320–3. Also useful is J. M. Barbour, *Trumpets, Horns and Music* (Lansing, 1964).
[6] See R. Topka, 'Der Hofstaat Kaiser Karls VI' (Ph.D. diss., University of Vienna, 1954), pp. 53–5, 103–6.
[7] See Brown, 'Caldara's', pp. 7–10.
[8] G. Heraeus, *Inscriptiones et Symbolia* (Vienna, 1723), n.p.

Table 2.2 *Hierarchy of feasts at the Viennese court*

	Hoffeste	Festtage der Heiligen
with trumpets	1. Galatage (celebrations of the imperial family) 2. *Toisonfeste* (attended by members of the Order of the Golden Fleece)	1. *Toison-Gottesdienste* (Marian and Apostolic Feasts) 2. *Pontifikal-Gottesdienste* (remaining feast days not ranked above)
without trumpets	3. *Gewöhnliche Andachten und Solemnitäten* (saints' days, processions to, and devotions in, various Viennese churches)	3. *Gewöhnliche Gottesdienste* (remaining Sundays and low times of Advent and Lent)

musical manifestations of the rocks and, in turn, of Charles's motto. The most telling musical example is Fux's opera *Costanza e Fortezza* (1723) where the overture is scored for an orchestra divided into two choirs.

From the early years of Charles's reign, the trumpeters and timpanists were listed in the *Hofstaat* under several different jurisdictions.[9] Presumably, the most prestigious were the *Musikalische Trompeter und Hörpaucker* (Trumpet and Timpani Players), a division of the *Kaiserliche Hof- und Kammermusici* (Imperial Court and Chamber Musicians), under the direction of *Hofkapellmeister* Fux. A second group, which overlaps with the *Hofkapelle* (Court Chapel), was the *Hof- und Feldtrompeter und Hörpaucker* (Court and Field Trumpet and Timpani Players), part of the *Obriststallmeisterstab und Hoffutter Amt* (Office of the Headquarters of Chief Riding Master and of Forage). In addition, trumpeters and timpanists attired in mail (*Hartschieren*) belonged to the *Kaiserliche Leibgarde*. Although the trumpeters and timpanists for the *Leibgarde* are not listed by name, they too probably overlapped with the *Hof- und Feld* group. Other players held further appointments: in the court of the widowed Empresses, and for *Exerciten* (Military Drilling). Finally, some players were *Hofscholaren* (Court Scholars) in that they served a two-year apprenticeship in preparation for full membership of one of the court organizations.[10]

---

[9] Published as part of *Kaiserlicher Hof- und Ehren Calender*, an annual publication for most of the century. A nearly complete run can be had from the holdings of the Österreichische Nationalbibliothek, the Stadtbibliothek Wien and the Haus-, Hof- und Staatsarchiv.

[10] R. Dahlquist, *The Keyed Trumpet and its Greatest Virtuoso, Anton Weidinger* (Nashville, 1975), p. 10.

The principal duties of these groups were musical (the *Hofkapelle*) and ceremonial (the *Stallmeister* and *Leibgarde*). But the main distinction between the two was one of administration and not function; at court during Charles VI's reign every appearance of the Emperor was ceremonial, even when an event was primarily musical, whether it be the performance of a birthday or nameday opera, music for the Emperor's table in the *Ritterstuben*, or for a liturgical celebration. According to Kilian Reinhardt's *Rubriche Generali* of 1727, in the liturgical sphere trumpets would provide *Intraden* or fanfares to punctuate the mass: at the beginning, in the middle before the 'Te ergo quaesumus', and at the end of the Te Deum; and as a response to litany-like texts used in processions.[11] This was in addition to whatever trumpeting occurred in the figural music for the mass itself. Trumpets might also be called for in the Gradual sonata.[12] In the *Ritterstuben*, instrumental music would be played in the gallery. Trumpets appear in the orchestra in the famous engraving of 1705 that portrays the swearing of oaths of allegiance to Charles as Archduke of Austria.[13] Such a musical environment must have been duplicated during the *Toisonfeste* which were attended by various members of the Order of the Golden Fleece.

The trumpet scoring was to some degree affected by the importance of the feast. For some of the *Hoffeste* and *Festtage der Heiligen* of the first order (see Table 2.2), two choirs of trumpets and timpani would be used. Each choir at its fullest would contain two *clarini*, whose range might extend to the twenty-sixth partial or g^3, and two *trombe*, who rarely exceeded the eighth partial or c^2, with the second player duplicating the tonic and dominant of the timpani.[14] Since the number of players during Charles's reign was always greater than the number of scored parts – thirteen to sixteen *Musikalische Trompeter* and never more than two timpanists – either the trumpet parts were at times doubled or the trumpeters were rotated in their duties. The question of doubling can also be posed for those works with a single choir of players or even just two players with timpani. Nevertheless, if doubling took place, there must have been some distinctions between solo and tutti, for many clarino passages would be difficult to render with two or more players.

This large group of players, with its own organization and hierarchy akin to a guild, guarded strongly that part of the repertoire that remained unnotated, passing it on to the new players as they entered the profession. Thus, it is impossible to determine with any degree of certainty whether during Charles's

---

[11] See Kilian Reinhardt, *Rubriche Generali per le Funzioni Ecclesiastiche Musicali di tutto l'Anno* (Vienna, 1727), A-Wn Suppl. Mus. 2503. A summary of its content is given in Ludwig Ritter von Köchel, *Die Kaiserliche Hof-Musikkapelle in Wien von 1543–1867* (Vienna, 1869), pp. 135–44.

[12] During Charles's reign this scoring was clearly exceptional, according to F. W. Riedel, *Kirchenmusik am Hofe Karls VI (1711–1740)* (Munich, 1977), pp. 210–21.

[13] See the plate in E.A. Bowles, *Musical Ensembles in Festival Books 1500–1800: An Iconographical & Documentary Survey* (Ann Arbor, 1989), p. 415.

[14] This style of playing is also known as 'principale', in contrast to modern usage of the word principal.

reign the main composers of the available repertoire, Johann Joseph Fux (1660–1741) and Antonio Caldara (c. 1670–1736), drew on the improvised (or unnotated) tradition for the fanfares that appear in their own overtures to dramatic works (Table 2.3). For example, the opening fanfares in Fux's *Le nozze di Aurora* (1722)[15] and *Costanza e Fortezza* (1723),[16] and Caldara's *Cajo Marzio Coriolano* (1717),[17] *La concordia de' pianetti* (1723)[18] and *Ornospade* (1727)[19] suggest such origins (Ex. 2.1, pp. 22–5).[20] Up to 1738 only one known Gradual sonata with trumpets survives.[21] Most Gradual sonatas were scored for strings and organ (those by Fux, Caldara and Corelli, for instance); the piece by Wenzel Raimund Birck (1718–63) from 1738 calls for one choir of trumpets with timpani and three-part strings. On close inspection, this single-movement sonata – an adagio followed by a thematically related allegro – is in reality a trio sonata with trumpet and timpani parts grafted on to the texture; they are entirely dispensable (Ex. 2.2, p. 26). According to Riedel, this work was first heard at the *Toison-Amt* on 28 October 1739, the *Festtage der Heiligen* for Simon and Judas, in the *Grosse Hofburgkapelle*.[22] Even though this is the only work with trumpets documented for use in the service between 1711 and 1740, one wonders if sinfonias to operas and oratorios were also used for festive liturgical celebrations in the *Hofkapelle* during Charles's reign.

The trumpet overtures themselves (Table 2.3) are almost entirely by Fux and Caldara with an occasional contribution by Georg Reinhardt (1715), Francesco Conti (1723), Giuseppe Bonno (1737), and Georg Reutter the younger (1736). The overtures by Fux and Caldara exemplify two separate traditions. Fux organizes his pieces in ways that seem to look backwards to the operatic overture of the seventeenth century, with hints of the canzona. *Pulcheria* (1708)[23] begins with an episodic alternation of allegro and adagio sections, continues with a presto fugue, and concludes with a cadential adagio (Ex. 2.3a, p. 27); *Gli ossequi della notte* (1709)[24] scored for two orchestras, repeats the opening section after

---

[15] A-Wn, Cod. 17262.
[16] E. Wellesz, ed. in *Denkmäler der Tonkunst in Österreich*, xxxiv–xxxv (Vienna, 1910).
[17] Gesellschaft der Musikfreunde, Vienna; Autograph 353.
[18] A-Wn, Cod. 17138.
[19] A-Wn, Cod. 17140.
[20] Fanfares, in contrast to signals, were apparently played by a full ensemble of two *clarini*, two *trombe* and timpani. Some of these are now edited: see L. Nowak, 'Studien zu einer Musiktopographie Niederösterreichs', *Jahrbuch für Landeskunde Niederösterreich*, xxix (1944–8), p. 406; A. Haller, 'Unbekannte Kostbarkeiten für Trompetenensemble' in *Brass Bulletin*, xxxviii (1982), pp. 15–24; and M. M. Schneider-Cuvay, E. Hintermaier and G. Walterskirchen, eds., *Aufzüge für Trompeten und Pauken* in *Denkmäler der Musik in Salzburg*, i (Munich, 1977). The presentation by J. Burghauser, *Staré České Fanfáry* (Prague, 1961) is so edited that the original sources and scoring are unclear.
[21] See Riedel, *Kirchenmusik*, p. 215.
[22] See Riedel, *Kirchenmusik*, p. 225.
[23] A-Wn, Cod. 17272. The most complete study of Fux's overtures is J. H. van der Meer, *J. J. Fux als Opernkomponist* (Bilthoven, 1961). See also D. Altenburg, 'Instrumentation in Zeichen des Hofzeremonials. Bemerkungen zur Verwendung der Trompete im Schaffen von J. J. Fux', in B. Habla, ed., *Johann Joseph Fux und die Barocke Bläsertradition* (Tutzing, 1987), pp. 157–68.
[24] A-Wn, Cod. 17998.

Table 2.3 *Trumpet Overtures to Dramatic Works 1685–1762*

Year	Composer	Title	Genre	Overture Title
1685	Draghi	Il sagrificio d'Amore	Serenata	Sonata
1697	Richter, Ferd.	Le promesse degli dei	Opera	Sonata
1705	Ariosti	Le profizie d'Eliseo	Oratorio	Sinfonia
1707	Badia	Napoli ritornata ai Romani	Componimento	Intrada
1708	Bononcini, Gio.	Il natale di Giunone	Componimento	Ouverture
1708	Fux	Pulcheria	Poemetto Dramatico	Intrada
1709	Fux	Gli ossequi della notte		Sinfonia
1709	Caldara	Il nome più glorioso	Componimento	Sinfonia
1715	Reinhardt	La più bella	Componimento	Intrada
1716	Fux	Angelica vincitrice di Alcina	Festa teatrale	Intrada
1717	Caldara	Cajo Marzio Coriolano		
1719	Fux	Elisa	Componimento teatrale	Intrada
1720	Caldara	Assalone	Oratorio	Introduzione
1721	Caldara	Ormisda	Dramma per musica	Introduzione
1722	Fux	Le nozze di Aurora	Festa teatrale	Sinfonia
1723	Fux	Costanza e Fortezza	Festa teatrale	Sinfonia
1723	Conti	Il trionfo della fama	Serenata	Sinfonia
1723	Caldara	La concordia de' pianetti	Componimento teatrale	Introduzione
1723	Caldara	Ester	Oratorio	Sinfonia
1724	Caldara	Gianguir	Dramma per musica	Introduzione
1725	Caldara	Il Venceslao	Dramma per musica	Introduzione
1725	Caldara	Il trionfo della religione	Oratorio, etc.	Introduzione
1726	Fux	La corona d'Arianna	Festa teatrale	Sinfonia
1727	Caldara	Ornospade	Dramma per musica	Introduzione
1728	Caldara	Mitridate	Dramma per musica	Introduzione
1728	Caldara/Reutter	La forza dell'amicizia	Dramma per musica	Sinfonia
1729/30	Caldara	Caio Fabbrizio	Dramma per musica	Introduzione
1731	Fux	Enea negli Elisi	Festa teatrale	Sinfonia
1732	Caldara	Adriano in Siria	Dramma per musica	Introduzione
1734	Caldara	Enone	Dramma per musica	Introduzione
1736	Reutter	La speranza assicurata	Serenata	Intrada
1736	Caldara	Achille in Sciro	Dramma per musica	Introduzione
1736	Caldara	Ciro riconosciuto	Dramma per musica	Introduzione
1737	Bonno	La gara del genio con Giunone	Serenata	Sinfonia
1749	Wagenseil	L'olimpiade	Dramma per musica	Sinfonia
1750	Wagenseil	Armida placata	Dramma per musica	Sinfonia
1750	Wagenseil	Vincislao	Dramma per musica	Sinfonia
1752	Bonno	L'eroe cinese	Dramma per musica	Sinfonia
1755	Wagenseil	Gioas, Re di Giuda	Oratorio	Sinfonia
1756	Wagenseil	Il roveto di Mosè	Oratorio	Sinfonia
1762	Wagenseil	Prometeo assoluto	Serenata	Sinfonia

Occasion	Key	Scoring
M Kurf. Maximilian Emanuel & Maria Antonia	C	2 Cl, 2 Ch of Strgs (2 Vi, 2 Va, B)
B Leopold I	C	2 Cl, 2 Tr, Tp, Strgs (1 Vi, 2 Va, B)
	D	2 Tr, Strgs a 4, Bssn
B Charles III (Charles VI)	C	2 Tr, Strgs a 5 (Vc, B), Obs,
B Amalia Wilhelmina	C	2 Tr, Tp, Strgs a 5 (Vc, B), Obs, Bssn
N Amalia Wilhelmina	C	Tr, Strgs a 4, Obs
N Amalia Wilhelmina	C	Orchestra in 2 Ch of 2 Tr, Strgs a 4, Obs
N Charles III (Charles VI)	D	2 Tr, Strgs a 4, Obs
N Elisabeth Christine	C	2 Cl, Tp, 2 Obs, Strgs a4
Birth of Leopold, Archduke of Austria	C	Orchestra in 2 Ch of 2 Cl, 2 Tr, Strgs a 4, Obs
B Elisabeth Christine	C	4 Tr, Tp, Strgs a 4, Obs, Bssn
B Elisabeth Christine	C	Orchestra in 2 Ch of 2 Cl, Tr, Tp, Strgs a 4
Lent?	C	2 Cl, 2 Tr, Tp, Strgs a 4, Bssn
N Charles VI	C	2 Ch of 2 Cl, 2 Tr, Tp; Strgs a 4, Obs, Bssns
M Maria Amalia, Archduchess of Austria	C	2 Cl, 2 Tr, Tp, Strgs a 4
C in Prague Charles VI & *B* Elisabeth Christine	C	Orchestra in 2 Ch of 2 Cl, 2 Tr, Tp, Strgs a 4, Flts, Obs
N Charles VI	C	2 Tr, Tp, Strgs a 4, Obs
B Elisabeth Christine	C	2 Cl, 2 Tr, Tp, Strgs a 4, Obs, Bssns
Lent?	C	Tr, Strgs a 4, Obs, Bssns
N Charles VI	C	2 Ch of 2 Cl, 2 Tr, Tp; Strgs a 4, Obs, Bssns
N Charles VI	C	2 Ch of 2 Cl, 2 Tr, Tp; Strgs a 4, Obs, Bssns
Festival of St Benedict	C	2 Cl, 2 Tr, Tp; Strgs a 4, Obs, Bssns
B Elisabeth Christine	C	2 Cl, 2 Tr, Tp; Strgs a 4, Obs, Bssns
N Charles VI	C	2 Ch of 2 Cl, 2 Tr, Tp; Strgs a 4
N Charles VI	C	2 Ch of 2 Cl, 2 Tr, Tp; Strgs a 4
B Elisabeth Christine	C	2 Ch of 2 Cl, 2 Tr, Tp; Strgs a 4
N Charles VI	C	2 Ch of 2 Cl, 2 Tr, Tp; Strgs a 4
B Elisabeth Christine	C	2 Ch of 2 Cl, 2 Tr, Tp; Strgs a 4, Obs, Bssns
N Charles VI	C	2 Ch of 2 Cl, 2 Tr, Tp; Strgs a 4
B Elisabeth Christine	C	2 Cl, 2 Tr, Tp, Strgs a 4
B Maria Theresia	C	2 Cl, 2 Tr, Tp, Strgs a 4, Obs, Bssns
M Maria Theresia & Francis of Lorraine	C	2 Ch of 2 Cl, 2 Tr, Tp; Strgs a 4
B Elisabeth Christine	C	2 Ch of 2 Cl, 2 Tr, Tp; Strgs a 4
B Maria Theresia	C	2 Cl, 2Tr, Tp, 2 Obs, Strgs a 4
B Maria Theresia	C	2 Cl, 2 Tr, Tp, 2 Obs, Strgs a 4
B Elisabeth Christine	C	2 Cl, Tp, 2 Obs, Strgs a 4
B Franz Stephan of Lorraine	C	2 Cl, Tp, 2 Obs, Strgs a 4
B Maria Theresia	C	2 Cl, 2 Tr, Tp, 2 Hr, 2 Obs, Strgs a 4
Lent	C	2 Cl, Tp, 2 Obs, Strgs a 4
Lent	C	2 Cl, Tp, 2 Obs, Strgs a 4
B & *N* Archduke Joseph?	C	2 Tr, Tp, 2 Obs, Strgs a 4

Abbreviations

- B – Birthday
- C – Coronation
- M – Marriage
- N – Nameday

Abbreviations

B – Bass	Flt – Flute	Tr – Trombe
Bssn – Bassoon	Hr – Horn	Va – Viola
Ch – Choir	Ob – Oboe	Vi – Violin
Cl – Clarino	Tp – Timpani	

Ex. 2.1 Opening fanfares from
(a) Fux, *Le nozze di Aurora* (1722)

(b) Fux, *Costanza e Fortezza* (1723)

(c) Caldara, *La concordia de' pianetti* (1723)

(d) Caldara, *Cajo Marzio Coriolano* (1717)

(e) Caldara, *Ornospade* (1727)

Ex. 2.2 Birck, Sonata (1739)

four other contrasting movements (Ex. 2.3b, p. 27); *Aurora* (1722)[25] is similar to *Pulcheria*; and *La corona d'Arianna* (1726)[26] repeats the first section after an adagio. Other overtures, such as *Angelica* (1716),[27] *Elisa* (1719),[28] *Costanza e Fortezza* (1723) and *Enea* (1731)[29], are closer to the textbook model of the Italian opera sinfonia; single movements are often episodic in structure, and either soloistic or fugal in texture. Despite these patterns, Fux's overtures are never predictable in their cyclic layout, though their dependence on fanfares, transitional and solemn slow sections for strings, dance styles and fugues seems to diminish the effect of their unusual and retrospective cycles.

In contrast, Caldara is more predictable. All his overtures are in two or three movements. The three-movement overture consists of a fast first movement in concertante style, a solemn second movement for strings in the relative minor ending on its dominant, and a finale for full orchestra in a march style. In the two-movement overture the slow second movement is followed by the opening chorus of the opera. In this layout, the first movement is almost always

---

[25] A-Wn, Cod. 17262
[26] A-Wn, Cod. 17270.
[27] A-Wn, Cod. 17281.
[28] A-Wn, Cod. 17228.
[29] A-Wn, Cod. 17274.

Ex. 2.3
(a) *Pulcheria* (1708)

1. Allegro 4/4   Adagio   Allegro   Adagio
   Tutti   Strings   Tutti   Strings
   8 bb.   4 bb.   14 bb.   10 bb.

2. Presto 4/4 – Fugue   Adagio
   ‖: Tutti Solo Tutti Solo Tutti :‖   Strings
   59 bb.   6 bb.

(b) *Gli ossequi della notte* (1709)

1. Allegro 4/4
   Alternation of two choirs and concertino group
   21 bb.

2. Adagio 3/2
   Strings tutti vs. concertino
   83 bb.

3. Allegro 4/4 – Fugue
   ‖: Tutti Solo Tutti Solo Tutti :‖
   56 bb.

4. Adagio 3/2
   Concertino
   8 bb.

5. Tempo di Menuetto
   ‖:   1st time: tutti   :‖:   1st time: tutti   :‖:   Tutti   :‖
         repeat: concertino   repeat: concertino
         8 bb.   8 bb.   8 bb.

6. = 1
   21 bb.

the more substantial in form and texture. Not only is a concertante texture shared between the two choirs of trumpets, but Caldara may also include solos for the strings. In some seven instances he includes a concertante trio of two oboes and bassoon (see Table 2.3, pp. 20–1). In Caldara's last opera overtures, the slow movements become less solemn, less transitional and more substantial, beginning with *Caio Fabbrizio* (1729)[30] and continuing with *Adriano in Siria* (1732),[31]

[30] A-Wn, Cod. 17148.
[31] A-Wn, Cod. 17162.

and *Ciro riconosciuto* (1736).[32] For another opera from 1736, *Achille in Sciro*,[33] Caldara produces a middle movement in repeated binary form that easily reminds one of what was to be the norm during the mid-century in Vienna (Ex. 2.4). The finales remain more constant in style, though some of the later ones are in the style and tempo of a minuet.

Perhaps the greatest convergence of trumpeting and art music in the reign of Charles VI occurred in connection with the court's journey to Prague in 1723 for the coronation of Charles and his wife, Elisabeth Christine, as King and Queen of Bohemia. Fux's *Costanza e Fortezza*, composed for the Empress's birthday as well as the coronation, was scored for an orchestra of two choirs, each with its own full complement of trumpets and timpani. For the Emperor's nameday on 4 November 1723 Francesco Conti composed *Il trionfo della fama*[34] with what for him was an expanded scoring of two trumpets and timpani, in addition to the usual strings, oboes and bassoons. In Znaim (Znojmo) on 19 November, during the return trip to Vienna, Caldara's *La concordia de' pianetti* was performed for the Empress's nameday. Scored for only a single choir of trumpets and timpani, the overture was probably a reflection of the rather improvised circumstances of the performance.[35]

Like the later works of Caldara, the overtures to *La speranza assicurata* (1736) by Georg Reutter[36] and *La gara del genio* (1737)[37] by Giuseppe Bonno are representative of the late Viennese Baroque. Both first movements operate according to the ritornello principle. The second movement of the Reutter is hardly of the solemn type usually found in Caldara; the violins in unison are accompanied by the basso continuo, and the piece concludes with a full cadence. Bonno's second movement (3/8, C minor) is headed 'Allegro assai ma piano sempre', which might well signify a programmatic content in the manner of a 'characteristic' movement. Reutter's finale is a 3/8 binary form suggestive of the mid-century symphony, while the dimensions of Bonno's finale are more like those of its first movement. Concerning the trumpet writing, Reutter displays an unabashed clarino idiom, while Bonno confines the clarinists' range to a peak of a^2. Lastly, Bonno releases the oboes from the older *colla parte* writing, giving them greater independence. In short, some aspects of the music look forward, while others are more conservative.

With the death of Charles VI in late 1740 many of the practices and proprieties of court life went into decline. Among these was the large complement of trumpeters. In 1739 there were fifteen trumpeters listed among the *Hof- und Feldtrompeter* and thirteen among the *Musikalische Trompeter*. By 1744

---

[32] A-Wn, Cod. 17177.
[33] A-Wn, Cod. 17179.
[34] A-Wn, Cod. 17222.
[35] See A. P. Brown, 'Caldara's', p. 17 for the report of this event in the *Wiennerisches Diarium* ('Anhang' to No. 94, 24 November 1723).
[36] A-Wn, Cod. 17980.
[37] A-Wn, Cod. 18276.

Ex. 2.4 Caldara, *Achille in Sciro* (1736), 2nd mvt

both groups had lost personnel: the *Hof- und Feld* was reduced to ten and the *Musikalische* to six. By 1776 the *Musikalische Trompeter und Hörpaucker* ceased to exist, and the *Hof- und Feld* contingent stabilized at six.[38] The reasons for this decline were many. The glories of the court life and the dynasty's accomplishments under Charles VI were sumptuous in the areas of art, architecture and musical theatre. But these accomplishments at home, as well as military operations abroad, were costly. When Maria Theresia succeeded to the throne,

[38] According to data gathered from the *Kaiserliche Hof- und Ehrencalender* with the accompanying *Hofstatt*.

the imperial treasury was in dire condition; she needed first and foremost to protect the Habsburg inheritance. Budgetary necessities resulted in economies affecting the *Hofkapelle*. In 1751 the court changed the administration of its musical establishment by providing *Kapellmeister* Georg Reutter with a relatively small budget for everything from salaries to music copying for the church. It increased some payments, while some were lowered and others redistributed.[39] The status of the five *Musikalische* trumpeters remained essentially the same, except that the lead player's compensation was reduced by one third. In later years, the trumpeters were to receive increases in salary, but only upon the death of a colleague. For example, when *Obertrompeter* (Chief Trumpeter) Franz Anton Küffel died on 22 May 1754, part of his salary of 600 florins was given in 50-florin increments to four of the remaining players, and he was not replaced, reducing the number of *Musikalische Trompeter* to four.[40]

Secondly, the ceremonies that dominated life under Charles VI were of less interest to Maria Theresia and of practically no interest to her son, Joseph II. Perhaps her authority was somewhat weakened by the fact that her consort, Francis of Lorraine, and not she, bore the title of Holy Roman Emperor. Additionally during her marriage she was fully occupied with ruling and childbearing, leaving little time left for court ceremony. Perhaps, too, the heavy obligations of protocol, which seemed to dominate court life under her father, were not suited to her temperament. After the death of the widowed Empress Elisabeth Christine in December 1750, the regular production of extravagant operas in the Fux tradition for the *Hoffeste* came to a virtual end. With her own widowhood in 1765, Maria Theresia took the mantle of perpetual mourning, which was hardly conducive to the kind of court celebrations practised before 1740.

Finally, the use of trumpets in the church was curtailed by an edict from Pope Benedict XIV dated 19 February 1749, that allowed only string instruments, bassoons and organ in church music.[41] In 1753 the church authorities in Vienna forbade the use of trumpets and timpani in the church, because of their theatrical associations.

While this decree was followed in the Viennese court chapels, it was only a temporary force in the parishes; Otto Biba has shown that by 1755 trumpets were again used at the church of the Piarist order of Maria Treu.[42] By 1767 trumpets and timpani returned to the court chapel and metropolitan church of

---

[39] The document is reprinted in L. Stollbrock, 'Leben und Wirken des k.k. Hofkapellmeisters und Hofkompositors Johann Georg Reuter [sic] jun.', *Vierteljahresschrift der Musikwissenschaft*, iii (1892), pp.180–4. For an overview of a portion of this decline see H. Haider-Pregler, 'Festopern am Wiener Hof in Theresianischer Zeit', in R. V. Karpf, ed., *Musik am Hof Maria Theresias* (Munich, 1984), pp. 41–50.

[40] According to documents in the Haus-, Hof- und Staatsarchiv (Vienna) this occurred in 1747 with the closing of the account of Joseph Hollandt (SR 99), and in 1754 with the death of Franz Anton Küffel (SR 102).

[41] See E.A. Wienandt, ed., *Opinions on Church Music* (Waco, 1974), pp. 67–8.

[42] O. Biba, *Der Piaristenorden in Österreich* (Eisenstadt, 1975), p. 113. See also O. Biba's discussion in 'Die Wiener Kirchenmusik um 1783', *Jahrbuch für Österreichische Kulturgeschichte*, i (1971), pp. 71–3.

St Stephen's to celebrate, on 14 June, the recovery from serious illness of Empress Maria Theresia. According to the indefatigable diarist Johann Joseph Khevenhüller-Metsch an edict was issued for a

Te Deum von dem Cardinalen in Gegenwart aller Cleriseien, Dicasterien und hohen Adels beiderlei Geschlechts zu St. Stephan auf das prächtigste und zwar mit verschiedenen Chör, Trompeten und Paucken um 10 Uhr gehalten, sondern dasselbe auch bei Hof in der Cammer-Capellen auf specialen Befehl des Kaisers Majestät Joseph II., welcher sich mit sämtlicher höchster Familie und denen Vornehmeren von Hof darbei eingefunden, von denen Hof-Capellanen nach 11 Uhr ebenfahls unter Trompetten- und Pauckenschall wiederhollet. Diese bruyante Musique wurde vor einigen Jahren auf Veranlassung des seeligen Cardinals Trautsohn edictaliter verbotten; allein bei gegenwärtiger so erfreulichen Epoque wurde von denen Stellen eingerathen und von dem Hof approbirt, daß bei denen Te Deum und dergleichen feierlichen Begängnussen, sonsten aber nicht, sich die Trompetten und Paucken wieder dörffen hören lassen; welche Verordnung bei dem Volck, so auf derlei Demonstrationen immer zu sehen pfleget, ein ungemaines Vergnügen erwecket hat.[43]

Te Deum by the cardinal in the presence of all the clergy, officials and high nobility of both sexes, to be performed in a most magnificent way with several choirs, trumpets, and drums at St Stephen's at 10.00; but also with the repetition of the same at the court in the court chapel. The court performance was by the command of the Imperial Majesty Joseph II, who was present together with his entire family and the higher nobility, and, when it was celebrated by the court chaplains after 11.00, it was with the same glorious sound of trumpets and drums. This noisy music was forbidden by edict several years ago at the command of the late Cardinal Trautsohn. However, in the present so pleasant epoch, it was advised by the same officials who had formerly forbidden it, and certified by the court, that the decree permitted trumpets and drums to be heard again only for the forementioned Te Deum, and accompanying ceremonials, also during similarly solemn ceremonies, but not otherwise, which order has generated an extraordinary delight among the people, as they always look forward to this kind of celebration.

However, Riedel believes that his decree affected only the performance of *Intraden* and did not concern concerted music.[44] Further evidence of the banning of trumpets and timpani is suggested by the sources for a series of Reutter's works, which were part of the St Stephen's music collection before they were acquired by the Gesellschaft der Musikfreunde. As in the *Hofkapelle*, the dates of performances were recorded on the covers of the parts (see Table 2.4). Only one of the works (A-Wgm XIII/2826c) clearly falls within the period forbidding trumpets and timpani in the service. But perhaps in this case, as well as in the other work titled 'Servizio di Tavola', the work was never used for a

---

[43] Rudoph Graf Khevenhüller-Metsch and H. Schlitter, eds., *Aus der Zeit Maria Theresias: Tagebuch des Fürsten Johann Josef Khevenhüller-Metsch*, vi (Vienna, 1917), p. 246. I thank Michelle Goetz for bringing this passage to my attention.
[44] F. W. Riedel, 'Liturgie und Kirchenmusik' in *Joseph Haydn in seiner Zeit* (Eisenstadt, 1982), p. 123.

Table 2.4 *Georg Reutter trumpet sinfonias*

	Title	Sources	Instrumentation	Performances
1.	Sinfonia (see Table 2.3, 1736)	A-HE (auto) A-Wgm XIII/8574	2 Ch of 2 Cl, 2 Tr, Timp; Strgs a 4	1753
2.	Sinfonia a due chori	A-HE (auto) A-Wgm XIII/8577	Orchestra of 2 Ch of 2 Cl, 2 Tr, Timp, Strgs a 4	1740–43
3.	Lateinisches dramatisches Stück	A-HE (auto)	Orchestra of 2 Ch of 2 Cl, 2 Tr, Tp, Strgs a 4	1743
4.	Servizio di Tavola	A-Wgm XIII/2826c (ed. DTÖ, xxxi)	2 Obs, 2 Cl, 2 Tr, Tp, Strgs a 4	1757–59
5.	Servizio di Tavola	A-Wgm XIII/8093	2 Obs, 2 Cl, 2 Tr, Tp, Strgs a 4	1769–71
6.	Intrada	A-Wgm XIII/8435	2 Cl, 2 Tr, Timp, Strgs a 4	1770
7.	Partitta a due chori	A-HE (auto)	Orchestra of 2 Ch of 2 Cl, 2 Tr, Tp, Strgs a 4	–

liturgical service, but rather in the *Ritterstuben* for one of the celebrations or public meals that might have taken place there. Evidence is also provided by two Caldara sonatas from the *Hofkapelle*: one was performed nine times between January 1746 and July 1753, the other six times between 1750 and May 1752.[45] Thus, what little evidence exists seems to support a broadly based ban on trumpets.

To a greater or lesser extent all these circumstances contributed to a decline in the trumpeting institutions at court and also to the clarino style, which was apparently not used by the *Hof- und Feldtrompeter*.[46] With the gradual demise of the *Musikalische Trompeter*, there was no reason to be a clarinist.

[45] The performance dates for two Caldara sonatas (A-Wn, Cod. 3616 and 3617) also support this view; they do not go beyond 1753.
[46] The evidence for this statement about trumpet music in Vienna played by the *Hof- und Feldtrompeter* is a single example of signals that survives from the time of Maria Theresia published in E. Rameis, *Die österreichische Militärmusik* (Tutzing, 1976), Abbildung 11. Only one of these signals moves into the clarino range. As late as 1799 the Viennese music dealer Johann Traeg was offering in his *Verzeichniss* (p. 104) 'Stücke die ein k.k. trompeter im Felde braucht' ('Pieces used by a Royal and Imperial Field Trumpeter'). Other signals that are published are much earlier; the major collections are found in G. Schünemann, ed., *Trompeter Fanfaren: Sonaten und Feldstücke. Nach Aufzeichnungen deutscher Hoftrompeter des 16./17. Jahrhunderts* in *Reichsdenkmäler deutscher Musik: Das Erbe deutscher Musik*, vii (Kassel, 1936). See also Schünemann, 'Sonaten und Feldstücke der Hoftrompeter', *Zeitschrift für Musikwissenschaft*, xvii (1935), pp. 147–70. See also the examples in Edward H. Tarr et al., 'Military Signals', in *The New Grove Dictionary of Music and Musicians*, ed. S. Sadie (London, 1980), xii, pp. 316–20.

Ex. 2.5 Reutter, ritornello from *Il Parnasso* (1738), 'Lo stuol che Apollo onora canti d'Elisa il vanto'

At the same time, court trumpeting achieved a pinnacle of virtuosity, as revealed by reports and in the works of Georg Reutter. Witness the following contemporary observation from the Kremsmünster monk Beda Planck about a trumpet aria he heard in a performance of Andrea Bernasconi's *Artarserse*, given on the nameday of Francis of Lorraine in 1746. Planck reported hearing an 'aria adagio' sung like an angel, and with a trumpet obbligato.

Herr Heinisch der berühmte Trompeter hat ein Solo zu dieser Arie geblasen, so künstlich und hoch, dass es menschlicher Weis fast nicht möglich hätte sein können, denn es ging die Trompete wie ein Flötel. Zum End dieser Arie schlug dieses Weibsbild einen so langen und lieblichen Triller, dass ich wirklich geglaubt, der Atem werde ihr nicht mehr kommen; und also machte auch einen ebenso langen und noch längeren Triller Herr Heinisch auf der Trompete mit ihr.[47]

[47] Quoted from Planck's diaries as published in A. Kellner, *Musikgeschichte des Stiftes Kremsmünster* (Kassel, 1956), p. 247.

Ex. 2.6 Reutter, Servizio di Tavola (1757–9) (A-Wgm XIII/2826c), 2nd mvt

Mr Heinisch, the famous trumpeter, performed a solo in this aria so artfully and high that it seemed almost beyond human capability, for the trumpet was more like a piccolo. At the end of the aria, this female sang such a long and lovely trill that I really believed she would run out of breath; she then performed a longer and still longer trill accompanied by Mr Heinisch on his trumpet.

Since there are neither trumpet parts nor a single trumpet aria in Bernasconi's opera, this 'aria adagio' must have been an insertion; no example fitting Planck's description has yet been discovered.[48] But his description does fit an aria by Georg Reutter, part of his *festa teatrale per musica*, *Il Parnasso* (1738), 'Lo stuol che Apollo onora canti d'Elisa il vanto' (Ex. 2.5, p. 33–7),[49] which may have been written with Johann Heinisch in mind. Its range extends from c^1 to g^3 – more than two-and-a-half octaves. Its top note (g^3) is heard numerous times and is approached diatonically and chromatically as well as by skip. Other examples demanding g^3 date as far back as Caldara's *I due dittatori* (1726).[50] Coincidentally, this was the year Heinisch began his two years of training as *Hofscholar*.[51]

[48] The 'aría adagio' is not part of the score of Bernasconi's *Artaserse* in the Bayerische Staatsbibliothek, Munich (Cod. Mus 151/1–3).
[49] A-Wn, Cod. 17986.
[50] A-Wn, Cod. 15903, aria for Quinto Fabio, 'Nulla bada destrier generoso'.
[51] According to the *Kaiserliche Hof- und Ehrencalender* for the years between 1745 and 1751.

Ex. 2.7 Reutter, Servizio di Tavola (1769–71) (A-Wgm XIII/8093), 3rd mvt

Table 2.5 *Independent symphonic trumpet works (excluding works by Reutter, Haydn, Mozart and Beethoven)*

Composer	Title (Source)	Scoring	Modern Catalogue	Date
Birck, Wenzel Raimund	Sonata (A-Wn)	2 Cl, 2 Tr, Tp, Strgs a 3	–	1738
Tuma, Franz Ignaz	Overture (H-G)	2 Cl, 2 Tr, Tp, Strgs a 3	Vogg deest	c. 1741–50?
	Sonata (D-ddr-Dlb)	2 Cl, 2 Tr, Tp, Strgs a 3	Vogg deest	c. 1741–50?
Wagenseil, Georg Christoph	Symphony	2 Cl, Tp, Strgs a 4	Kucaba C7	b. 1757
	Symphony	2 Cl, Strgs a 4	Kucaba C10	c. 1750–60?
	Symphony	2 Cl, Tp, 2 Ob, Strgs a 4	Kucaba C12	b. 1761
Ordonez, Carlo d'	Symphony	2 Cl, Tp, 2 Ob, 2 Hr, Strgs a 4	Brown 1:C9	b. 1775
	Symphony	2 Ch of 2 Cl, Tp; 2 Ob, 2 Hr, Strgs a 4	Brown 1:C10	1760s?
Ziegler, Joseph Paul	Symphony (A-M)	2 Cl, 2 Tr, Tp, Strgs a 4	–	b. 1767
Steffan, Joseph Anton	Concerto for Organ	2 Cl, 2 Tr, Tp, Strgs a 4	Svetkova 97	b. 1763

Writing like that in Reutter's arias makes J. S. Bach's Second Brandenburg Concerto, with two approaches to g³ on a trumpet in F, seem less daunting.

Comparable demands on the trumpeters are found in other works from Georg Reutter's pen, works that remained in the repertoire until 1771 (see Table 2.4, p. 32). Nos. 2 and 7 on the list obviously hark back to some of Fux's opera overtures for multiple instrumental choirs, although without the old canzona-type forms. No. 3 can be dated 1743 on the basis of a performance on 6 December reported in the *Wiennerisches Diarium*. Some 210 participants had performed a three-hour *Lateinisches Schauspiel* on the subject of Emperor Constantine: 'The music was by the Royal Majesty's Composer, Georg von Reutter' ('Die Musik war von Ihrer königl. Majestät Compositor Hrn. Georg von Reutter').[52] It uses the double choirs of trumpets and timpani of the opera overtures during Charles VI's reign. Nos. 4, 5 and 6 reflect two important aspects of Viennese trumpet playing: first, the availability of only one choir of trumpets from the 1750s to the 1770s, and second, the continued existence of at least two players still practising the clarino style into the 1770s despite the general decline of the style. Exx. 2.6 (pp. 38–9) and 2.7 (pp. 40–1) from the two works termed 'Servizio di Tavola' reveal sustained as well as technical display. Though Reutter's music has been denigrated – Burney said he was without taste or invention[53] – Joseph Haydn probably came to know Nos. 1–3, if not the other works from this tradition.

Belonging more to Caldara's approach are a couple of works by Franz Tuma (1704–74), presumably written during or after the period 1741–50 when he was Kapellmeister to the widowed Empress Elisabeth Christine (Table 2.5, p. 42). The sonata, which survives in a nineteenth-century source form Dresden,[54] has a structure similar to that of a Caldara overture: a quick first movement with solo/tutti alternation and even a central fugato, a solemn slow movement in 3/2 for strings ending with a cadence on its dominant, and a final allegro which departs from the Caldara model in that it is of almost equal substance to the first movement. The clarino writing in the finale, though never extending beyond c³, is notable for allowing the players to introduce passages that lean towards both the dominant and subdominant; that is they call for f♯² and b♭² (Ex. 2.8). The 'Overture' from Györ follows the French model (Ex. 2.9, p. 46) and concludes with a polonaise for strings.[55] Here the trumpet writing is less demanding (the range is from c¹ to g²), but it is still heavily soloistic. If both these works were for the chapel of Elisabeth Christine and if the size of her musical retinue had not changed since the 1720s, they would have been easily

---

[52] *Wiennerisches Diarium*, 18 December 1743.
[53] See C. Burney, *The Present State of Music in Germany, the Netherlands and United Provinces* (2 vols., London, 1775), p. 361.
[54] Dresden, Sächsische Landesbibliothek Mus. 2968-0-500.
[55] Györ, Káptalandomb T.8. Neither this nor the work cited in note 54 is listed by H. Vogg, 'Franz Tuma als Instrumentalkomponist' (Ph.D. diss., University of Vienna, 1951).

Ex. 2.8 Tuma, Sonata (c. 1741–50?) (Vogg deest), 3rd mvt

Ex. 2.9 Tuma, Overture (ca. 1741–50?) (Vogg deest)

||: [Slow]   :|| Fuga 3/8   Adagio 3/4   Fuga da capo
C major   A minor V
                                        cadence:

accommodated by the available resources, for the chapel had three *Hoftrompeter*[56] and two unnamed players for her *Leibgarde*; both works require only one choir of two *clarini*, two *trombe* and timpani.

The works of Reutter and Tuma look backwards to Fux and Caldara. Those few overtures/sinfonias by Wagenseil and Bonno – both from a generation later – are more up-to-date for a mid-century composer. Bonno's overture to *L'eroe cinese* (1752),[57] for the birthday of Maria Theresia, has a hybrid scoring of one full choir of trumpets with timpani and what we regard as the standard classical orchestra of two independent oboes (exchanged for flutes in the second movement), two horns and strings. Except for one isolated bar of diffident florid writing the trumpet choir gives no hint of the older trumpeting tradition. Neither does Bonno's overture to *La gara del genio* (1737), where the clarino range is even more conservative; all three movements are substantial and closed,

[56] As listed in the *Kaiserliche Hof- und Ehrencalender* for 1726 and 1727.
[57] A-Wn, Cod. 18265.

and their forms are not clearly based on ritornello or sonata principles. Here is a work torn between the Baroque tradition of the trumpet sinfonia/overture and the style of its time.

Wagenseil's overtures/sinfonias to *L'olimpiade* (1749) and *Armida placata* (1750)[58] are even less adventurous than Bonno's works in their trumpet writing, even though *L'olimpiade* calls for one full trumpet and timpani choir. But whereas Bonno vacillates between ritornello and sonata principles, Wagenseil clearly tips towards a sonata structure but, as expected in an overture, without repeats. Both central movements are formally complete and closed, while the Tempo di Menuet movements use part forms. But one should not assume that for Wagenseil the clarino style was completely dead, for a symphony in C major from before 1757 (Kucaba C7)[59], scored for *clarini*, timpani and strings, extends the first clarino to c^3, but without any florid or soloistic passages and with only one hint of a fanfare (Ex. 2.10).

With Wagenseil (1715–77) and Bonno the old-style trumpet symphony in Vienna seems almost to be a forgotten tradition. Florid writing, extremes of range and boastful use of multiple trumpet choirs are no longer heard in imperial Vienna. Of the two dozen symphonies and two dozen overtures written during the 1760s and early 1770s by the court composer, Florian Leopold Gassmann (1729–74), only five of the overtures associated with Vienna have trumpet parts; three are in D major and none has prominent trumpeting. Not one of Gassmann's concert symphonies from the 1760s uses trumpets.[60] But to call them 'concert symphonies' may be inappropriate; perhaps these works by Gassmann are more properly chamber works in which a bold style is eschewed.

This trend away from brilliance in court music may not have coincided with public taste during the era of Maria Theresia and Joseph II. If we are to believe a rather sarcastic writer in the Viennese *Realzeitung der Wissenschaften, Künste und Kommerzien* for 1777 trumpeting in the theatre was still commonplace.

Geschmack an der Musik, den wird uns wohl niemand absprechen. Gluck und andere grosse Meister, die hier genährt, geehrt, bewundert werden, deren Hörsäle niemals leer stehen, immer die Zuschauer nicht fassen, sind Zeuge davon. Wann nun ein Mann aus Ober- oder Niedersachsen sich schleunig vor die Thüre eines unsrer Uftertheaters, zum Beyspiele vor die Thüre des *** Schauspielsaales, versezt sähe, wenn er die Einladung zur prächtigsten musikalischen Akademie angeheftet fände. Die Neugierde triebe ihn hinein. Pauken und Trompeten beärbten und Unschlittdampf aber erstickte ihn. Würde er wohl recht haben, wenn er deshalb den Wienern ein wenig ekle Nase und eben so wenig ekle Ohren andichten wollte?[61]

---

[58] A-Wn, Cod. 18234 and 18021.
[59] The symphony is edited by J. Kucaba in *Georg Christoph Wagenseil, Fifteen Symphonies*, in *The Symphony 1720–1840*, B/iii (New York, 1981), pp. 149–80.
[60] According to G. R. Hill, *A Thematic Catalog of the Instrumental Music of Florian Leopold Gassmann* (Hackensack, 1976).
[61] 'Theatral-nachrichten, Vierzigster Brief', *K.k. Allergnädigst privilegirte Realzeitung der Wissenschaften, Künste und Kommerzien 1777*, p. 190.

Ex. 2.10 Wagenseil, Symphony (Kucaba C7), 1st mvt

Taste in music, no one will deny us that. Gluck and other great masters who are nourished, honoured and admired here, whose productions are never empty and are always oversubscribed, are indicative of this. If a man from Upper or Lower Saxony were to find himself suddenly transported to the front door of one of our down-and-out theatres, for example to the door of the *** Theatre, where he'd find posted the invitation to the most illustrious concert, curiosity would drive him in. But timpani and trumpets would numb him, and the tallow candle smoke would choke him. Would he be right if he were therefore to ascribe to the Viennese little sense of smell and, likewise, little sense of hearing?

Though fanfares were still heard in theatres, after c. 1770 the overtures and symphonies preserved only the key of C major and the associated martial style with fanfare rhythms and flourishes.

Notable exceptions to this characterization are two symphonies in C major (Brown I: C9 and 10) by the Viennese composer Carlo d'Ordonez (1734–86),[62] certainly composed before 1775 and probably from the 1760s. In its scoring Symphony C10 imitates the old opera overtures for the *Gala Festtage*, but in a scaled-down version; instead of two full choirs, each choir now consists of a pair of *clarini* and timpani with a standard late eighteenth-century orchestra of oboes, horns and four-part strings. The trumpet writing includes conspicuous fanfares and mildly florid passages (Ex. 2.11, pp. 52–5). Most notable are the 'double stops' in the timpani part. The form of a movement is a synthesis of

[62] See A.P. Brown, *Carlo d'Ordonez (1734–1786): A Thematic Catalogue* (Detroit, 1978), pp. 30–33.

ritornello and sonata procedures (Ex. 2.12, p. 56), but without repeats of exposition and development/recapitulation; it comes close to that found in Wagenseil's *L'olimpiade* (1749).[63] The 'Andante più tosto adagio' is an aria for solo oboe and three-part strings with cadenzas at the end of the exposition and recapitulation. The finale duplicates the approach of the first movement.

Symphony C9 is, for the early 1770s, a thoroughly up-to-date piece with standard scoring plus a pair of trumpets and timpani. The first movement begins and concludes with a slow section of fanfares and flourishes, framing a central allegro that contains developed references to the introductory material. Such a frame and the totally soloistic nature of the fanfares hark back to Fux and Caldara. After an andantino for strings, Ordonez's finale, strongly shaped by sectional colours, again recalls Caldara's much briefer third movements. Where Caldara's finales were often marches, Ordonez uses a gavotte imbued with martial style and timbre. This highly accomplished symphony must have satisfied a nostalgia for the past as well as the eighteenth-century preference for the new. According to the copy from Svaty Jur in Slovakia, this symphony was used appropriately for the Festival of the Three Kings.

Ordonez's two symphonies are direct derivatives of the Viennese trumpet sinfonia tradition. In the works of Joseph Haydn (1732–1809), who was brought up on the repertoire at St Stephen's, reminiscences are more difficult to pinpoint except that in some works the C major affect remains. Of Landon's fifteen examples mentioned at the beginning of this essay, Nos. 37 and 63 should probably be eliminated from the subgenre since both lack authentic trumpet and timpani parts. In addition, both works, as well as No. 20, do not possess the requisite ceremonial character of fanfares and flourishes, and do not have the brilliance of sound fostered by an extended upward range. In Symphonies Nos. 32, 33 and, possibly, 38 a brilliant clarino sound is present, particularly if one accepts the hypothesis that C alto horns were used with *clarini* and timpani.[64] If these works were for horns in C basso, they not only would lose much of their brilliance but would gain a muddied texture which does not accord at all with the C major tradition. Finally, the *clarini* parts in Symphonies Nos. 32 and 33 rise to c^3 and b^2 respectively (Ex 2.13, pp. 58–61); they are clearly exceptional among Haydn's early symphonies. Thus, Haydn's symphonies from the time before he entered the service of the Esterházy family seem to ignore many of the traditional features of trumpet writing. If these pieces have a mid-century connection, it is probably with a work like Wagenseil's Symphony C7 (see Ex. 2.10, pp. 48–50); but it must be emphasized that the imperial court composer's clarino parts are much more exposed and demanding than Haydn's. Thus, Haydn represents another step away from the clarino style.

[63] A-Wn, Cod. 18234.
[64] The hypothesis is questioned by P. Bryan in 'The Horn in the Works of Mozart and Haydn: Some Observations and Comparisons', *Haydn Yearbook*, ix (1975), pp. 222–8.

Ex. 2.11 Ordonez, Symphony (1760s?) (Brown I:C10), 1st mvt

THE TRUMPET OVERTURE AND SINFONIA IN VIENNA 55

Ex. 2.12 Ordonez, Symphony (Brown I:C10), form of 1st mvt

Exposition

P	T	1S	2S	K
Ritornello		Episode		Ritornello
Fanfare	Brilliant	Singing	Brilliant	Fanfare
Trumpets	Tutti	Strings a 3	Strings a 4	Tutti
I		V		V
b. 1	b. 9	b. 20	b. 27	b. 35

Development

K	T	N
Ritornello		
Fanfare vs. Brilliant →		Brilliant
I		vi
b. 42	b. 45	b. 61

Recapitulation

P	S	T	2S	P
Ritornello	Episode			Ritornello
Fanfare	Singing	Brilliant	Brilliant	Fanfare
Trumpets	Strings a 3		Strings a 4	Tutti
I	I			
b. 69	b. 77	b. 81	b. 85	b. 103

Symphonies Nos. 41, 48, 50 and 60 represent a new type of trumpet piece in which the brass scoring is assigned to C alto horns only; during this period there were no trumpets on the Esterházy payroll.[65] Of this group, symphonies Nos. 41 and 50 barely hint at characteristic material: in No. 41 only seven bars in the exposition (bb. 12–18) and recapitulation, and in No. 50 only the slow introduction. Symphony No. 48, known as the 'Maria Theresia', probably because it was performed during her visit to Eszterháza in 1773 but almost certainly composed earlier,[66] is the most regal of the works for C alto horns. Fanfares with a corona figure, flourishes and orchestral hammerstrokes pervade substantial portions of the first movement (Ex. 2.14, pp. 62–3) and are not entirely absent from the minuet and finale. The symphony contains a full range of expression in its first movement, mixing majestic moments with darker

---

[65] This does not mean that trumpeters were not used as part of the *Hof- und Feld* contingent at the Esterházy court. Whether these players ever participated in orchestral performances is an open question.

[66] According to the Joseph Elssler copy in the Matica Slovenská in Martin, Slovakia. A facsimile of the orchestral parts was published by the archive in 1982.

passages (bb. 12–17, 53–63). No. 60, the incidental music to the Regnard play *Le distrait*,[67] is filled with satirical ceremonial fanfares that appear in the first, second, fourth and fifth movements of this six-movement symphony; its popularity was such that Haydn referred to it in later years as 'old tripe' ('den alten Schmarn').[68] In later sources, all three of these symphonies contain trumpet and timpani parts, only some of which may be authentic. Authentic or not, their existence reveals the perceived character of these works.

A third Haydn type emerges in the 1770s; the trumpeting and ceremonial character is wedded to the idiom of the symphony as it existed during the last quarter of the eighteenth century. Beginning with Symphony No. 56 and continuing with Nos. 69, 82, 90 (finale) and 97, Haydn is able to preserve a trumpeting character in a context that is stylistically more diverse.

It is a mistake to associate trumpeting and ceremonial music only with the imperial key of C major, for the Italian trumpet key of D major with its own associations is hinted at in Symphonies Nos. 70 and 96. By the 1790s Haydn extends the character of works in C and D to other keys. For example, in Symphony No. 94 ('Surprise') Haydn originally conceived the trumpet writing for instruments in G, and wrote out such parts for the first movement before re-writing them in C. The original parts in G lend the first movement an almost Baroque brilliance. In 1796 Haydn composed the Trumpet Concerto in E♭ (Hob.VIIe: 1) for a keyed trumpet developed by the Viennese trumpeter Anton Weidinger, who had risen through the court ranks as a *Hofscholar* with the court *Oberhoftrompeter* Peter Neubold.[69] Here, the Trumpet writing brings together two previously irreconcilable styles: fanfares based on the overtone series, and cantabile writing using both diatonic and chromatic materials in the *principale* register. At the same time, Haydn also revived a motive that was one of the favoured Viennese Baroque clarino figures (Ex. 2.15, p. 64). However, it is played neither by the strings nor by the trumpet at the extreme of its range, but rather in the area between the *principale* and clarino registers.

Mozart's true trumpet symphonies came relatively late, even though both he and his father Leopold had written concertos; Wolfgang's concerto, now lost, dates from his first visit to Vienna in 1767 and is associated with the city's Waisenhaus. For Mozart, C major in orchestral music was a key diminished in importance by D major, which likewise contained fanfares and flourishes. It was not until the move to Vienna in 1781 that he exploited C major with its attendant trumpeting and ceremonial character in symphonic music. Though Symphony No. 34 (K338) was the last composed in Salzburg, it was – if the

---

[67] See the explication of the relationship of symphony and play by R. A. Green, '"Il Distratto" of Regnard and Haydn: A Re-examination', *Haydn Yearbook*, xi (1980), pp. 183–95; and E. Sisman, 'Haydn's Theater Symphonies', *Journal of the American Musicological Society*, xliii (1990), pp. 311–21.
[68] See H. C. Robbins Landon, *Haydn: Chronicle and Works. Haydn: The Late Years 1801–1809* (London, 1977), pp. 262–3.
[69] R. Dahlquist, *The Keyed Trumpet*, p. 10.

Ex. 2.13
(a) Haydn, Symphony No. 32, 1st mvt

(b) Haydn, Symphony No. 33, 1st mvt

Ex. 2.14 Haydn, Symphony No. 48, 1st mvt

Ex. 2.15 Haydn, Trumpet Concerto (Hob.VIIe: 1), origins of figure from 3rd mvt

Haydn, Trumpet Concerto

Ordonez, Symphony C10

Reutter, Servizio di Tavola

Reutter, Clarino Concerto

Reutter, *La speranza*

Reutter, Chorus of Soldiers from *Ciro in Armenia*

Birck, Regina Coeli

Tuma, Sonata

hypotheses are correct – the work Mozart used repeatedly during his first year in the imperial city.[70] And K338 is Mozart's first convincing example of a trumpet symphony of a type Haydn had been composing from c. 1773. Fanfares and flourishes become established motifs in the first movements of Symphonies Nos. 35 in D (K385, 'Haffner'), 36 in C (K425, 'Linz'), 38 in D (K504, 'Prague'), 39 in E♭ (K543) and 41 in C (K551, 'Jupiter'), as well as in the symphonically conceived piano concertos, K415, K467, K503 and K537.

The 'Jupiter' symphony (K551) has been subjected to a panoply of analyses and observations dealing with its formal, contrapuntal and other properties. I view the first movement and finale, with their fanfares and flourishes, as belonging to a trumpeting tradition. The emphasis placed on the contrapuntal aspects of the finale has obscured the dual tradition of its closing material, which serves as a recurring refrain at the end of the primary (bb. 19–35), transition (bb. 65–73) and closing (bb. 136–57) sections of the exposition (Ex. 2.16). Each time the material recurs, it has greater contrapuntal momentum, progressing from pure fanfare, to imitation, and then in canon, stretto and inversion. One can also view this as an effort to recapture the effect of multi-choired groups of trumpets responding to proclamations.

Mozart's last opera, *La clemenza di Tito*, composed for the coronation festivities in Prague of Leopold II, conforms to the new Emperor's preferred taste. It was Leopold who was to re-establish a company in Vienna to perform opera seria,[71] and the choice by the Bohemian estates of an old Metastasio libretto as the basis of a coronation opera was no accident. It was also no accident that the work is filled with old imperial trappings that hark back to the era of Charles VI; it is C major with fanfares, flourishes and pealing bells that begin the evening. Again, it was perhaps no accident that – in modern parlance – the recapitulation of the overture is reversed, a structure that reminds one of the ritornello tendencies of the old trumpet overtures. Much about *Tito* indicates that Mozart was familiar with its tradition as a *dramma per musica* extending back to its first setting by Caldara in 1734.

Beethoven's First Symphony (op. 21) has been shown by Carl Schachter to be in some ways modelled on Mozart's 'Jupiter'.[72] An early review in the *Allgemeine musikalische Zeitung* complained that the symphony was 'more a wind band piece than orchestral music' ('mehr Harmonie, als ganze Orchestermusik'),[73] a statement that in part reflects the prominence of horns, trumpets

---

[70] See, for example, N. Zaslaw, *Mozart's Symphonies: Context, Performance Practice, Reception* (Oxford, 1989), p. 361.

[71] According to J. A. Rice, 'Emperor and Impresario: Leopold II and the Transformation of Viennese Musical Theater, 1790–92' (Ph.D. diss., University of California, Berkeley, 1987), especially pp. 57–89. A complete documentary summary is found in H.C. Robbins Landon, *1791: Mozart's Last Year* (London, 1988), pp. 102–21.

[72] C. Schachter, 'Mozart's Last and Beethoven's First: Echoes of K.551 in Op. 21', in C. Eisen, ed., *Mozart Studies* (Oxford, 1991), pp. 227–251.

[73] *Allgemeine musikalische Zeitung*, iii (15 October 1800), col. 49.

Ex. 2.16 Mozart, 'Jupiter' Symphony (K551), 4th mvt

and timpani. It should no longer be necessary to view the C major trumpeting portions of Symphony No. 5 as having anything to do with music in post-revolutionary France; a tradition closer to home would serve the historical cause more persuasively. In fact, the beginning of the Fifth Symphony's finale could easily be related to the march-like conclusions of Caldara's trumpet sinfonias/overtures. Also belonging to this military trumpeting style are the piano concertos in C, G and E♭. The finale to the G major concerto (op. 58) features a conflict between its C major fanfare refrains and its home key of G major.

Finally, Beethoven's C major overture, *The Consecration of the House* (op. 124), composed in 1822, presents an all-encompassing statement of imperial musical taste, displaying nearly every musical emblem of the old Austrian Monarchy: resounding chords to test the acoustics of the Josephstädter Theater, a solemn march with dotted rhythms, trumpet fanfares with rushing scales in the bassoons, and flourishes that evolve into a double fugue. The occasion of its first performance, on the eve of the Emperor's birthday, brings to mind the overtures to operas by Fux and Caldara that celebrated the namedays and birthdays of Charles VI and Elisabeth Christine. Thus, Beethoven's overture brings history full circle. Op. 124 almost certainly brought the same ceremonial message to audiences in early nineteenth-century Vienna as the trumpet overtures, sonatas and the like had a century earlier to the subjects of Charles VI.

3

The early Classical violin concerto in Austria

CHAPPELL WHITE

The focus of this essay is on solo violin concertos produced by Austrian composers between the middle of the eighteenth century and c. 1780.[1] I will attempt to place the early Classical Austrian concerto in relation to others of the time, to discover its special characteristics and, finally, to suggest possible reasons for the secondary position it occupies in music of this time. The discussion will centre on those aspects which seem of specific importance to the genre: texture, tutti–solo relationship, the exhibition of virtuosity, and form. In all of these elements, but most especially in form, the development from Baroque to Classical has added interest because of the position occupied in the older style by the violin concerto; it is the only mature, well-established instrumental genre of the late Baroque that survived through to the Classical period.

The evidence about this limited repertory comes from the works of fifteen composers and some fifty concertos.[2] The number is small for a period of thirty years, compared to Austrian output in other instrumental genres; but the Austrian violin concerto was not an international type, nor was it favoured by some of the most illustrious Austrian composers. While Austria exported symphonies it imported violin concertos, brought into its repertory by numerous touring virtuosos. The concertos of these visitors, while by no means representing a different musical language, will be of concern here largely for comparison. It should be said, however, that geographical and political divisions are often arbitrary; there are other composers, especially those of other middle European areas, who share specific Austrian characteristics – such men, for example, as Joseph Riepel (1709–82) in Regensburg and Antonio Rosetti (c. 1750–92) at Wallerstein.

[1] Most of the material presented here resulted from research done for a larger study. Readers interested in more detailed evidence, as well as a wider geographical and historical organization, are referred to the author's *From Vivaldi to Viotti: A History of the Early Classical Violin Concerto* (Philadelphia, 1992).
[2] The composers are M. G. Monn (1717–50), Wagenseil (1715–77), Schlöger (1722–66), Starzer (1726/7–87), Asplmayr (1728–86), Joseph Haydn (1732–1809), Michael Haydn (1737–1806), Dittersdorf (1739–99), Vanhal (1739–1813), Hofmann (1738–93), Ordonez (1734–86), Mozart (1756–91), Pichl (1741–1805), L. Tomasini (1741–1808) and Lamotte (?1751–?81).

At mid-century the violin concerto was still basically an Italian form, enthusiastically cultivated throughout much of Europe. As the development of instrumental music moved inexorably northward and Italian violinists increasingly left home for the prosperous northern cities and courts, the centre for the violin concerto began to shift. In late 1764 and early 1765, after a lapse of nearly twenty years, two sets of violin concertos – six by Johann Stamitz (1717–57), six by Pierre Gaviniès (1727–1800) – were published in Paris. These were the first in an increasing flow of Parisian publications, and the city quickly became the focal point for the violin concerto. A cosmopolitan type of violin concerto emerged, created by composers of various nationalities who were drawn to Paris both by its famous public concerts and by publication opportunities. In this cosmopolitan Parisian concerto, national characteristics were in large part subsumed into an international early Classical style.

Texture, however, is one of the more persistent of national characteristics in the early Classical violin concerto; the marked contrast in this aspect of style is between the Italian and north German concerto. The Vivaldian solo concerto had established as a virtual principle that the orchestra should not obscure or compete with the soloist in the solo episode. As the accompaniment of bass alone faded in popularity in the 1750s, Giuseppe Tartini (1692–1770) established in his late concertos the extreme of the reduced accompaniment in the new style: two violins only – no viola, no bass; and equally as marked as the resulting thin sonority was the lack of significant, varied rhythmic activity in the accompaniment.

Only a few Italians outside Tartini's immediate circle followed him to such a consistent extreme. Although two-part accompaniment is a frequent intermittent choice with all Italian composers, the conventional Italian accompaniment, even through to the 1780s, consists of three parts – two violins and bass. Violas, like winds if they are present, rest in all solo passages. This was the normal full accompaniment for such composers as Pugnani (1731–98), who began in the 1750s, and Giornovichi (c. 1740–1804), whose last concerto appeared in the mid-1790s; and it is characteristic even in Italian concertos written for, and often published in, northern centres. A striking example of this persistence is seen in its consistent use in the two violin concertos of Luigi Tomasini, whose entire career was spent as Haydn's associate at the Esterházy court.

The difference between Italian and north German texture does not hinge on learned fugal polyphony – that is uncommon everywhere in the early Classical concerto. The difference is that north Germans frequently include violas in a four-part accompaniment, and this thicker sonority contains more important rhythmic figures and, occasionally, even motivic material. The most influential of the north German composers in this respect was Franz Benda (1709–86), violinist at the court of Frederick the Great.

The texture of Austrian concertos stands between the two extremes of Italian and north German practice, and it tends to be more varied than either. The influence from the north — and Benda's concertos are well represented in Austrian collections — blends with the traditional influence from the south. Austrian composers exhibit a typically Italianate concern for the clarity of the solo line, marking the contrast especially at the beginning of a solo section; but changes in sonority and in rhythmic patterns as well are an important resource for variety. A thin, airy background with decisive rhythmic punctuation may contrast with a thicker, more continuous background in a fashion limited only by the composer's imagination. A simple passage from Mozart's first concerto furnishes a characteristic illustration (Ex. 3.1).

Wind instruments do not play a major role in the early Classical violin concerto. Their use in tutti is conventional and limited, and they seldom play in the solo passages.[3] With the publication of Gaviniès's six concertos in 1765, two oboes and two horns become the standard for Parisian publications; but since the parts are almost always *ad libitum*, even if assigned a brief melody in a tutti passage, their significance is limited. Austrian concertos, surviving almost entirely in manuscript, are more likely to be for strings alone. Dittersdorf's seventeen concertos, for example, probably date from the early 1760s to perhaps as late as 1775. Four include oboes and horns, three include horns without oboes; the other ten (not all of which survive) are for strings only. Chronology seems to have little to do with the addition of winds, and we can only assume that their inclusion was determined by the local situation. As illustrated in Haydn's two (possibly three) violin concertos (Hob.VIIa: 1, 3 and 4), it is not uncommon for manuscripts to include winds in one location and omit them in another. Aside from occasional substitution of flutes for oboes, winds other than pairs of oboes and horns are quite rare until well into the 1780s.[4]

Closely related to the stylistic element of texture is the relationship between tutti and solo. (I refer here not to the repetition of melodic material but to brief alternations, usually in the form of tutti interjections into essentially solo sections.) Short alternations were sometimes an effective element in Vivaldi's style; but the tendency of the early Classical style to produce a markedly sectional structure did not encourage quick interchange, and the practice almost disappears in the more progressive Italian concertos of the 1750s and 1760s.

In north Germany, the older practice of flexible tutti–solo interchange continued. Probably the most telling use of the brief tutti interjection occurs with the creation of a brief, prominent motive that returns as a kind of motto at

---

[3] The most striking and most numerous exceptions to this convention are found, not surprisingly, in the concertos of Mozart.

[4] The limitations of instrumentation and of accompaniment sonority persisted in Paris at least through the 1780s. There is some evidence that Vienna may have preceded Paris in the expansion of the violin concerto orchestra. See White, *From Vivaldi to Viotti*, p. 65.

Ex. 3.1 Mozart, Concerto in B♭ (K207) (1773), 1st mvt

significant points in the solo passages. More common, but less significant structurally, is the interjection of a bar or two of tutti to create some form of punctuating division between phrases.

For many critics who value the special medium of the concerto, flexibility in the relationship between tutti and solo is an essential element, for in that relationship lies the potential of confrontation. Shifts from equal co-operation to subservience, even to combat, are a potent source for drama. In so far as this element is preserved in the violin concerto through the 1770s, it happens largely in Austria. The second generation of Benda's most successful students – those who appeared internationally in the 1770s, his son Friedrich Wilhelm (1745–1814), his nephew Friedrich Ludwig (1746–92), Carl Haack (1760–1827) and Joseph Fodor (1751–1828) – show no interest in exploiting a dramatic or intimate relationship between tutti and solo. Like the second generation of Mannheim violinists, they adopt the cosmopolitan Parisian style in which, brilliant though the orchestra may be in tutti sections, the purpose of the structure is to provide an effective frame for the solo.

The Austrian composers are not untouched by this widespread view of the purpose of a concerto, but the best of them – Joseph Haydn, Michael Haydn, Dittersdorf, Pichl and above all Mozart – did not forget the potential of a varied relationship between tutti and solo. Returning tutti cadences and connecting passages are frequent. One finds occasional instances of echoes between orchestra and solo, of solo providing accompaniment to the orchestra, and of interest equally divided. While no other composer comes close to Mozart in the variety of the tutti–solo relationship, it is obvious that such imaginative interaction as seen in Ex. 3.2 represents only the best of a practice common in Austrian concertos.

Ex. 3.2 Mozart, Concerto in G (K216) (1775), 1st mvt

The exhibition of virtuosity is essential to the solo concerto, and to none more so than the solo violin concerto. Yet we should not mistake the nature of eighteenth-century virtuosity as being concerned exclusively with the overcoming of difficulties. For the violinist, as for the singer, the production of tone is an element in display; and in the early Classical style, the ability to charm the listener was as important as the ability to astonish.

The evolution of technique in the early Classical violin concerto is not a steady progression towards greater difficulties. On the contrary, the early forays into galant style in the violin concerto are markedly easier than examples of late Baroque virtuosity. We may turn again to Tartini for illustration. His early concertos, while not so extreme as Locatelli's famous caprices, show characteristic Baroque difficulties, and they exploit the upper range at least to a^4 – i.e. seventh position. His late concertos, with much less elaborate figuration, do not go above third position.

Tartini is extreme in his renunciation of difficulties, but the trend towards technical simplicity is general in the 1750s and much of the 1760s. Virtuosity as the conquest of amazing technical difficulties returns with a vengeance in the person of Antonio Lolli (c. 1725–1802), the true eighteenth-century precursor of Paganini. Everywhere he played, Lolli was met with astonishment and sensational success, but always there was a negative reaction too. Vienna, which among the great capitals heard him first, welcomed him warmly in 1763, but some people had doubts. Dittersdorf, who later became Lolli's close friend, probably summed up the reactions of the best musicians. When told he must imitate Lolli, he replied 'God forbid! . . . I must do exactly the opposite, and try to cut a better figure in the adagio through good solid playing and expression' ('Behute Gott! . . . Ich muss gerade das Gegenteil tun, und durch solides Spielen und Ausdruck in Adagio abzustechen suchen').[5]

Lolli's influence was nevertheless widespread. Most violinists may have been unwilling or unable to follow him to that extent, but they could not ignore his success with audiences. Yet in the Austrian courts and monasteries, and even in Vienna where private or semi-public concerts never occupied the central position that was held in Paris by the fully public Concert Spirituel and Concert des Amateurs, the impact of technical exploits was less than in the French capital. Austrian concertos, without renouncing virtuosity, remained conservative (Ex. 3.3).

Ex. 3.3 Starzer, Concerto in F (c. 1775), 3rd mvt

Display in the Baroque concerto had been carried out in large part through ornamentation, either written or improvised, and in the familiar sequential expansion of the so-called *Fortspinnung* technique. Improvised embellishment of melodies continued to some degree in the new style, but declined in importance; and *Fortspinnung* gave way to melody and passage work. It was in this tendency of the early Classical style to separate and clearly differentiate between melodic sections, on the one hand, and transition and closing sections, on the other, that composers found a means for technical display. These sections of rapid figurative, non-motivic passage work became the structural points at which brilliant difficulties could be exploited. Thus, the ability to make these

---

[5] N. Miller, ed., *Karl Ditters von Dittersdorfs Lebensbeschreibung*, Lebensläufe, Biographien, Erinnerungen, Briefe, xii (Munich, 1967), p. 126.

passages both brilliant and functionally interesting is one of the most essential talents of the successful composer of violin concertos.

Often the degree of difficulty in passage work is determined not simply by the extremity of the range or by the occasional phrase that is technically awkward; rather, it is dependent on the length of the passage work and the proportion that lies in the upper register. It is in this connection that Austrian composers appear rather restrained. The upper limit of the instrument in virtuoso concertos was commonly a^4 (seventh position), often extended to c^5 and occasionally even to e^5; but the extreme upper register may be reserved for a climactic ending, and the scope of passage work may be distinctly limited. It is these limitations that separate the conservative display of most Austrians from the extremes of Lolli and his imitators and, to a lesser extent, from the brilliance of such French virtuosos as Saint-Georges (1739–89). In Lolli, passage work all but overwhelms melody, and the display remains in the upper range for line after line. In Haydn, Dittersdorf, Vanhal, Mozart, Pichl and other Austrians of lesser talent, extremes are limited and made to function within a calculated balance of musical elements (Ex. 3.4).

Ex. 3.4 Dittersdorf, Concerto in A (before 1773) (Krebs deest)

I turn, finally, to form. This is not the place for a detailed account of the interesting development of first-movement form in the violin concerto. Suffice it to say that the early Classical period is marked by the gradual growth of sonata-form principles and their eventual integration with the old ritornello principles. By the 1760s, we can identify the widely used conventional form inherited from Vivaldi: four tutti sections in the key sequence of tonic, dominant, relative minor to tonic, and tonic, separated by solo sections. For the purpose of this essay, I will make only three brief points on the relationship of this form to the Classical sonata form developed concurrently in other genres.

First, concerning thematic material: while it is indisputable that tonality is the basis of Classical form, it is also true that thematic material increasingly played an articulating role in the structure. In concerto form, repetition of the opening motive in the dominant helped move the ritornello form towards binary form; its repetition in all four tutti passages, as was common in the 1750s and even later, preserved to some extent the basic role of the ritornello in the articulation of the large form. As these decisive thematic repetitions in the tutti passages became less popular, the emphasis moved closer to a sonata form that was complete in the solos, with the tutti providing framing introduction and closing sections.

Second, concerning development: whatever we may consider as basic principles of sonata form, the central section of the form is usually marked by the use of familiar motives in a developmental texture. This characteristic is foreign to most early Classical concertos. The second solo, corresponding to the 'development' section, may begin (as in binary form) with the principal motive in the dominant but, increasingly, this becomes less common. The central section is characteristically constructed from new material, often presenting more than one new melody. Modulation to the relative minor or relative of the dominant is usual, but fragmentation and further tonal instability are rare.

And third, concerning recapitulation: two principles are usually thought to be involved in recapitulation, the simultaneous return of the tonic and the opening theme, and the transposition from dominant to tonic of some portion of the subsidiary material. Throughout the thirty-odd years of the early Classical period these principles are ignored or applied variously; in the violin concerto, the recapitulation is the last of sonata form principles to be conventionalized.

The following simple diagrams show three first movements, each by a different composer. The upper line represents the material, the second shows tutti or solo, the third the tonal plan, the fourth bar numbers, and the fifth correlation with sonata form.

Haydn, Concerto in C (Hob.VIIa: 1) (?c. 1761–5)

a	b	c	a	d	e	b'	c	a	b"
T			S			T		S	
I	V	I	I	V		V		V ii	–
1	16	29	40	57	82	101	113	124	137

'Exposition' .... 'Development'

e	e	a	d	e	b'	c
	T		S		T	
vi	vi–V	I	I		I	
188	195	205	231	246	261	275–85

.... 'Recapitulation' ....

Gaviniès, Concerto in A, Op. 4 No. 5 (published in 1764)

a	b	a	a'	c	b	a'		
T			S	T	S		T	
I	I	I	I	V	V	V–iii–vi	vi	
1	20	46	51	77	111	137	193	

'Exposition' .... 'Development'....

a	b'	a	
	S	T	
I	I	I	
195	197	239	247–51

'Recapitulation'.................

Simon Leduc, Concerto in C, Op. posth. (c. 1772–7)

a	b	a	c	d	a	e	f	b	a
T	S			T	S				T
I	I	I–V	V	V	V	vi	I	I	
1	29	54	76	88	117	133	155	182	216–22

'Exposition' .... 'Development' 'Recapitulation'

Haydn's movement, early though it is, could almost serve as a textbook model of concerto form. The second and third tuttis do not use the opening motive; in the recapitulation, the clear double return belongs to the solo and all the material in the dominant key is transposed; and while the technique in the second solo is far from that in a mature Haydn symphony, it comes close to true development. In this movement, the defining force of the form has to some extent moved from tutti to solo, with the tutti assuming the role of introduction, transition and closing sections.

Gaviniès also uses closing material in the second tutti; like Haydn, he opens the second solo with the first theme, as in binary form, but continues with unrelated passage work. His recapitulation, with its very brief reference to the first theme, is not so decisive as Haydn's, the resolution being most strongly felt at the solo transposition of subsidiary material. Leduc (c. 1745–77) omits the modulating tutti, a design quite rare in an Austrian or German concerto. All three tuttis in the Leduc concerto state the opening theme, with the last one following the transposition in solo of a subsidiary melody, in sonata-form terms a reversed recapitulation. And Leduc's modulating second solo ('development') presents two new melodies.

The two French composers were talented creators and competent craftsmen; their shaping of form is neither confused nor old-fashioned. These movements simply reflect the lack of firmly established conventions at some critical points in the design: some aspects of the resulting flexibility could be demonstrated also in the concertos of the Stamitz brothers, Giornovichi and even the first concertos of Viotti (1755–1824).

Not all Austrian composers, and not Haydn himself in his rather later A major concerto, move consistently towards the sonata-form principles that are implied in his C major concerto. Under the cosmopolitan Parisian influence, the trend in Austria is towards thematic variety rather than concentration. Nevertheless, and despite the lack of consistent evolutionary progress, Austrian composers are those most likely to bring the first-movement form into close relationship with sonata form. Mozart's first movements may again be the model: clear ritornello-sonata forms including recapitulation, but with new material in the 'development'. Concertos by Wenzel Pichl show quite similar characteristics, and a few by other composers, including a notable example by Asplmayr (D major, manuscript in the Gesellschaft der Musikfreunde, Vienna), show unusual thematic concentration.

For a long time in the development of the Classical concerto the first and last movements were considered to be in the same structure; the difference, if any, was in the character of the movement. The finale often had a close relationship to one of the conventional dance types. The consequent simplicity of melodic style might affect the large structural design; melodic repetition in the tutti might be more common than in the first movement, and melodic contrast more common in the solos. Thus, while the basic design of the four-ritornello form remained, the structure moved, not so much towards sonata form, as towards what later analysts were to call a modulating rondo.

Nevertheless, composers probably saw a distinct separation between the traditional ritornello finale and the rondo finale. The rondo was introduced into the Parisian violin concerto in the very late 1760s, possibly from London. It quickly became a fashion, and by 1771 the older type was a rarity in French publications. The rondo reached the Austrian concerto somewhat later. The case of Mozart is illustrative. His first concerto (K207), now known to be from 1773, has a ritornello finale; the other four (K211, K216, K218 and K219), composed in 1775, have rondos; slightly later, Mozart replaced the finale of his first concerto with a modern rondo (K269).

Of course, the vogue for the rondo in Austria in the middle 1770s was not confined to the concerto, and there were influences other than the specifically French. But there is evidence that the fashion of the rondo in the violin concerto came directly from Paris. Austrian finales of the ritornello type, if not derived from a moderate dance such as the minuet, were usually in a faster tempo than the first movement. The French rondo, on the other hand, was typically an allegretto; its refrain was simple, tuneful, squarely regular in structure, closely related to the style of popular French song. Simplicity was also typical of the overall structure: clear sections, contrast rather than unity of material, limited modulations, no tendencies towards what is termed sonata-rondo form. These characteristics are obvious in a number of Austrian rondo finales (Ex. 3.5).

Ex. 3.5 Pichl, Concerto in B♭ (Amsterdam, c. 1779), 3rd mvt

But the Parisian influence is tempered. Even this simple, regularly structured melody from Pichl has more variety than the majority of Parisian rondo themes. Michael Haydn's single rondo finale in his A major concerto (MH207, c. 1773/5) shows the typical simple structure; but it is a presto tempo, it greatly exceeds the French rondo in length, and it incorporates a sonata-like recapitulation of episodic material in the final refrain. As for Mozart, his rondos have something of the French character and simplicity, but in each of the final three concertos, at least one episode contains a contrast that is nothing less than startling.

The slow movement shows some parallels with the formal developments in the finale, but no particular type dominates as does the rondo finale after its establishment in Paris. The Italian slow movement was often devoted entirely to the solo violin accompanied, not by bass alone as was common earlier, but by reduced strings – often Tartini's favourite two violins. These Italian solos were generally brief, binary in form, and monothematic. Among the Germans, the ritornello form continued to be favoured and contributed to the tendency towards longer slow movements. There were seldom more than three ritornellos, however, and even more markedly than in the first movement the form was binary. The structure is comparable to a small aria (an arietta or cavatina) and by the 1760s it is often bi-thematic. Whether or not we should call it a small sonata form may depend on the presence or absence of a central section corresponding to a development and on the degree of conformity to recapitulation principles.

In the first years of Parisian publications after 1765, the slow movements were cast in one or other of these two types, or some mixture of the two. The length generally tended towards Italian preference for brevity. About 1770 another type of slow movement emerged in Paris: the *romance*. This word became somewhat ambiguous in the nineteenth century, but in 1770 it still referred quite specifically to a simple type of French song. In instrumental music these songs could serve as the basis for variations or a rondo form. Pichl had introduced the *romance* into the Austrian symphony as early as 1766 in a symphony in E♭,[6] and Haydn's variations on a *romance* in Symphony No. 85 ('La reine') are well known. Violinists, perhaps surprisingly, shunned variations in the concerto and used only a ternary or (rarely) a five-part rondo form.

The simplicity and the regularity of both small and large structures in the *romance* represent an extreme of the galant style for the slow movement. It was fashionable with visiting virtuosos in Paris, but much less so with native French composers. Austrian concerto writers, with the single exception of Franz Lamotte, did not go to Paris and apparently did not use the *romance* at all in the years up to c. 1780. For the violin virtuoso, the *romance* must have been closely associated with Paris, something for visitors to use as a polite tribute to their hosts. Not until the mid-1780s did the *romance* exert an appeal for Austrian composers who were not directly concerned with Parisian fashion.

Thus Austrian violinists stayed mainly with aria-like sonata structures for their slow movements, occasionally reverting to the Italianate solo. While the fashion for the bare simplicity and regularity of the *romance* affected their melodic style to some extent, a brief comparison of two openings illustrates that differences remained (Ex. 3.6). For the finest examples of the type of movement most characteristic of Austria, one should turn again to the last three violin concertos of Mozart.

Why does the violin concerto in Austria occupy such a secondary position during this period? A sizeable percentage of all eighteenth-century violin concertos was written by virtuosos for their own performance, but very few of the Austrian concerto writers were primarily violinists throughout their careers. On our list of fifteen, at least four, not counting Mozart, were best known as keyboard players: Monn, Wagenseil, Schlöger and Michael Haydn. Mozart's resistance to the career of a violin virtuoso is well documented. Dittersdorf, the most prolific, was certainly a virtuoso performer, but the growth of his reputation after his early years was based on his symphonies, his stage works, and his success as a leader. Vanhal, Starzer and Asplmayr were violinists; but the first ceased professional performance quite early and lived by composition, teaching and publication, while the other two concentrated on ballet music. Both Pichl and Tomasini earned their livelihood by playing the violin and were evidently excellent technicians, but neither achieved nor, indeed, sought

---

[6] This symphony was later published in Paris as the work of Dittersdorf (Krebs 41). M. G. Grave, 'First-movement Form as a Measure of Ditterdorf's Symphonic Development' (2 vols., Ph.D. diss., New York University, 1977), ii, p. 531. Date from the catalogue of Pichl's symphonies in *The Symphony 1720–1840. Reference Volume: Contents of the Set and Collected Thematic Indexes* (New York and London, 1986), p. 417, no. 6.

Ex. 3.6
(a) Giornovichi, Concerto No. 5 in E (Paris, before 1777), 2nd mvt

(b) Pichl, Concerto in B♭ (Amsterdam, c. 1779), 2nd mvt

international reputation. Franz Lamotte is the only internationally famous virtuoso in this group. A Netherlander by birth, he came to Vienna as a young man and became first violinist in the *Hofkapelle*. Burney called him the best soloist in Vienna.[7] But his first concertos, typical examples of cosmopolitan Parisian style, are publications resulting from appearances in Paris in 1775 and in London. He never returned to Vienna.

The violin concerto had little attraction as amateur salon music; its market was necessarily limited, and its distribution often depended on performance by the composer himself. Dozens of Austrian symphonies were published in Paris by composers who never left home, but such was not the case for the violin concerto. The late development of music publication in Austria and, probably, Vienna's lack of an established concert series, such as the Concert Spirituel in Paris, must have had a dampening effect on the production of violin concertos.

[7] P. Scholes, ed., *Dr. Burney's Musical Tours* (2 vols., London, 1959), ii, p. 125.

A more general reason for the limited interest of Austria's most illustrious composers may have been the stylistic tradition of the violin concerto. Growing as it did from a mature Baroque form, the violin concerto was still stylistically conservative relative to the symphony, the keyboard sonata and the string quartet, all genres associated from their beginnings with the new style. It was perhaps not only the rising prestige of the symphony and the marketability of chamber music that attracted the most original composers to these genres; it may also have been an outlook that encouraged new and imaginative solutions, an outlook lacking in the violin concerto.

Despite its secondary place internationally and its limited importance in the total repertory of Austrian instrumental music, the early Classical violin concerto of Austria has features that are both individual and enriching in comparison with the most favoured international type. These features include more varied texture and tutti–solo relationship, a less stereotyped finale and a stronger tendency towards progressive symphonic form. Its repertory contains, in addition to the three acknowledged masterpieces of Mozart, some of the most attractive examples of the time, pieces worthy of occasional revival in the limited modern repertory of violin concertos. And finally, the view provided by the violin concerto of early Classical style developing in an established Baroque form is of rare historical interest.

PART II

Traditions in sacred music

4

Haydn's *Missa sunt bona mixta malis* and the *a cappella* tradition

DAVID WYN JONES

For over 200 years Haydn's *Missa sunt bona mixta malis* (Hob.XXII: 2) was an unknown composition. The discovery of the autograph in 1983 cleared up a number of mysteries concerning the work, previously known only from its inclusion in two thematic catalogues associated with the composer, the *Entwurf Katalog* and the *Haydn Verzeichnis*.[1] First: it emerged that the work was a fragment rather than a complete setting of the text of the mass; Haydn completed a Kyrie movement and the Gloria as far as the clause 'Gratias agimus tibi' before, apparently, abandoning the composition. Second: the fragment was composed in 1768. Third: as some scholars had suspected, it was not a work for vocal forces and orchestra but an *a cappella* mass, scored for SATB chorus and continuo.

Whereas it is Haydn's only mass of this type it can be set alongside two later church compositions by the composer scored in a similar way, the offertory motet 'Non nobis, Domine' (Hob.XXIIIa: 1) and the 'Libera me' (Hob.XXIIb: 1★).[2] Together they constitute a very small part of Haydn's output but all three belong to a persistent tradition of *a cappella* liturgical music in eighteenth-century Austria.

A cappella music was performed at two particular periods in the church year, Lent and Advent, when instrumental accompaniment was deemed inappropriate. Through the century the repertoire was either newly composed or taken from a long accumulation of such pieces. The first modern author to discuss this repertoire was Karl Gustav Fellerer who, referring to the music as being in the 'Palestrina style', dealt with nearly fifty composers in eighteenth-century

---

[1] The autograph, together with music sketches and letters by Beethoven, Rossini, Schumann, Mendelssohn and others, was discovered in a farmhouse in Northern Ireland in 1983. The material was sold at Christie's auction house, London, on 28 March 1984. The mass is now in private possession.

I would like to record my thanks to Otto Biba for his ready assistance in the preparation of this essay.

[2] Neither of these works can be dated accurately. 'Non nobis, Domine' was composed before 1786; see D. W. Jones, 'A Spanish Source for Haydn's 'Non nobis, Domine'', *Haydn Yearbook*, xvii (1992), pp. 167–9. The 'Libera me' survives in only one source and it is possible that it was copied rather than composed by Haydn: see work-list in 'Haydn, Joseph', *The New Grove Dictionary of Music and Musicians*, ed. S. Sadie (London, 1980), viii, p. 361.

Italy and Germany, as well as Austria.[3] More recently, for Vienna, Friedrich Riedel has shown that the tradition can be traced back to the early seventeenth century when several codexes of Renaissance polyphonic music were acquired by the *Hofkapelle*.[4] For the early eighteenth-century Riedel records performances of *a cappella* works by Palestrina (c. 1525–94), Allegri (1582–1652, the famous Miserere), Legrenzi (1626–90), Ziani (c. 1653–1715), Fux (1660–1741), Alessandro Scarlatti (1660–1725), Caldara (c. 1670–1736), Reinhardt (1676/7–1742) and Palotta (c. 1688–1758). Of the modern composers who found a convenient liturgical location for the perpetuation of the Golden Age of Polyphony the most significant was Fux. He composed several dozen such works including five settings – possibly more – of the mass.[5] His Missa canonica (K7), composed in 1719, was especially esteemed; it was widely distributed, Michael Haydn copied it in 1757[6] and Joseph Haydn, too, owned a manuscript copy of the work.[7] More important than any single work, however, was Fux's treatise, *Gradus ad Parnassum* (1725), in which the composer sought to define the style in a way that was to influence its development in Austria throughout the eighteenth century. Perhaps the familiar terms 'Palestrina style' and 'stile antico' are unfortunate ones, in that they suggest a wholly conservative approach, as if the composer was writing in an alien, archaic style. For Fux, however, it was an up-to-date challenge. The 'stylus a capella', as he called it, is one of three contemporary styles of composition defined in the *Gradus*, to be set alongside 'stylus recitativus' and 'stylus mixtus', three styles that are introduced to the student once he has worked his way through the theoretical part of the treatise.[8] Fux subdivides the 'stylus a capella' into two: for voices only, and with organ and other doubling instruments; the latter 'enjoys more freedom of modulation and singing, and of structure' ('qui major, & modulandi, & canendi, vagandique gaudet libertate'). Thus 'stylus a capella' unites the old tradition of polyphony with newer features, in particular the possibility of using basso continuo. The music is modern in that it is usually in major and minor keys and not modal, has a strong sense of functional harmony, particularly towards cadences and, consequently, a permissive attitude towards the use of

---

[3] K. G. Fellerer, *Der Palestrinastil und seine Bedeutung in der vokalen Kirchenmusik des achtzehnten Jahrhunderts* (Augsburg, 1929).
[4] F. W. Riedel, *Kirchenmusik am Hofe Karls VI. (1711–1740). Untersuchungen zum Verhältnis von Zeremoniell und musikalischem Stil im Barockzeitalter* (Munich and Salzburg, 1977), pp. 72–145.
[5] Riedel, *Kirchenmusk*, p. 133.
[6] *Denkmäler der Tonkunst in Österreich*, 1/i (Vienna, 1894), p. 141.
[7] Listed in Johann Elssler's catalogue of Haydn's music library and I. Sauer's inventory of Haydn's estate. H. C. Robbins Landon, *Haydn: Chronicle and Works. Haydn: the Late Years 1801–1809* (London, 1977), p. 313, p. 402.
[8] J. J. Fux, *Gradus ad Parnassum* (Vienna, 1725); modern facsimile in *Monuments of Music and Music Literature*, 2nd series, xxiv (New York, 1966), pp. 239–79. I have used S. Wollenberg's valuable translation: J. J. Fux, '*Gradus ad Parnassum* (1725): Concluding Chapters', *Music Analysis*, xi (1992), pp. 215–43. For an assessment of this neglected portion of Fux's treatise see S. Wollenberg, 'The Unknown "Gradus"', *Music and Letters*, li (1970), pp. 423–34.

sequence and the use of the tritone as part of a dominant seventh or diminished seventh sound. Although Fux does quote some examples in the *Gradus* in which the pulse is notated in crotchets the more usual notation was in minims. The principal points of indebtedness to the old tradition are, of course, the predominantly vocal sonority and the imitative texture.

The 'stylus a capella' as defined by Fux was cultivated throughout the eighteenth century and well into the next, providing a continuous performing tradition that links Palestrina with the *a cappella* output of Bruckner.[9] The repertoire can be divided into two broad groups: single, short homophonic movements, typically used for the Proper of the Mass, and contrapuntally ambitious settings in several movements of the Ordinary and, occasionally, other lengthy liturgical texts such as that of the requiem. Table 4.1 presents a list of 'stylus a capella' masses by composers active in Haydn's lifetime; his *Missa sunt bona mixta malis* is clearly part of this tradition. Seven of the representative masses contain 'a cappella' (or a variant) in their title, others reflect the polyphonic ambition of the work by including a reference to counterpoint, while others refer to the time of year ('Quadragesima', Lent) when they were performed. In practice sources often transmit different titles for the same work, or combine two or more kinds of title.

For more detailed consideration, I have chosen two 'a capella' masses from the mid century by composers whose music was well known to Joseph Haydn: Georg Reutter the younger, Haydn's teacher at St Stephen's in Vienna; and Gregor Werner, Haydn's predecessor as Esterházy Kapellmeister and for five years until his death in 1766 a colleague.

Reutter's 'a capella' mass (Hofer 4) survives as a set of parts in the Österreichische Nationalbibliothek, Vienna (H.K. 785). The title page indicates that it was first performed on 2 March 1744, the second Sunday in Lent. Underneath this date is a long list of subsequent performance dates: 21 March 1745 (third Sunday in Lent), 12 December 1745 (second Friday in Advent), 14 March 1748 (fifth Sunday in Lent), 21 March 1751 (fourth Sunday in Lent), 27 February 1763 (second Sunday in Lent) and then the year only from 1770 through to 1775. Thus, in a period of thirty-one years the mass was performed on at least twelve occasions. Joseph Haydn must have known the work intimately; as a choirboy in St Stephen's he would very likely have sung at its first performance in 1744, and in as many as three subsequent performances until he left in 1749 or 1750. Most of the performances were during Lent, so that there is no Gloria movement. In addition to multiple choral parts (three of each) the extant source material has contemporary parts for organ, cello and double

---

[9] In 1823 Beethoven suggested that his Missa Solemnis might be performed '*a la cappella*' (letter of 25 March 1823: E. Anderson, trans. and ed., *The Letters of Beethoven* (3 vols., London, 1961), iii, p. 1022). Given Beethoven's familiarity with the 'stylus a capella' tradition, the composer is not suggesting the possibility of performing the work unaccompanied (an absurd impossibility) but with the support of continuo, the organ providing the orchestral part.

Table 4.1 *A cappella masses composed in the period c. 1740–1800*

Georg Reutter the younger (1708–72)
  Missa brevis . . . senza Gloria a 4 Voci Capella (Hofer 3)
  Messa â 4 da Capella (1744, Hofer 4))
  Missa a Capella in C (Hofer 6)
See N. Hofer, 'Thematisches Verzeichnis der Werke von Georg Reutter jun.', in 'Die beiden Reutter als Kirchenkomponisten' (Ph.D. diss., University of Vienna, 1915).

Gregor Werner (1693–1766)
  Missa contrapunctata in C
  Missa Lydia
  Missa in Contrapuncto
  Missa pro Quadragesima alla Capella
  Missa Quadrages
From thematic catalogue in H. Dopf, 'Die Messenkompositionen Gregor Werners' (Ph.D. diss., University of Innsbruck, 1956).

Georg Wagenseil (1715–77)
  Missa à 4^{tro} dà Capella (ÖNB Mus. Hs. 16431)
See R. Philipp, 'Die Messenkompositionen der Wiener Vorklassiker G. M. Monn und G. Chr. Wagenseil' (Ph.D. diss., University of Vienna, 1938).

Johann Georg Albrechtsberger (1736–1809)
  Missa in C (A.II.2)
  Missa pro hebdomada sancta/Missa romana (A.II.5). Modern edition by K. Pfannhauser (Vienna, 1946)
  Missa quatuor vocum/Missa canonica (A.II.6)
  Missa in G (A.II.7)
From thematic catalogue in D. Schröder, *Die geistlichen Vokalcompositionen Johann Georg Albrechtsbergers. Hamburg Beiträge zur Musikwissenschaft*, xxiv (Hamburg, 1987).

Michael Haydn (1737–1806)
  Missa Sanctae Crucis a 4 Voci in Contra punto (1762, MH 56, Klafsky I/16). Modern edition by K. Pfannhauser, *Österreichische Kirchenmusik*, vii (Vienna, 1949).

Leopold Hofmann (1738–93)
  [Missa] Alla: Cap. ^{la} N°1 (ÖNB, 18.717)
See thematic catalogue in H. Proházka, 'Leopold Hofmann und seine Messen', *Studien zur Musikwissenschaft*, xxvi (1964), pp. 79–139.

Antonio Salieri (1750–1825)
  Missa Stylo a Cappella (1767). Modern edition by O. Biba, *Kirchenmusik der Wiener Klassik*, iii (Altötting, 1987).

bass, a total of fifteen parts. However, the title page indicates that the source once had twenty-four parts plus a score ('Partes 24 et Sparte'); the missing parts may have consisted of additional choral parts but perhaps some instrumental parts too, such as *colla parte* trombones and/or strings. The following pertinent dialogue from Fux's *Gradus* points to the options available in the performance of 'stylus a capella' music.[10]

Joseph. Quum in hoc stylo instrumenta quoque cooperatores sint, quid de illis agendum? Haud ignoro, Tubas ductiles cum Alto, & Tenore in Unisono consonare solitas esse: sed quid Fidibus tribuendum?

When instruments also participate in this style, what must be done with them? I am not ignorant of the fact that trombones are usually sounded in unison with the altus and tenor: but what part is given to the stringed instruments?

Aloys. Et primis, & secundis Fidipus in hoc stylo à Capella cum Cantu in unisono incedendum esse affirmo.

I declare that in this 'a Capella' style the first and second violins should both proceed in unison with the cantus.

Table 4.2 summarizes the structure of Reutter's mass. It is in *alla breve* metre throughout with only one change of basic tempo, for the 'Et incarnatus' section

Table 4.2 *Reutter: Messa à 4. da Capella . . . 1744*

Kyrie	Kyrie	¢	F	a4	27 bars
	Christe	¢	d	a4	42 bars
	'Kyrie da Capo'	¢	F	a4	27 bars
Gloria	[no Gloria movement]				
Credo	Credo	¢	F	a4	67 bars
	Et incarnatus (Un poco adagio)	¢	d	a4	26 bars
	Crucifixus (Tempo ordinario)	¢	F	a4	195 bars
Sanctus	Sanctus	¢	F	a4	47 bars
	Osanna	¢	F	a4	59 bars
Benedictus	Benedictus	¢	F	a4	25 bars
	Osanna [da capo]	¢	F	a4	59 bars
Agnus Dei	Agnus Dei	¢	F	a4	73 bars
	Dona nobis	¢	F	a4	71 bars

[10] Fux, *Gradus*, p. 272. For doubling practice in sacred music generally see O. Biba, 'Die Wiener Kirchenmusik um 1783', *Jahrbuch für Österreichische Kulturgeschichte*, i/2, Beiträge zur Musikgeschichte des 18. Jahrhunderts (Eisenstadt, 1971), pp. 70–1.

Ex. 4.1 Reutter, Messa â 4 da Capella
(a)

(b)

(c)

of the Credo. The following 'Tempo ordinario' is the prevailing one throughout the mass. Equally restricted is the key structure. Apart from D minor for 'Christe eleison' and 'Et incarnatus est', it is firmly rooted in F major.

In contrapuntal practice the approach is, as one might expect, the one most familiar to modern listeners from the masses of the Renaissance and codified in Fux's *Gradus*. Each clause of the text is associated with a new point of imitation. Short passages of the Ordinary such as the Kyrie, 'Agnus Dei' and 'Dona nobis pacem' are set in extended passages of counterpoint; the Credo, on the other hand, with its many clauses, is less consistently imitative and, on occasions, is homophonic; it does, however, end with a lengthy 'Amen' section. The examples quoted in Ex. 4.1 (pp. 94–6) show the range of writing in Reutter's mass. The Kyrie opens with a full four-part exposition on a traditionally constructed subject of a rising fourth followed by a descent in crotchets; the lowest sounding voice is accompanied by the organ, the cello and double bass entering with the bass voice at bar 8 (Ex. 4.1a). The 'Et incarnatus est' in the Credo is homophonic with the expressive harmonic language embracing a single diminished seventh as well as some dominant sevenths (Ex. 4.1b). Throughout the mass there is not even a hint of modal writing; indeed the end of the Credo, with its dominant pedal and unwinding of the imitative texture, affirms F major in a thoroughly modern manner (Ex. 4.1c). The work may be founded on the old polyphonic tradition but it is not reverentially *antico*.

To anyone approaching this work by Reutter from the tradition of the instrumental mass of the time, one movement is surprisingly perfunctory. In masses with orchestral accompaniment the Benedictus is often the most indulgent movement with lengthy orchestral passages, solo writing for the voices, sometimes obbligato instrumental writing and a good deal of verbal repetition.[11] The reverse is true in this 'a capella' mass. With only twenty-five bars the section is the shortest in the mass and is completely dwarfed by the succeeding 'Osanna'. Since the mass was composed for Lent a penitential rather than luxurious setting of the text was obviously appropriate.

Werner's 'Missa contrapunctata a 4 voci alla Capella' (the first in Table 4.1) dates from 1756. Werner had been Kapellmeister at the Esterházy court since 1728 and church music of all types constituted the bulk of his output, performed at the court chapel and also in the church of St Martin in Eisenstadt with which Werner seems to have had a close connection. He is thought to have studied with Fux in Vienna in the 1720s, and a copy of *Gradus ad Parnassum* with annotations by Werner has survived.[12] His output of liturgical

---

[11] See B. MacIntyre, *The Viennese Concerted Mass of the Early Classic Period* (Ann Arbor, 1986), p. 422, pp. 445–68.

[12] O. Pausch, *Die Herkunft Gregor Joseph Werners mit einer Studie über Musiktheoretische Lehrbücher aus dem Besitz des Meisters. Veröffentlichungen der Kommission für Musikforschung*, ed. F. Grasberger, xvii (Vienna, 1975). H. Dreo, 'Die fürstliche Esterházysche Musikkapelle von ihren Anfängen bis zum Jahre 1766', *Jahrbuch für Österreichische Kulturgeschichte*, i/2, *Beiträge zur Musikgeschichte des 18. Jahrhunderts* (Eisenstadt, 1971), pp. 80–115.

music in the 'stylus a capella' is extensive, making him the most important composer of such music after Fux. As well as five masses there are several settings of the Salve Regina and other smaller works.

The parts of the present work, originally from the Esterházy archives, are in the Országos Széchenyi Könyvtar, Budapest (Ms Mus III: 36).[13] The title 'Missa contrapunctata a 4 voci alla Capella' continues 'con Basso Generale e Violone' and there are, accordingly, parts for organ continuo and for violone; there is no cello part and no evidence of doubling instruments. Only one part per voice exists. There is no Gloria movement, as in most of Werner's 'a capella' masses. As Table 4.3 shows, the scale of the work is similar to that of the Reutter; to obtain a fair picture the totals in the Credo need to be doubled to allow Werner's use of 4/2 to be compared with Reutter's 2/2. But, as one might expect from a composer practised in the 'stylus a capella' and more committed to the Fux tradition, this work is more varied and resourceful than Reutter's mass. There is some variety of metres: the mass begins in 3/2 before moving to 4/2 in the Credo and thereafter Werner mixes the two. Likewise, there is a range of tempo markings: the main tempo is an implicit 'tempo ordinario',

Table 4.3 *Werner: Missa contrapunctata â 4 voci alla Cappella . . . 1756*

Kyrie	Kyrie	3/2	C	a4	25 bars
	Christe	3/2	a–V/C	a3	13 bars
	'Kyrie ut sopra'	3/2	C	a4	25 bars
Gloria	[no Gloria movement]				
Credo	Credo	4/2	C–G	a4	41 bars
	Qui propter	4/2	G–C	a3	11 bars
	Et incarnatus (Largo)	3/2	–d	a4	16 bars
	Crucifixus (Lente)	4/2	–F	a4	14 bars
	Et resurrexit (Vivace)	3/2	C	a4	69 bars
Sanctus	Sanctus (Larghetto)	4/2	C	a4	8 bars
	Pleni sunt coeli (Andante)	4/2	C	a4	9 bars
	Osanna (Vivace)	3/2	C	a4	20 bars
Benedictus	Benedictus (Molto moderato)	4/2	a–C	a4	16 bars
	'Osanna ut sopra' (Vivace)	3/2	C	a4	20 bars
Agnus Dei	Agnus Dei (Andante)	4/2	C–G	a4	33 bars
	Dona nobis (Vivace moderato)	4/2	C	a4	16 bars

[13] There is a score prepared by C. F. Pohl in the Gesellschaft der Musikfreunde, Vienna (I.35471). This source is listed in the thematic catalogue in H. Dopf, 'Die Messenkompositionen Gregor Werners' (Ph.D. diss., University of Innsbruck, 1956), but not the parts from the Esterházy archives.

changing to Largo for 'Et incarnatus est', 'Lente' (*sic*) for 'Crucifixus' and, perhaps most surprising in this *a cappella* idiom, Vivace for 'Et resurrexit'. Similar contrasts between slow and fast are to be found in the Sanctus, Benedictus and Agnus Dei. There is, too, greater variety in the vocal scoring with two sections being set for three-part voices, 'Christe' and 'Et incarnatus est'. The principal key of the mass is C major but contrasting tonalities are more effectively deployed than in the Reutter mass; in particular, the Benedictus begins in A minor before moving to C major for the return of 'Osanna'; and the Agnus Dei moves to the dominant key. Indeed, the way in which the Andante of 'Agnus Dei' reaches G major and then takes off in a Vivace moderato tempo in C major for 'Dona nobis pacem' is distinctly modern – Haydnesque one might say, except that plenty of other composers were doing it – and shows a willingness to accommodate influences from the contemporary instrumental mass.

Werner is a more resourceful contrapuntist than Reutter. The opening of the Kyrie is rhythmically more intricate than any passage in the Reutter; the octaves in bar 4 between tenor and alto are a rare solecism (Ex. 4.2a). As in the Reutter, the 'Et incarnatus' section is chordal and chromatic, featuring a couple of Neapolitan sixths (Ex. 4.2b). 'Dona nobis pacem' (Vivace moderato) presents a convincing display of animated counterpoint with, five bars before the end, an effective *subito piano* (Ex. 4.2c). As in the Reutter the Benedictus is a brief movement, but its opening reveals a departure from the continuous imitative or homophonic texture that is the norm in the mass; over an independent walking bass for the organ (marked 'solo') pairs of voices declaim the text four semibreves at a time (Ex. 4.2d). The style of the Werner is altogether more diverse than that of the Reutter.

Haydn's contribution to the 'stylus a capella' tradition dates from 1768, twenty-four years after the Reutter and twelve after the Werner. From the title page of the autograph (Plate 4.1, p. 104) it is clear that Haydn's original title for the work was the traditional one, 'Missa a 4^{tro} voci alla Cappella'; 'Sunt bona mixta malis' was added later and placed as if to form part of the title.[14] In this guise it was entered into the *Entwurf Katalog* (p. 2) and from there into the *Haydn Verzeichnis* (p. 23). There is no indication on the title page of the nature of the instrumental support; the music itself has the customary four-part chorus with a fifth stave labelled 'Organo'.[15]

Though the work is only a fragment it shows some interesting differences from the Reutter and the Werner (Table 4.4). First, the 124 bars of the Kyrie

---

[14] Alois Fuchs, who must have seen the autograph early in the nineteenth century when it was owned by Artaria, noted the separation of title and subtitle See A. van Hoboken, *Joseph Haydn, Thematisch-bibliographisches Werkverzeichnis*, ii (Mainz, 1971), p. 72.

[15] A modern edition prepared by H. C. Robbins Landon and D. W. Jones is published by Editions Mario Bois (Paris, [1992]).

Ex. 4.2 Werner, Missa contrapunctata
(a)

HAYDN'S *MISSA SUNT BONA MIXTA MALIS* 101

(b)

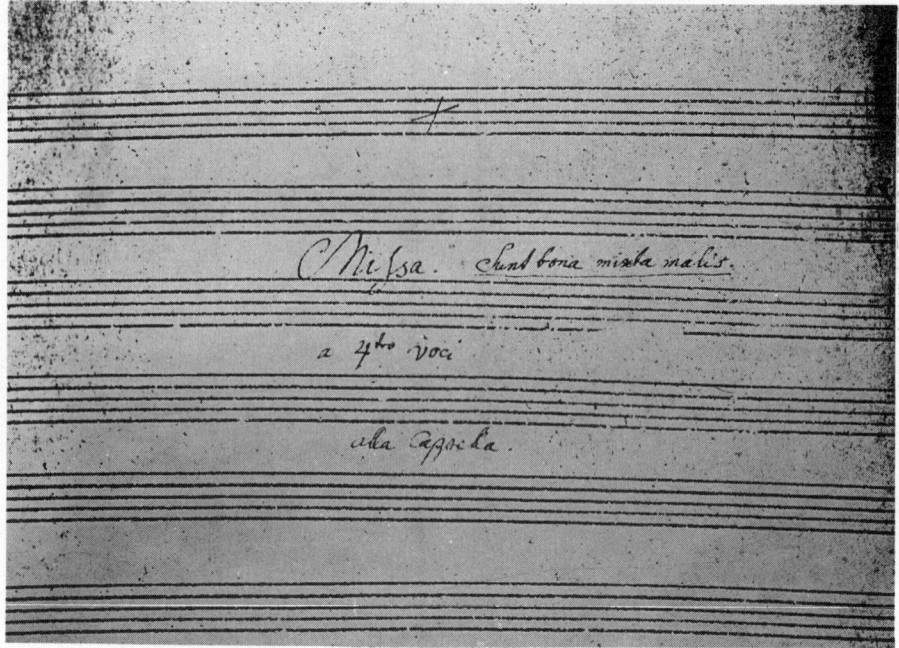

Plate 4.1 Portion of title-page of Haydn's *Missa sunt bona mixta malis*

Table 4.4 *Haydn: Missa a 4tro voci alla Cappella . . . 1768*

Kyrie		¢	d	a4	124 bars
Gloria	[to Gratias agimus tibi]	¢	d	a4	190 bars

movement promise a work on a large scale, twice, if not three times the size of the Reutter or the Werner. Second, it has a Gloria movement, which suggests that it was composed with Advent rather than Lent in mind. Third, in keeping with the scale of the work, the Kyrie is a through-composed movement in three clear stages and not the *da capo* structure found in the Reutter and Werner. Each of the three clauses is set to a new contrapuntal motif and each clause is separated by a short linking passage for organ alone, making rather routine use of sequence; Ex. 4.3a (p. 106) quotes the passage linking the end of 'Christe' to 'Kyrie'.

The Gloria adopts the approach found in the Credo movements of the masses of Reutter and Werner, that is polyphony that tends towards homophony, rather than the pervasive counterpoint of the Kyrie movement. The willingness of Reutter and, especially, Werner to embrace a more modern idiom is evident in Haydn's work too. Ex. 4.3b (p. 107) is from near the opening of the Gloria, a predominantly homophonic passage that takes in a Neapolitan sixth in bar 9. Later in the movement the mixture of idioms is even more striking. The clause 'Laudamus te' is set to a traditional motif of a descending fifth but as the music becomes more homophonic it becomes more rhetorical also, with repeated diminished seventh harmonies and two unexpected silences (Ex. 4.3c, p. 108–9). This is a long way from Palestrina and a considerable way from Fux, Reutter and Werner too.

Haydn's fragment ends with the clause 'Gratias agimus tibi'. Though Haydn's work is not heavily indebted to either the Reutter or the Werner, the two earlier works do suggest how Haydn might have continued. The Kyrie and Gloria are both in *alla breve* time and the setting of the 'Gratias' takes the form of an extended contrapuntal paragraph of eighty-seven bars ending with a strongly articulated cadence in A minor. Almost certainly, 'Qui tollis' would have been chordal rather than imitative, and probably in triple time; perhaps a return to *alla breve* and imitation would have occurred at 'Quoniam'. The Benedictus would probably have been a short movement but, given the brief linking passages for the organ in the Kyrie and Gloria, might Haydn have written an independent part for the organ in the Benedictus, in the way suggested by Werner? Finally, would Haydn have expanded on the contrast between 'Agnus Dei' and 'Dona nobis pacem' found in the Werner, exploiting chromatic harmony, and varying speed and dynamic to maximize the expressive content? All this is speculation of course. But there is sufficient evidence in the fragment to suggest that Haydn was being ambitious rather than cautious, progressive rather than conservative.

The annotation 'sunt bona mixta malis' ('the good mixed with the bad') must be seen against this stylistic background. I have suggested elsewhere that the annotation was a self-critical, ironic assessment of an attempt to compose in an atypical style. This was the traditional usage of the remark and can be set alongside other wry comments by Haydn, such as the 'nihil sine causa' on the autograph of the Baryton Trio Hob.XI: 109 and the German 'in Schlaff geschrieben' on the Horn Concerto (Hob.VIId: 3).[16] Like Reutter and Werner, Haydn was attempting to seek the common ground between his normal style and the 'a capella' tradition, that is fulfilling Fux's view that the 'stylus a capella' was not an exercise in musical archaism but a considered compromise between the old and new. Haydn clearly felt that he had not been entirely successful, there were good things such as the well-crafted fugal expositions and stretto sections, and weaker things such as the perfunctory organ links; and passages like Ex. 4.3c (pp. 108–9) reveal not so much a compromise as an indigestible mix of idioms.

---

[16] H. C. Robbins Landon and D. W. Jones, *Haydn: His Life and Music* (London, 1988), p. 143. On the composer's fondness for short Latin expressions see also E. K. Borthwick, 'The Latin Quotations in Haydn's London Notebooks', *Music and Letters*, lxxi (1990), pp. 505–10.

Ex. 4.3 Joseph Haydn, Missa sunt bona mixta malis

(a)

HAYDN'S *MISSA SUNT BONA MIXTA MALIS*

(b)

(c)

There is a mass by Werner, written c. 1762, that carries the same title, 'Missa sunt bona mixta malis'. It is a work for the common church forces of two violins, continuo and voices. The parts from the Esterházy archives are now in the Országos Széchenyi Könyvtar, Budapest (Ms Mus III: 19) and it is clear from them, at least, that 'sunt bona mixta malis' was not added later. While it shows that at least two people in the Esterházy court used the remark 'sunt bona mixta malis' in the 1760s, it also exemplifies a fondness in Werner's masses for whimsical titles: others include 'Missa alla Zoppa' (occasioned by the syncopated opening of the Kyrie), 'Missa quasi vero', and 'Missa hic labor hoc opus est' ('this is the task, this the toil').[17] Haydn's mass was composed two years after Werner's death, both the subtitle and its significance reflecting the influence of the old Esterházy Kapellmeister.

Apart from the year of composition, 1768, there is no further information on Haydn's autograph about the circumstances of the mass's composition. Since the work has a Gloria movement it is reasonable to postulate that it was intended for Advent rather than Lent in 1768, though performances of masses with a Gloria movement were allowed on certain days in Holy Week. This

---

[17] Manuscript parts of Missa alla Zoppa in Országos Széchenyi Könyvtar, Budapest (Ms Mus III: 45); remaining works from H. Dopf, 'Die Messenkompositionen Gregor Werners', p. 219. I am grateful to E. Kerr Borthwick for identifying the source of 'hic labor, hoc opus est', a slight misquotation of 'hoc opus, hic labor est' from Virgil's *Aeneid* (6. 129).

accords well with what is known about Haydn's output that year; the early part of the year was taken up with the important 'Applausus' cantata and the late summer with the opera *Lo speziale*. But for whom was the work intended? Since Haydn was now full Kapellmeister, assuming responsibility for church music at the court following Werner's death in 1766, and there was a strong local tradition of 'stylus a capella' music, it seems reasonable to suggest that it was composed for the Esterházy court or, perhaps, the church of St Martin in Eisenstadt, the church with which Werner had been associated. But church music was no longer at the centre of musical activity at the Esterházy court and its resources were already in decline. Haydn did compose several important items of church music at this time – the first Missa Cellensis (Hob.XXII: 5), the Stabat Mater (Hob.XXbis), the 'Grosseorgelsolomesse' (Hob.XXII: 4), the 'Applausus' cantata (Hob.XXIVa: 6), the Salve Regina (Hob.XXIIIb: 2) and the Missa Sancti Nicolai (XXII: 6) – but only two of these works can be associated with the Esterházy court, the Missa Sancti Nicolai and the Salve Regina. At least one work (the cantata) was commissioned from outside and at least one (the Stabat Mater) is known to have been performed in Vienna. Indeed, Haydn seems to have maintained active contact with church establishments in Vienna during the first decade of his service at the Esterházy court. Werner in the famous letter of complaint (1765) about Haydn noted that the young composer allowed church music from the Esterházy library 'to go out to all the world' ('so gehen nun auch die meisten Kirchen-Musicalien in alle Welt aus'); in the same letter, Werner alludes to his own practice of supplying music to churches in Vienna 'since Vienna at present has a considerable lack of church composers' ('weilen dermalen die Wienstadt von denen Kirchen-Compositoren ziemlicher Maßen evacuiret worden').[18] Perhaps Haydn's 'a capella' mass was intended for Vienna rather than Eisenstadt.

In keeping an open mind about the circumstances of composition a further aspect needs to be considered, not necessarily a substitute for performance in Eisenstadt or Vienna, but complementary. Although the 'stylus a capella' was a living practical tradition, constantly updated and adapted, it remained rooted in the Fux ideal, enunciated in *Gradus ad Parnassum*, that such music, being the product of the best of the ancient and modern, was the work of a fully fledged composer, one who had worked through basic theory and species counterpoint and who was now ready to tackle the foothills of Parnassus. Leopold Hofmann's mass (listed in Table 4.1; see p. 92) is almost certainly his first, composed c. 1760; Michael Haydn copied out Fux's Missa canonica at the age of twenty; and Salieri's *a cappella* mass (also listed in Table 4.1) was his first composition, written at the age of seventeen following a period of study with Gassmann, a

---

[18] Werner's letter of October 1765 to Prince Nicolaus Esterházy. D. Bartha, ed., *Joseph Haydn, Gesammelte Briefe und Aufzeichnungen* (Basel, Paris and London, 1965), pp. 52–3. English translation in H. C. Robbins Landon, *Haydn: Chronicle and Works. Haydn: the Early Years 1732–1765* (London, 1980), pp. 418–19.

study that is known to have included Fux's *Gradus*.[19] This element of instruction and improvement features in the background to Haydn's 'stylus a capella' work too. During the 1750s and 1760s Haydn studied in most thorough detail the celebrated treatises of the day, those by Mattheson and C. P. E. Bach, as well as Fux's *Gradus*. These had a profound and pervasive effect on the composer's style in the 1760s and early 1770s, particularly in encouraging greater use of counterpoint. For Haydn, whose symphonies, quartets, baryton trios and church music reveal in varying degree his increasing contrapuntal skill, this 'a capella' mass is still a very self-conscious work. That it represented a didactic Parnassus rather than an artistic Parnassus explains why it was, indeed, 'bona mixta malis'.

[19] R. Angermüller, *Antonio Salieri; sein Leben und seine weltlichen Werke unter besonderer Berücksichtigung seiner 'großen' Opern. Schriften zur Musik*, xvii (Munich, 1974), ii, p. 11.

5

Johann Baptist Vanhal and the pastoral mass tradition

BRUCE C. MACINTYRE

Johann Baptist Vanhal (1739–1813) was among the most prolific and highly regarded composers of masses during the second half of the eighteenth century. Indeed, in all kinds of church music Vanhal was a major contributor at this time. As Alexander Weinmann noted in his thematic catalogue of the composer.

Die große Zahl der Kirchenwerke Wanhals weist ihn als uneigennützigen Künstler aus, mit ihnen war wohl auch damals kein finanzieller Erfolg zu erzielen. Als gläubiger Katholik war er mit diesen in der ganzen alten Monarchie bekannt und geschätzt, wie zahlreichen Fundorte deutlich beweisen.[1]

The large number of Vanhal's church compositions shows him to be an unselfish artist, [for] even then there was no financial success to be achieved with them. As a faithful Catholic he was known and esteemed with these [works] throughout the entire old Monarchy, as the numerous source locations clearly prove.

Large numbers of Vanhal's masses are preserved in manuscript copies located in German, Austrian and, especially, Czech and Slovak archives. This extensive dissemination reflects an aspect of the composer's career that is seldom recognized.

Vanhal the instrumental composer was extremely productive and talented. He was recognized and highly praised by his contemporaries. In *A General History* (1776–89) Charles Burney, who had met Vanhal in Vienna in 1772, praised the composer's 'spirited, natural, and unaffected symphonies'. He considered Vanhal an 'excellent composer' whose quartets and other pieces for violins 'deserve a place among the first productions, in which unity of melody, pleasing harmony, and a free and manly style are constantly preserved'.[2] Reporting on travels through Austria in 1781 Friedrich Nicolai, a Berlin bookdealer and man of letters, remarked how (after Joseph Haydn) Vanhal and Leopold Hofmann (1738–93) had contributed most 'to the development of a better musical taste

---

[1] A. Weinmann, *Themen-Verzeichnis der Kompositionen von Johann Baptiste Vanhal*, Wiener Archivstudien, vol. xi (2 parts, Vienna, 1987[?]), part 1, p. iv. Weinmann indicates (part 2, p. 194) that, in addition to countries of the former Austro-Hungarian Empire, Poland has numerous copies of Vanhal's sacred music.
[2] C. Burney, *A General History of Music: From the Earliest Times to the Present Period* (4 vols., London, 1776–89); ed. F. Mercer (London, 1935), ii, p. 958.

in Austria' ('zur Bildung eines besseren musikalischen Geschmacks in Oestreich').[3] As late as 1796, in his *Jahrbuch der Tonkunst von Wien und Prag*, Johann Schönfeld spoke kindly of 'one of our oldest composers [then aged fifty-seven] who, so it seems, is going out of fashion with us' ('einer unserer ältesten Kompositoren, welcher aber, wie es scheint, dermalen bei uns aus der Mode kommt'). Schönfeld went on to note, however, that things were different outside Austria where Vanhal's works were 'still very highly treasured' ('wo man noch immer seine Werke sehr hoch schätzt').[4]

In recent years there has been renewed interest in Vanhal's instrumental music. Several of his seventy-six symphonies have been published and are being recorded in stunning performances that have begun to explicate Vanhal's popularity with his contemporaries.[5] In the course of preparing my study of the Viennese concerted mass, I was struck by a parallel exuberance and originality in most of the composer's masses, but particularly in his *Missa Pastoralis* in G major, the work to be discussed in more detail here.[6]

Current research indicates that Vanhal composed approximately fifty masses. The early nineteenth-century lexicographer Dlabacž, who knew and interviewed Vanhal for his *Künstler-Lexikon* of 1815, reported only twenty-five 'large and small masses' ('große und kleine Messen') in a lengthy and detailed work-list.[7] Milan Poštolka's work-list for the *New Grove Dictionary* (1980) attributed as many as sixty masses to Vanhal,[8] while Weinmann's more recent thematic catalogue (1987) enumerates forty-seven masses in the following keys.[9]

Key	Weinmann (1987)
C	11
D	9
E♭	6
F	5
G	7
A	4
B♭	5
Total	47

[3] F. Nicolai, *Beschreibung einer Reise durch Deutschland und die Schweiz im Jahre 1781* (Berlin and Stettin, 1784), iv, p. 527.
[4] J. F. von Schönfeld, *Jahrbuch der Tonkunst von Wien und Prag* (Vienna and Prague, 1796); rpt, ed. O. Biba (Munich and Salzburg, 1976), pp. 64–5.
[5] P. Bryan, ed., *Johann Vanhal: Six Symphonies*, Recent Researches in the Music of the Classical Era, xvii (Madison, Wisconsin, 1985), p. vii documents the recognition of Vanhal's symphonic output by modern scholars. Another recent publication of symphonies is Bryan's edition of five works in *The Symphony 1720–1840*, ed. B. S. Brook (New York, 1981), Series B, vol. x.
[6] In December 1989, on the occasion of the 250th anniversary of Vanhal's birth, I had the opportunity to rehearse and perform this mass with my chorus at Brooklyn College, New York.
[7] G. J. Dlabacž, 'Wanhall, Johann Baptist' in *Allgemeines historisches Künstler-Lexikon für Böhmen und zum Theil auch für Mähren und Schlesien* (Prague, 1815); rpt, ed. P. Bergner (Hildesheim, 1973), iii, cols. 324–7.
[8] M. Poštolka, 'Vanhal, Johann Baptist', in *The New Grove Dictionary of Music and Musicians*, ed. S. Sadie (London, 1980), xix, p. 524.
[9] Weinmann, *Verzeichnis*, part 2, group XIX, pp. 197–213.

My own researches have added and subtracted some masses so that the actual total is about fifty – no small number at that time.[10] In comparison, Joseph Haydn composed only some fourteen masses, his brother Michael some thirty masses and Wolfgang Mozart some sixteen complete masses.

This sizeable number of masses is rather surprising since, as far as we know, after his teenage years in Bohemia, Vanhal had no regular church music position. Was it private piety, the forgetfulness of old age, or Vanhal's reported 'extraordinary modesty ('außerordentliche Bescheidenheit') that kept the fifty-six-year-old composer from relating the full extent of his mass output to Dlabacž in 1795? Of Vanhal's Viennese contemporaries only the older Franz Tuma (1704–74), with about sixty–five masses, and Georg Reutter the younger (1708–72), with about seventy-two masses, matched or exceeded that size of output.[11] Perhaps this extraordinary productivity in sacred rather than secular music was one reason for Schönfeld's description of Vanhal as 'aus der Mode' in 1796. In a front-page obituary that appeared in the *Allgemeine musikalische Zeitung* Friedrich Rochlitz notes how Vanhal devoted his compositional talents almost exclusively to church music in later years, after his recovery from mental illness. 'He wrote many masses, offertories, Salve Reginas etc., several requiems and a large number of smaller works' ('Er schrieb viele Messen, Offertorien, Salve Regina etc., einige Requiem, und eine grosse Anzahl kleinerer Kirchenstücke').[12] On the basis of two of Vanhal's masses (a short mass in G and a long mass in C), Rochlitz then praises his church music.

Nach dieser schätzbaren Arbeit zu urtheilen, hatte W. in seinen spätern Jahren an Geist und Kunst keineswegs verloren – wie man aus späteren Instrumental-Compositionen behaupten möchte; er hatte vielmehr in jeder Hinsicht gewonnen. Die Ideen sind hier eigenthümlicher, Geist, Sinn und Geschmack zeigen sich würdig, und die Arbeit ist weit gründlicher, auch in Absicht auf Contrapunct und Fuge, als man ihm, selbst nach seinen besten Symphonien aus früher Zeit, zutrauen möchte.[13]

Judging from this valuable work [in church music], Vanhal in his later years lost nothing in imagination and art – as one might maintain with his later instrumental compositions; in every respect he had gained much more. Here the ideas are more original; imagination, understanding, and taste are respectable, and the work is far more

---

[10] As a continuation of earlier studies I have been preparing a thematic locator for the Viennese mass of the late eighteenth century. Thus far, Weinmann's total of forty-seven can be increased by three because I have added six masses not listed in Weinmann's catalogue (three in C, two in D and one in B♭) and substracted three masses that have other attributions. Future researchers might also consult H. C. Robbins Landon's personal Vanhal thematic catalogue begun in 1951 and mentioned in *Haydn: Chronicle and Works. Haydn at Eszterháza 1766–1790* (London, 1978), p. 389, n. 1.

[11] See tabulations in B. MacIntyre, *The Viennese Concerted Mass of the Early Classic Period* (Ann Arbor, 1986), pp. 8, 84 and 89. According to H. Federhofer in *The New Grove Dictionary* (vii, p. 46) Johann Joseph Fux (1660–1741) composed about eighty masses. Fux, Tuma and Reutter were, of course, part of an older generation of Viennese composers.

[12] J. F. Rochlitz, 'Johann Wanhall', *Allgemeine musikalische Zeitung*, xvi (1814), col. 38.

[13] *Ibid.*

thorough (also with respect to counterpoint and fugue) than he is given credit for even in his best symphonies from the earlier period.

None of Vanhal's masses can be dated exactly; there are no known autograph scores. Several masses have only a *terminus ante quem* deduced from a dated copy.[14] Those masses that I have inspected bear dates running from 1778 to 1797, with the majority falling in the early 1780s, the time when Vanhal had already recuperated from his mental illness and was living chiefly in Vienna (with some travels to Varaždin in Croatia and elsewhere).[15] Already behind him were his two years of exposure to Italian music and musicians (1769–71) when, as Dlabacž reports, Vanhal 'studied composition after the best models' ('studierte daselbst die Komposizion nach den besten Mustern') in order to gain the necessary deeper 'aesthetic understanding of the style of the Italian masters' ('die fernere Geschmacksbildung nach italienischen Meistern nötig wäre').[16] Another indicator of the popularity of Vanhal's masses is the fact that two of them were published by Steiner of Vienna in 1818.[17] Publication of masses, even then, was still a rarity, particularly when a composer was no longer living.

In his recent dissertation on the pastorella and pastoral mass, Mark Germer has noted that Geoffrey Chew in 1968 was 'the first to recognize the importance of pastoral as a stylistic mode in the sacred music of the Austro-Bohemian baroque'.[18] As Chew's articles for the *New Grove Dictionary* relate, the main impetus for pastorales and pastoral sacred pieces in central Europe came from seventeenth- and eighteenth-century Italy. Composers like Corelli and Durante created a vocabulary of motifs associated with Christmas Eve, and these motifs 'eventually became the common property of all European music'.[19] In other words, the motifs were incorporated into Christmas Eve service music, whether in the mass itself, in the accompanying instrumental music, or in a pastorella.

As is commonly known, pastorellas were para-liturgical compositions based on the announcement of the nativity and the arrival of the shepherds as described in the second chapter of Luke. Pastorellas were especially popular in rural churches on Christmas Eve.[20] In an article on south German pastorellas, Otto Biba notes how pastorellas created an effective link between the ancient

---

[14] Writing about Vanhal's sacred music overall, Weinmann (*Verzeichnis*, part 2, p. 194) similarly notes how dated copies are in a minority and that such dates provide only a *terminus ante quem*. He also confirms that there are very few extant, certified autograph scores for Vanhal (part 1, pp. xii, xv) and practically none for his sacred music (part 2, p. 196).

[15] For biographical details see Bryan, ed., *Johann Vanhal: Six Symphonies*, pp. vii–viii; also Poštolka, 'Vanhal', pp. 522–5.

[16] Dlabacž, 'Wanhall', col. 325.

[17] These published masses are C8 and G5 in Weinmann, *Verzeichnis*, and V284 and V285 in RISM Series A/1.

[18] M. Germer, 'The Austro-Bohemian Pastorella and Pastoral Mass to c. 1780' (Ph.D. diss., New York University, 1989), p. 119; cf. G. Chew, 'The Christmas Pastorella in Austria, Bohemia and Moravia and its Antecedents' (Ph.D. diss., University of Manchester, 1968).

[19] G. Chew, 'Pastorale' in *The New Grove Dictionary of Music and Musicians*, ed. S. Sadie (London, 1980), xiv, p. 291.

[20] Germer, 'Pastorella', p. 389; cf. Chew, 'Pastorella' in *The New Grove Dictionary*, xiv, p. 296.

biblical accounts and the imaginations of modern participants and listeners.[21] Reciprocal influences among all the Christmas Eve musical genres were quite strong; in fact, Germer describes hybrid pastoral masses in which certain elements of the pastorella (e.g. parts of its text and related musical motifs) invade a mass setting. As Germer writes, 'Just as the Central-European pastorella evolved in large measure out of popular devotions at the crib, the pastoral mass in some quarters drew so near to the pastorella tradition as to become inseparable – and indistinguishable from it.'[22] Biba suggests that pastoral motifs originated in the pastorella (where there were specific connections between text and music) before being carried over into settings of the Ordinary of the mass and, even later, the Proper of the mass (where only the general mood of nativity events could be conveyed).[23]

Pastoral masses of the eighteenth century were usually treated as a special type of concerted mass in their archival cataloguing. Many contemporary inventories listed *missae pastorales* separately from masses for the rest of the church year.[24] This segregation reflected not only their liturgical association with Advent season and Christmas Eve but also the unique nature and targeted style of most pastoral masses.

Manuscripts entitled 'Missa pastoralis', 'Missa pastoritia', 'Missa pastorella' 'Missa nativitatis' etc. usually imply but do not necessarily guarantee the use of pastoral musical devices from this period.[25] Despite the widespread use of these motifs and topoi, not all composers of masses with a pastoral title used them; many masses for Christmas Eve were straightforward works in a style no different from that used on other solemn occasions.[26]

The complete history of the *missa pastoralis* has yet to be written. We still have no clear idea how many were composed during the eighteenth century when the popularity of such masses was blossoming. More archival studies are needed; the RISM Series A/II project of manuscript indexing will certainly help.[27] By the start of the nineteenth century the quantity of new pastoral masses had mushroomed, and the genre had become a favourite of many Catholic churches throughout central Europe.[28] Pastoral masses written by Abbé Vogler

---

[21] O. Biba, 'Süddeutsche Weihnachtsmusik', *Musica Sacra*, xcvii (1977), p. 411.
[22] Germer, 'Pastorella' p. 389.
[23] Biba, 'Süddeutsche Weihnachtsmusik', pp. 412–13, 420.
[24] Germer, 'Pastorella', p. 258. Pastorellas, too, were catalogued separately from other genres of sacred music; Biba, 'Süddeutsche Weihnachtmusik', p. 411.
[25] Germer, 'Pastorella', p. 257.
[26] It should be noted that the title for a particular mass often varied from copy to copy so that we are not always certain of the composer's original title (see MacIntyre, *Concerted Mass*, p. 5). My experience, however, has been that pastoral titles for masses stick (i.e. they tended to be passed on whenever a new copy of a pastoral mass was made).
[27] Germer ('Pastorella') lists only sixty-five masses in a catalogue in his dissertation. No explanation is given why several pastoral masses by Boog, Donberger, Grasl, Klima, F. Schmidt, Seuche and Vogler have not been listed.
[28] See A. A. Dimpfl, 'Die Pastoralmesse' (Ph.D. diss., University of Erlangen, 1945), pp. 86–8.

Table 5.1 *Pastoral traits in eighteenth-century masses*[a]

I   Overall sound

- A[b] Tender, gentle, 'sweet', simple, rustic and direct
  1. Without high drama
- B[b] Emphasis upon choral/orchestral homophony
  1. Pastoral fugatos, when present, are 'more tuneful than erudite' (M. Germer, p. 269)
- C[b] Some passages in unison (simplicity; 'naive piety')
- D[b] Paired voices in 'dialogue' alternation
- E Use of woodwinds, often with solo obbligatos
  1. Flutes or oboes
- F Use of horns
- G Use of 'Christmas' instruments or folk instruments
  1. E.g., tuba pastoralis, oboe da caccia
- H[b] Restrained use of dynamics ('peace on earth')
  1. Occasional echo effects (f–p)
  2. Endings often soft and subdued

II   Harmony

- A[b] Drones in imitation of bagpipes
- B[b] Pedal points
- C[b] 'Rustic' dissonances set up by drones and pedal points
- D[b] Extended passages alternating I and V
- E[b] Frequent parallel thirds and sixths
- F[b] Use of a 'pastoral' key (G? D? C?)

III   Melody

- A[b] Emphasis on the lyrical, flowing, graceful and conjunct
- B[b] Song-like regularity of phrases (even-numbered)
- C[b] Triadic motives
- D[b] Motives of 'rocking' or alternating thirds
- E Imitative motives
  1. Herding horncalls
  2.[b] Annunciatory fanfares
  3.[b] Chirping birds
- F[b] Lullaby (*ninna*) style for some movements
- G[b] Dance-like tunes for some movements or passages
- H[b] Allusion to exotic scales of folksong
- I Short descending passages with chromatic steps
- J Quotation or paraphrase of extant tunes ('vernacular interlude')

IV   Rhythm

- A Lilting compound metres (6/8, 6/4, 12/8)
- B[b] Triple metres (3/8, 3/4, 3/2)

C^b	Rustic, dance-like duple metre (2/4)
D^b	Moderately flowing tempos
E^b	Short rhythmic formulae in alternating groups of two and four bars (additive phrase structures)
F	Scotch snaps
V	Text
A	Removal of texts inappropriate for the season
B	Interpolation of vernacular texts

a Based on descriptions by G. Chew, A.A. Dimpfl, M. Germer and E. Tittel, these are possible traits, not omnipresent ones.
b Device found in Vanhal's *Missa Pastoralis in G*.

(1749–1814), Diabelli (1781–1858), Hummel (1778–1837) and Lindpaintner (1791–1856) and many others were popular and widely disseminated, while several such masses from the eighteenth century continued to be performed.[29]

Vanhal apparently wrote only one pastoral mass: the *Missa Pastoralis* in G.[30] Composed no later than 1782, the work not only shows that Vanhal employed some of his best techniques from instrumental genres in his church music, but also serves as a fine example of the composer's ingenuity in using many of the devices typical of pastoral masses. Today the work is preserved in four manuscript sources, two in Vienna, one in Prague and another, with parts dated February 1782, in Brno.[31] The mass is remarkable for its bounty of musical devices typical of the pastoral style popular at Christmas Eve in Bohemian rural parishes during the second half of the eighteenth century. These pastoral devices not only allow a mass to echo musically the nativity event but also promote a coherent unity for the mass cycle.

In reviewing Vanhal's treatment of pastoral traits, we begin with the overall sound of a pastoral work (see section I in the list given in Table 5.1).[32] The adjectives tender, gentle, sweet, simple, rustic and direct easily apply to Vanhal's *Missa Pastoralis* (I/A in Table 5.1). In the Kyrie, for example, such adjectives

---

[29] Biba ('Süddeutsche Weihnachtsmusik', p. 411) adds the following nineteenth-century composers of pastoral masses: Schiedermayr (1779–1840), Kreutzer (1780–1849), Kniže, (1784–1840) and Kempter (1819–71). The firm of Böhm & Sohn (Augsburg) has recently published pastoral masses by Diabelli and Kempter.

[30] XIX: G4 in Weinmann, *Verzeichnis*.

[31] The following sources are given in Weinmann, *Verzeichnis*: Vienna, Österreichische Nationalbibliothek, Mus. Hs. 926, 'Missa pastorell in G . . . Del Sign. Giov. Wanhall' (acquired in 1908 from the Gilg Collection); Vienna, 9th district, Pfarrarchiv Roßau; Prague, University Library, 59 R 1275, 'Missa Pastoralis in G . . . Auth. Wanhal' (with two flutes, two horns, no trumpets). The work is found also in Brno, Moravské Múzeum, Hudebné Historické Oddelení, Ms. A.3051, Giov. Vanhal: 'Missa Pastoralis' (from the Vyskov collection; two parts are dated February 1782). The ÖNB copy has been used for the examples in this essay. The mass is M65 in the catalogue of Appendix C in MacIntyre, *Concerted Mass*, p. 669.

[32] All roman and arabic numbers refer to those in Table 5.1. For related observations about the *stylus rusticanus* and the eighteenth century see G. Chew's essay in this volume, pp. 133–93.

Ex. 5.1

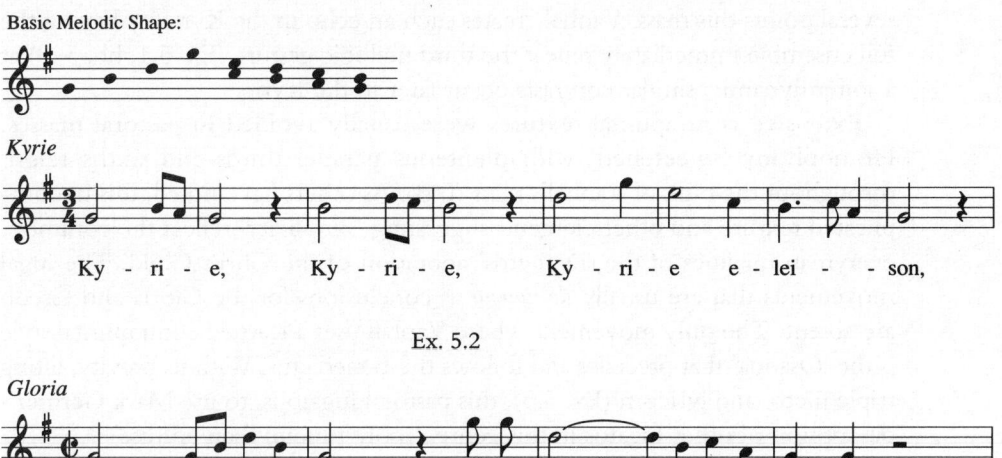

Ex. 5.2

Ex. 5.3

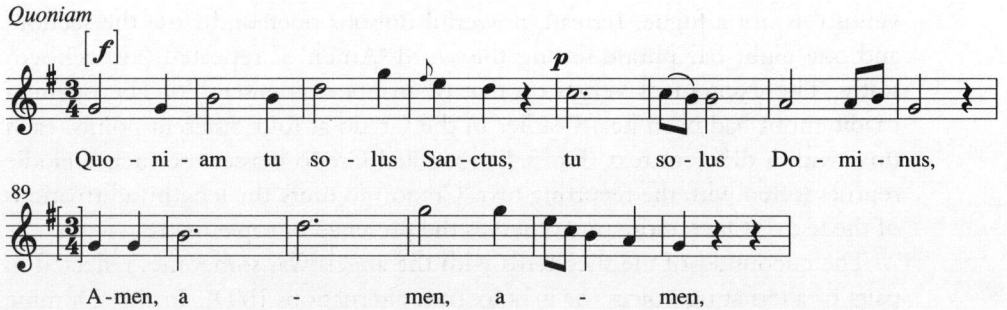

are particularly appropriate. Many of the other traits listed in Table 5.1 combine to create the tender, gentle and folk-like lyricism that characterizes this opening movement, whose main theme is quoted in Ex. 5.1. We encounter the delicately lilting triple metre that characterizes much of this mass and is representative of the proclivity for triple metres in pastoral works (IV/B). The pace is relatively relaxed; indeed, the tempo of this and several movements of the mass is allegro moderato. There is not the high drama that could be created by sustained instabilities or sudden contrasts in the harmony, melody, texture etc.; the only genuinely dramatic contrasts of the work are generated later by some quasi *Sturm und Drang* effects in the 'Qui tollis' and 'Crucifixus'. The opening of Haydn's *Missa Sancti Nicolai* (1772), a pastoral Kyrie in 6/4 metre and also in G major, similarly suggests the tender and gentle atmosphere of the Advent season for which it was written.

Echo effects were also part of the pastoral heritage (I/H1) and occur at several points this mass. Vanhal creates such an echo in the Kyrie by having the full ensemble immediately repeat the third melodic gesture (Ex. 5.1, bb. 5–8) at a softer dynamic; similar contrasts occur later in the Kyrie.

Extensive contrapuntal textures were usually avoided in pastoral masses. Homophony 'sweetened' with plenteous parallel thirds and sixths reigns throughout the bulk of Vanhal's mass (I/B). As others have noted, this uncomplicated texture and other elements suggesting 'simplicity' reflect the common, everyman qualities of the shepherds' adoration of the Christ Child. The fugal movements that are usually *de rigueur* as conclusions for the Gloria and Credo are absent. The only movement where Vanhal uses a learned contrapuntal style is the 'Osanna' that precedes and follows the Benedictus. With its brevity, lilting triple metre and lyricism (Ex. 5.5), this pastoral fugato is, to use Mark Germer's description of other fugatos in this genre, 'more tuneful than erudite'.[33]

Near the beginning or end of a section (or movement) Vanhal often requires the entire ensemble to sing and play in unison. Such striking unison acclamations were also part of the pastoral tradition (I/C) and, according to Ernst Tittel, may have symbolized the 'naive piety of the shepherds'.[34] Unlike the closing section of most Credo movements of the period, Vanhal's 'Et vitam venturi' is not a fugue. Instead, powerful unisons open and close the section, and one eight-bar phrase setting the word 'Amen' is repeated (i.e. echoed) softly. The excitement verges on that of an operatic ensemble. The opening triadic motif had been heard earlier in the Credo at four different points, each time with a different text (Ex. 5.4); so-called Credo masses use such melodic reprises (often with the recurring text 'Credo') to unify the lengthy affirmations of the text.[35] Once more one observes the presence of triple metre.

The encounter of the shepherds with the angels was sometimes reflected in pairs of alternating voices, or in solo/tutti alternations (I/D). In the 'Domine Deus' section from Vanhal's Gloria the soprano and alto soloists enter into a close dialogue of parallel thirds and sixths. Solo/tutti alternations in dialogue are used effectively in the final section of the mass, the 'Dona nobis pacem', to which we shall return later.

The orchestra for Vanhal's mass is rather small: two oboes, two trumpets in C, timpani, strings (including violas) and organ continuo. The trumpets and timpani befit the solemnity of the occasion and, as Biba has noted in pastorellas of the period, suggest the exultation and joy of the shepherds.[36] As in his other masses, Vanhal uses the oboes as vocal reinforcement, rather than for pastoral solos recalling the piping shepherds (I/E, F and G).[37]

[33] Germer, 'Pastorella', p. 269.
[34] E. Tittel, 'Die Wiener Pastoralmesse', *Musica Divina*, xxiii (1935), p. 194.
[35] For Credo masses see MacIntyre, *Concerted Mass*, pp. 361–2.
[36] Biba, 'Süddeutsche Weihnachtsmusik', pp. 413 and 417.
[37] The author has not had the opportunity to examine the use of pastoral flutes and horns in the manuscript of the work located at the University of Prague; see note 31 above.

Ex. 5.4

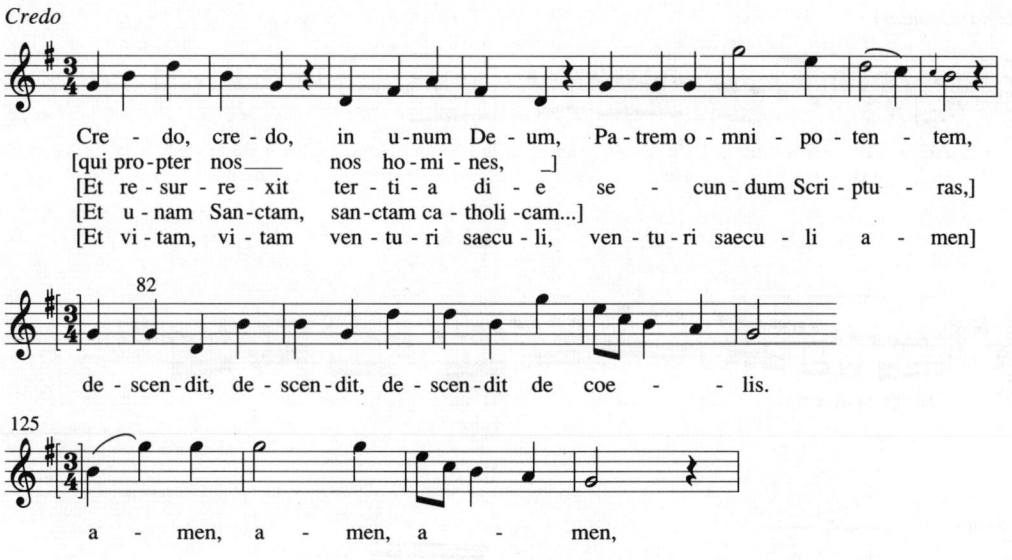

Ex. 5.5

Ex. 5.6

Ex. 5.7

Ex. 5.8

Ex. 5.9

Ex. 5.10

Ex. 5.11

Aside from the occasional echo effect, the use of dynamics was restrained in most pastoral masses, including this one (I/H). Most endings and some beginnings are *piano*, except perhaps for the final two or three cadential chords.[38]

Simplicity and stasis characterize the harmony of pastoral masses. Bucolic drones and pedal points frequently recall the bagpiping of shepherds (II/A and B). In Vanhal's mass the violins usually fiddle away at a repetitive dance tune above such drones, tunes that always contain complete triads (see Exx. 5.12–5.20). Vanhal's Kyrie (Ex. 5.1, p. 119) opens above a pedal point on G that lasts for five bars; such harmonic inactivity is an apt musical parallel to the message of 'peace on earth'. Later in the Kyrie (bb. 36ff) sopranos, violins and oboes play a repetitive rustic tune above the seven-bar drone sustained by the rest of the ensemble (Ex. 5.13 shows the repeated melodic cell). Here Vanhal demands quite a high tessitura from the sopranos in the chorus (phrases start on high A) and uses motifs of rocking thirds.

By their nature such drones and pedal points often generate biting dissonances that enliven the rustic tone of the work (II/C). For example, there are the harmonic clashes in the 'adoramus' portion of the Gloria; for an

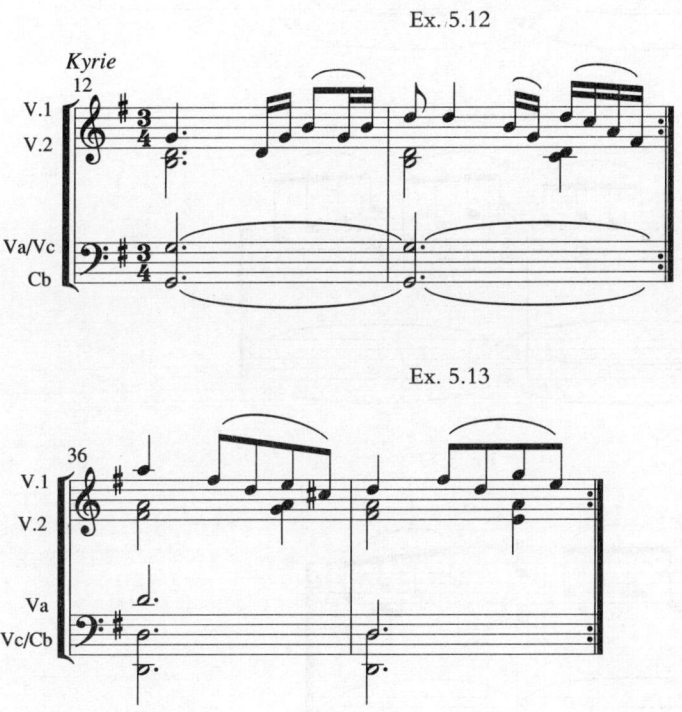

Ex. 5.12

Ex. 5.13

---

[38] In Vanhal's mass, however, surprise *forte* markings and accents such as *sf* and *fp* do help to intensify the 'storm and stress' aspects of the 'Qui tollis' and 'Crucifixus' sections.

Ex. 5.14

Ex. 5.15

Ex. 5.16

Ex. 5.17

Ex. 5.18

Ex. 5.19

Ex. 5.20

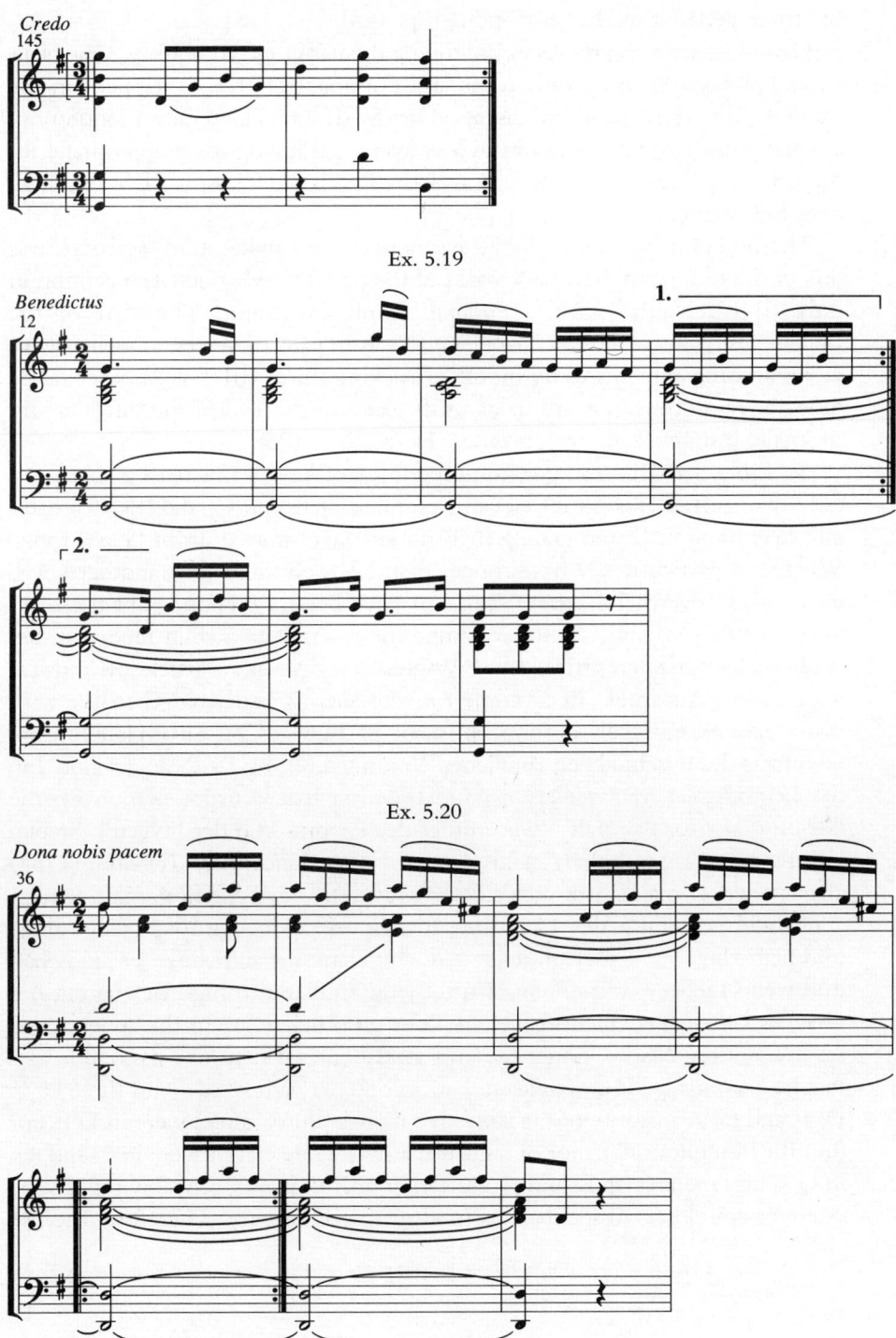

entire bar (b. 22) the ensemble sustains a dominant seventh sonority against the tonic pedal of the basses (Ex. 5.14, p. 124).

Harmonic stasis also results from limiting the harmonic vocabulary. One hears extended passages using only tonic and dominant chords, as happens in the example from the 'Quoniam' discussed below (II/D). This almost monotonous alternation of two chords results in a swaying and lulling effect appropriate for the ceremonial rocking of the crib associated with the Christmas Eve midnight mass in Bohemia.

The predominance of melodies harmonized in parallel thirds or sixths was one of the more common trademarks of the pastoral style since its inception in Italy (II/E). Vanhal's *Missa Pastoralis* is no exception. The start of the Benedictus teems with sweet parallel intervals in pairs of voices, as well as with violin accompaniments using motifs of rocking thirds (III/D). Another fiddle tune above a drone is heard in its usual place, at the end of the introductory ritornello just before the voices enter (Ex. 5.19, p. 125).

As Table 5.2 demonstrates, the predominant key of this mass is G major; only two movements out of eleven ('Domine Deus', in C, and 'Et incarnatus est', beginning in D and ending in B minor) take us away from G as a tonic. Whether a particular key has stronger pastoral associations than another key is debatable. Nevertheless, there seems to have been a preponderant use of G major for Advent and Christmas compositions. As Rita Steblin reports in her study of key characteristics, Abbé Vogler in 1779, in an article on musical expression ('Ausdruck' in *Deutsche Encyclopädie*, ii) associated G major with 'naive actions, especially of innocent rustic pleasures' ('Die naive Handlungen, besonders des unschuldigen ländlichen Vergnügens'); by 1812 Vogler noted in the *Vergleichsplan der Neumünsterorgel in Würzburg* that G major 'was always the favourite key for pastorals' ('war immer der Favorit-Ton der Idyllen'). Steblin also reports how Schubart in his *Ideen zu einer Ästhetik der Tonkunst* (1784) characterizes G major with such adjectives as rustic, idyllic, lyrical, calm, tender, gentle and peaceful ('Alles Ländliche, Idyllen und Eklogenmäßige, jede ruhige und befriedigte Leidenschaft, jeder zärtliche Dank für aufrichtige Freundschaft und treue Liebe, – mit einem Worte, jede sanft und ruhige Bewegung des Herzens läßt sich trefflich in diesem Tone ausdrücken').[39] In the appendix to his dissertation, Mark Germer presents a catalogue of sixty-five pastoral masses that he examined.[40] It is significant that over 80 per cent were in just three keys: D, C and G. A majority of the sixty-five masses (thirty-three) were in D major (not the ubiquitous C major of regular masses), while eleven were in C and ten in G. This emphasis on D and G, instead of only C major, probably reflects the desire of composers to set apart pastoral masses as a genre. Therefore, the use

---

[39] R. Steblin, *A History of Key Characteristics in the Eighteenth and Early Nineteenth Centuries* (Ann Arbor, 1983), pp. 274–5.
[40] Germer, 'Pastorella', pp. 442–62.

Table 5.2. Vanhal's *Missa Pastoralis in G*

Text incipit	Tempo	Metre	Keys	Bars	Misc.
Kyrie	Allegro moderato	3/4	G	164	w/ SATB soli
Gloria	Allegro moderato	¢	G	65	
Domine Deus	Andante molto	3/8	C–V/G	131	w/ SA soli
Quoniam	Allegro	3/4	G	100	
Credo	Allegro moderato	3/4	G	93	
Et incarnatus	Adagio	2/4	D–b	33	w/ SATB soli
Et resurrexit	Allegro moderato	3/4	G	150	
Sanctus	Adagio –	3/4	G–D	22	
Pleni	Allegro	2/4	G	19	
Osanna	Allegro	3/8	G	38	
Benedictus	Andante	2/4	G	104	
Osanna	Allegro	3/8	G	38	
Agnus Dei	Adagio	3/4	g–V/g	47	
Dona nobis pacem	Allegro moderato	2/4	G	116	w/ SATB soli
			Total length	1,120 bars	

Ensemble: SATB soloists, SATB chorus, two oboes, two clarini, timpani, two violins, viola [obbligato], contrabass, organ

of certain pastoral keys seems another plausible characteristic (II/F), and Vanhal has here used the rustic G major, a key that Haydn too uses in two possible Advent masses and in some of his pastorellas.[41]

Melodies in this mass are typically lyrical, flowing, graceful and conjunct (III/A), as several examples have already shown. Often we hear the persistent regularity of phrasing associated with folk music, dance and vernacular

---

[41] There are two possible masses for Advent by Haydn: the doubtful *Missa brevis alla capella Rorate coeli desuper* (Hob.XXII: 3, before c. 1751) and the *Missa Sancti Nicolai* (Hob.XXII: 6, probably for St Nicholas Day, 6 December 1772). Both masses are in G major. Haydn's pastorella works in G major include 'Mutter Gottes, mir erlaube' (Hob.XXIIId: 2) and 'Ei, wer hätt ihm das Ding gedenkt' (Hob.XXIIId: G1).

Christmas songs (III/B). Phrases tend to be built of repeated rhythmic motifs and to have even numbers of bars. For example, at the opening of Vanhal's Credo, a couple of two-bar gestures (Ex. 5.4. bb. 1–2 and 3–4, p. 121) is followed by a series of four-bar phrases (bb. 5ff). Here again one observes repeated triadic motifs that pastoral masses frequently used (III/C), perhaps as a suggestion of the fanfares heralding the arrival of the Christ Child (III/E/2). As Biba has noted, triadic melodies recall also the harmonic series of open notes on natural instruments such as the horn or trumpet.[42]

Some examples have already been presented for the rocking alternating thirds that often shape the melodies in Vanhal's *Missa Pastoralis* (III/D; see Exx. 5.13, p. 123, and 5.19, p. 125). When speeded up, such rocking thirds take on a bucolic air reminiscent of fluttering leaves in the trees or the chirping of birds (III/E/3). One of the orchestral ritornellos in Vanhal's Gloria seems to create this effect (bb. 28–31, just after 'Glorificamus te') and recalls similar chirping devices in earlier programme pieces by Vivaldi and others.

The tender style used in Italian *ninne* or Christmas lullabies is often alluded to in the slower movements of pastoral masses (III/F). The beginning of Vanhal's Sanctus best represents this style. Here the two upper voices slowly rock back and forth in parallel thirds, suggesting the rocking crib of tradition. This is not the typical Sanctus glorifying a powerful *deus majestatis* with great fanfares and choral acclamations; it is indeed a lullaby (Ex. 5.21). Such *Kindelwiegen* or cradle-rocking style in these masses probably came from the pastorella tradition dating back to the seventeenth century.[43]

As already suggested, rustic folk dance inspires some of the little fiddle tunes often heard above a sustained drone or pedal point in these pastoral works (III/G, see Exx. 5.12–20, pp. 123–5). The start of the 'Quoniam' section at the end of the Gloria similarly uses a fiddle tune of short, repeated motifs outlining tonic and dominant chords to close the orchestral ritornello of the movement (Ex. 5.17, p. 124). Exx. 5.22 and 23 present excerpts from contemporary pastoral masses by Jiří Linek (1725–91) and Jan František Novák (d. 1771) that have similar dance-like tunes in their accompaniments. Ex. 5.24 shows the same kind of triadic fiddle tunes in Haydn's pastorella 'Ei, wer hätt ihm das Ding gedenkt' (Hob.XXIIId: G1).

Pastoral works from Austro-Bohemian lands sometimes alluded to the exotic scales of certain folk songs (III/H). In Vanhal's 'Quoniam', when the voices sing 'altissimus Jesu Christe' in unison, one hears a chromatic Lydian fourth that momentarily lends a Slavic flavour to the movement (Ex. 5.8, p. 122).[44]

---

[42] Biba, 'Süddeutsche Weihnachtsmusik', p. 416. Biba's examples of triadic themes from Vanhal's pastorella 'Christus natus est nobis' are strikingly similar to those in this mass.

[43] *Ibid.*, p. 418.

[44] The so-called 'Night Watchman's song' from Bohemia is one of the most famous examples of a vernacular Christmas song that uses the raised fourth degree; see G. Chew, 'The Night-Watchman's Song Quoted by Haydn and Its Implications', *Haydn Studien*, iii (1974), pp. 106–24.

JOHANN BAPTIST VANHAL AND THE PASTORAL MASS TRADITION 129

Ex. 5.21

Ex. 5.22 Linek, Missa Pastoralis in D

Ex. 5.23 Jan František Novák (d. 1771), Missa Pastoralis, *Kyrie*

Ex. 5.24 Joseph Haydn(?), 'Ei, wer hätt ihm das Ding gedenkt?'

Since Vanhal used elements of Czech folksong in other works, it would not be surprising to discover that a few Czech tunes are concealed in this mass.[45]

Most of the rhythmic characteristics of the pastoral mass have already been touched upon briefly: use of duple, compound or triple metres, moderate tempos and additive, balanced phrase structures (IV/A–E). As the outline in Table 5.2 (p. 127) clearly shows, triple metre prevails in Vanhal's mass. An excellent example of the use of 2/4 metre for its dance-like qualities is the 'Dona nobis pacem' which concludes this mass in a most ebullient manner. Its opening theme (Ex. 5.11a, p. 122) uses an unusual, albeit catchy syncopated motif somewhat reminiscent of the American folksong 'Shoo fly, don't bother me'. This theme then serves as a kind of refrain for a structure that resembles an instrumental rondo or an operatic *vaudeville* finale. Certain repeated melismas sung by the chorus on the word 'pacem' sound out of place but perhaps reflect a rustic kind of drunken joy at Christmas time (Ex. 5.11b). The soloists sing in the usual parallel thirds, and the solo/tutti alternations recall the give-and-take of pastoral dialogues mentioned earlier (I/D). Biba has noted how dance-like rhythms in pastorellas effectively mirror the joy of the shepherds.[46] Vanhal's 'Dona nobis' ends gently with a soft choral-orchestral drone beneath another fiddle tune.

Vanhal does not change the liturgical text of the Ordinary by omitting passages which are out of character with the joyful season or by interpolating vernacular texts, as was sometimes the case in other pastoral masses of the day. Germer calls such insertions 'vernacular interludes'.[47] Perhaps Vanhal was too much of an urban composer to include such interludes which, apparently, were common in masses written for rural parishes.

Comparing Vanhal's masses with those by his contemporaries, one is struck by the almost obsessive formal clarity in Vanhal. Rarely does the text dictate the order of musical events, as was so often the case with prolix liturgical texts

---

[45] On folksong in Vanhal readers are referred to O. Loulová, 'Das tschechische Volkslied in Werke von Jan Křtitel Vaňhal' in *Internationale Mozartkonferenz* (Prague, 1956), pp. 70–2.
[46] Biba, 'Süddeutsche Weihnachtsmusik', pp. 416–17.
[47] Germer, 'Pastorella', pp. 342–4.

such as the Credo. Using his experience as an instrumental composer Vanhal lets the musical elements organize and unify a movement, rather than allowing the text to be the only master of form. Sonata, ritornello and rondo-like forms are found in the present work.

Formal unity exists at several levels, both within and between movements of this pastoral mass. Not only is each movement carefully structured around a few recurring themes and motifs, but the entire mass cycle exhibits a high degree of thematic unity supported by more than just the monogenic pastoral devices and recurring tunes. As in at least two of Vanhal's symphonies (Bryan B♭1 and g2),[48] the principal themes of several movements seem moulded from the same basic idea (see Exx. 5.1–6, p. 119, p. 121). Its essential shape, which appears above Ex. 5.1, arches upwards from g^1 through a triad to the octave (g^2) before gradually descending back to the tonic g^1 (or, alternatively, the third degree). Some listeners might hear this basic outline as reminiscent of the Advent hymn 'Wachet auf'.

Another potentially unifying idea is the turning, conjunct scale motif ('X') shown in Exx. 5.7–11c (pp. 121–2); after the Kyrie we often hear it as part of a ritornello that signals the end of a section. This rather comprehensive formal cohesiveness was innovative for its day, yet would perhaps have been too obvious and mechanical for a Joseph Haydn. However, coupled with a certain raw rustic vigour in rhythm, melody, harmony and colour, the formal integrity supports Vanhal's place as a progressive composer of concerted masses.

Vanhal's *Missa Pastoralis* cannot really be compared with the masses of Joseph Haydn. Haydn never wrote a mass specifically for Christmas Eve, but he did write masses for the Advent season which, when compared with Vanhal's contribution, are restricted in their use of pastoral devices. Haydn's masses are also less repetitive in their phrasing, and there is much greater harmonic variety than in Vanhal's mass. Perhaps Haydn considered that over-reliance upon pastoral devices would be a hindrance to his creativity and free expression – a compositional blueprint that could easily result in a mediocre or bland setting.

We should not forget that the two composers came from different sides of the Danube: Haydn from Lower Austria's Rohrau, to the south-east of Vienna, and Vanhal from a Bohemian village, Nové Nechanice, that was probably in close contact with the traditions of the rustic Czech pastorella. Also, unlike Haydn, Vanhal spent some two years south of the Alps where he would have been directly exposed to the Italian Baroque pastoral traditions. We should remember, too, that Haydn and Vanhal were writing their masses for different patrons, institutions and occasions. Nevertheless, Vanhal was an enterprising composer for his day, and in his masses as well as his symphonies he lived up to

---

[48] The catalogue numbers are from *The Symphony 1720–1840*, ed. B. S. Brook (New York, 1981), Series B, x. M. Poštolka ('Vanhal', p. 523) also notes Vanhal's reliance upon 'similarity of thematic material both within and among movements'.

his reputation as a 'proto-Romanticist'.[49] He, Abbé Vogler, Linek, Novák and others helped prepare the way for the Romantic composers of the early nineteenth century who carried the pastoral mass to its zenith.

Vanhal's *Missa Pastoralis* thus exemplifies the progressive side of concerted mass writing in Austria in the 1770s and 1780s. Along with impressive formal clarity, the tonal unity and the increased use of dance-like metres and rhythms, the work presents the solemn mass Ordinary in fewer movements than earlier extended masses. There are no movements for solo voices only; the solo sections are regularly incorporated into the choral movements (e.g. 'Kyrie', 'Domine Deus', 'Et incarnatus' and 'Dona nobis' in Table 5.2, p. 127). In addition, oboes are part of Vanhal's church orchestra (not just in this mass and not just for their pastoral connotations), and the viola has taken on an obbligato role.

To what extent the common devices of pastoral masses directly affected the style of all concerted masses we shall never know with certainty. Nonetheless, the manner in which the pastoral style helps to simplify, consolidate and unify a mass makes the genre a significant catalyst in the gradual change from the sprawling, multi-movement number mass of the Baroque to the more concise, symphonic and unified mass at the end of the eighteenth century. Commenting on the new blend of styles in Austro-Bohemian pastoral masses up to c. 1780, Mark Germer has perceptively noted that this was 'More than a miscellany of stylistic devices . . . what was successfully propagated in the north was the tendency to balance the sobriety of the ecclesiastical style with a calculated simplicity and directness of expression'.[50] In his *Missa Pastoralis* in G Vanhal inventively explores the traditional pastoral devices to which he had been exposed in his native Bohemia, and he combines them in a compelling, unified and attractive fashion that entices us to hear other masses by this significant contributor to the sacred repertoire in Austria at the end of the eighteenth century.

[49] Bryan, ed., *Johann Vanhal: Six Symphonies*, p. ix.
[50] Germer, 'Pastorella', p. 269.

6

The Austrian pastorella and the *stylus rusticanus*: comic and pastoral elements in Austrian music, 1750–1800

GEOFFREY CHEW

In his monograph on Haydn's symphonies, H. C. Robbins Landon has emphasized Haydn's allusions to 'exotic' Eastern European folk music in his works.[1] Different composers had different ideas about the use of material of this sort in eighteenth-century Austria, but Haydn cannot have been exceptional in his familiarity with it. In view of the surviving evidence and contrary to expectation, most of these musical allusions seem not to have been drawn directly from the orally transmitted folksong of town and countryside, which began to be comprehensively documented only in the nineteenth century, but from a written musical repertory transmitted in monasteries and parish churches throughout the Habsburg realms and in Catholic areas even further afield. The so-called 'pastorella' is one of the principal genres in this repertory.[2] Though it is, strictly speaking, 'art music', it relies for its genre definition on its allusions to a limited number of melodies and styles which symbolize – and may or may not literally correspond with – aspects of folk music.[3] Maintaining links with the repertory of allusions seems to have been much more important than the literal quotation of folk melodies, and often produced comic effects; and the importance of this process in late eighteenth-century Austrian church music and comic opera is the subject of this essay. The illustrations of comic opera below are drawn only from the late operas of Mozart, which offer a broad range of possibilities; but if the net had been cast more widely – in particular, with the inclusion of Haydn's operas, but possibly also of instrumental music – a yet more diversified view would, of course, emerge.[4]

[1] H.C. Robbins Landon, *The Symphonies of Joseph Haydn* (London, 1955), pp. 263–5; *Supplement to The Symphonies of Joseph Haydn* (London, 1961), pp. 46–7.
[2] For literature, see especially G. A. Chew, 'The Christmas Pastorella in Austria, Bohemia and Moravia and its Antecedents' (2 vols., Ph.D. diss., University of Manchester, 1968); J. Berkovec, *České pastorely* (Prague, 1987); M. Germer, 'The Austro-Bohemian Pastorella and Pastoral Mass to c. 1780' (Ph.D. diss., New York University, 1989).
[3] A preliminary discussion of this aspect can be found in Chew, 'The Christmas Pastorella', where the allusions are termed 'allusive clichés' and listed, but not exhaustively.
[4] See G. A. Wheelock, *Haydn's Ingenious Jesting with Art: Contexts of Musical Wit and Humor* (New York: Schirmer Books, 1992); also my review of this monograph, in *Music & Letters*, lxxv (1994), pp. 77–82.

Since the pastorella repertory is still not well understood, a very summary account of its history before 1750 may be useful. It must first have appeared around 1680–90, most likely as a by-product of small-scale dramatic productions presented by boys in monastic schools each Christmas; there is evidence of its use by Jesuits, Piarists and other teaching orders.[5] One of its most influential early patrons appears to have been Paul Esterházy, who in 1711 published some examples in his *Harmonia caelestis*.[6] As an ally of the Habsburgs he had as one of his principal concerns the recatholicization of those areas of Central Europe still infected by Protestantism.

From the outset, the pastorella normally took one of two distinct forms, strophic *ariae* normally with ritornellos and accompanied at least by violins and bass, and more extended miniature cantatas comprising three or four movements (solo arias, duets, recitatives and choruses, usually concluding with a short chorus). (The literature contrives to suggest both that the strophic form evolved into the miniature-cantata form and vice versa.[7] Neither suggestion has any foundation, as far as I am aware.) Pastorellas were composed by Viennese court composers in the early eighteenth century (Fux 1660–1741, Caldara c. 1670–1736, Reinhardt 1676/7–1742 and others) in both these forms.

The general nature of the repertory may be illustrated from an early multi-movement pastorella by J. G. Reinhardt; Ex. 6.1 reproduces the incipits of each movement.[8]

Pastorellas by their nature, like other varieties of pastoral, set up taxonomies, that is, differentiated systems, of musical style; their range is most clearly seen in the miniature-cantata variety. At the least, a simple 'country' style is distinguished from a more elaborate 'courtly' or 'city' style, but in Ex. 6.1 there is a threefold scheme; the moderately 'serious' style of the first aria, No. 1, contrasts not only with a markedly 'rustic' pastoral style in the two shepherds' choruses (Nos. 2 and 5), but also with an 'elevated' pastoral style in the D minor aria, No. 4, which is evoked with the plaintive chalumeau, an instrument probably representing the pastoral reed ('tenuis avena', 'calamus agrestis') of the first *Eclogue* of Virgil.[9] This

---

[5] See G. A. Chew, 'Die Vorgeschichte der mitteleuropäischen Pastorella und des stylus rusticanus im 17. Jahrhundert', in *Die Musik des 17. Jahrhunderts und Pavel Josef Vejvanovský: Symposium, Kroměříž 6.–9. September 1993*, (Brno, 1994), pp. 79–85.

[6] Paul Esterházy, *Harmonia caelestis seu moelodiae per decursum totius anni adhibendae ad usum musicorum* (n.p. [Vienna], 1711); modern edition: F. Bónis, ed. (Kassel, 1972ff); cf. M. Domokos, 'Paul Esterházy: Harmonia caelestis 1711', *Studia musicologica Academiae Scientianum Hungaricae*, x (1968), pp. 129–51.

[7] These views are represented, respectively, by J. Bužga, 'Oratorium, F: Tschechische Sonderformen', *Die Musik in Geschichte und Gegenwart*, x, col. 156–8, and O. Biba, 'Süddeutsche Weihnachtsmusik', in *Musica sacra*, xcvii (1977).

[8] All music examples in this paper (except from Mozart) are previously unpublished. The source for this work is an early eighteenth-century manuscript from the private collection of the late Dr K. Pfannhauser, to whom I am grateful for making it accessible to me.

[9] Virgil, *Eclogue* 1:1–2: 'Tityre, tu patulae recubans sub tegmine fagi / silvestrem tenui musam meditaris avena'; the 'humble reed', 'tenui avena', referred to here becomes a 'rural pipe', 'calamus agrestis', at line 10: the word 'calamus' is, of course, cognate with 'chalumeau'.

Ex. 6.1 J. G. Reinhardt, Pastorella in F 'Zum Freuden erwachet' (c. 1730)

No. 1. Aria (Angel, Soprano), 'Zum Freuden'

No. 2. Chorus Pastorum, 'Was hören wir Hirten'

THE AUSTRIAN PASTORELLA AND THE *STYLUS RUSTICANUS* 137

No. 3. Recitativo (Angel, Soprano), 'Fürchtet euch nicht'

No. 4. Aria (Angel, Soprano), 'Laßet euch'

No. 5. Chorus Pastorum, 'So wollen wir Hürten'

Chorus: Allabreve

instrument was favoured in Austrian pastoral music around the turn of the century. A copy of this work at Wilhering, cited by Biba, replaces the chalumeau with a trombone; the substitution cannot, of course, be authentic.[10]

The markedly 'rustic' style of the shepherds' choruses in this piece characterizes many of the more extended of the early pastorellas, even though it scarcely touches pieces in other genres by the same composers; the rustic style found in a pastorella by Fux[11] in a copy dated 1725 is unknown in his output otherwise.

Even in the earliest pastorellas, this rustic style may be distinguished from the more traditional, well-known Italianate pastoral style, established for the most part in the late Renaissance, with siciliano rhythms, 6/4 (or from the eighteenth century 6/8) time, and melodies in conjunct thirds and sixths in a Larghetto or equivalent tempo. The Austrian equivalents by contrast include fast 2/4 time, unison passages, melodies with broken-chord figuration, 'Lydian' sharpened

[10] See Biba, 'Süddeutsche Weihnachtmusik', p. 414.
[11] J. J. Fux, Pastorella 'Pastores pastores evangelizo vobis', in a manuscript copy from the collection originally at the Benedictine monastery of Rajhrad (Raigern), Brno, Moravian Museum, Music Division, A 12324; edited in Chew, 'The Christmas Pastorella', ii.

fourths, and other unusual chromaticism. Some features, such as extended pedal points, are common to both idioms.

Furthermore, the 'Austrian' rustic style (analogously to the Italian) could be used in more or less emphatic forms, sometimes in juxtaposition with the Italian pastoral style. Thus subtle stylistic taxonomies could be set up within pieces, and these are one of the hallmarks of the genre. In his monograph on Czech pastorellas, Jiří Berkovec has had the happy inspiration of inventing the pseudo-Baroque rhetorical term *musica rusticalis*, an obvious analogue of 'musica cameralis' and 'musica theatralis', for passages in pastorellas in a 'rustic' style. At the risk of appearing pedantic (but also with the advantage of remaining closer to the contemporary terminology of W. C. Printz, further discussed below), one might correct Dr Berkovec's Latin and refer to this rustic style as the *stylus rusticanus*. To recognize this style helps to explain the exotic allusions which Robbins Landon noticed in Haydn, for they are invoked precisely in order to set up taxonomies of style within pieces; the purposes of doing so are, of course, not necessarily the same on every occasion. Indeed the *stylus rusticanus* is not restricted to pastorellas: it appears in some of the vernacular intermezzi of Central European opera (for example, those to F. A. Míča's *L'origine di Jaromeriz in Moravia* of 1730), and a little later in such works as Bach's Peasant Cantata (BWV 212) of 1742 – a classic example in which several styles, ranging from the *stylus rusticanus* to the most 'elevated', are juxtaposed.

The *stylus rusticanus* originated, like the pastorella, but perhaps independently of it, in the late seventeenth century. One of its earliest witnesses is the late seventeenth-century theorist Wolfgang Caspar Printz, writing at Sorau in Lusatia (Lausitz), then an eastern German town and now in Poland; his *Phrynis Mitilenæus oder Satyrischer Componist* (1696) satirizes musical styles which he emphatically says are acceptable only to tavern musicians (*Bier-Fiedler und Schergeiger*).[12] Printz enters the ancient debate about the criteria for judging music, and adduces evidence that ignorant listeners are satisfied with the *stylus rusticanus* to argue against the exclusive use of the judgement of the ear (rather than that of the intellect) to discern the quality of music.[13] He recounts an overnight stay at a place in Siberia:

Da waren zween Bier-Fiedler / die machten eine solche Harmonie, daß mir die Ohren vier Wochen lang davon wehe thaten / massen der Bassiste ins Wesen hinein schrobete / wie es ihm einkahm / also / daß er fast nichts / als lauter Dissonanzen machte / und gemeiniglich eine Secunde über oder unter dem Thon / so mit dem Discant eine Octav resoniret / aushielte. Nichts desto weniger gefiele denen Bauern diese Music so trefflich wohl / und wurden darvon so lustig / daß ich gedachte / sie würden die Stube umbkehren.

[12] See Wolfgang Caspar Printz, *W. C. Printzens . . . Phrynis Mitilenæus, oder satyrischer Componist, welcher, vermittelst einer satyrischen Geschicht, die Fehler der ungelehrten . . . Componisten höflich darstellet* (Dresden and Leipzig, 1696), especially part iii.
[13] For the passage on which this discussion is based, see Printz, *Phrynis Mitilenæus*, part iii, pp. 84–6.

There were two tavern musicians, who played such harmony as made my ears ache for four weeks, since the violone player struck up in the ensemble simply as he wished, so that he played hardly anything except dissonances, and generally sustained notes a degree above or below the note which would have made an octave with the violin. All the same, this music pleased the peasants there so extremely well, and they became so jolly hearing it, that I thought they were going to break up the room.

On the basis of this and other anecdotes he sets up an interesting taxonomic system of four types of musical ear (*Gehör*) corresponding to different musical styles and different groups of listeners. This supplies a more focused contemporary theoretical formulation of the taxonomic systems already exemplified above in early pastorellas, and illustrates the type of conceptual apparatus that no doubt underlay the use of the *stylus rusticanus* at every stage of its history. He distinguishes:

1. a 'Siberian ear' (*Syberianisches Gehör*), possessed by 'Siberian' listeners ('Syberianer'), who will tolerate any sound that is made, totally without discrimination;
2. a 'rural ear' (*Bäurisches Gehör*), possessed by 'country' listeners ('Rusticaner'), who cannot tolerate dissonances but accept any other musical solecism without demur;
3. a 'civilized ear' (*Höffliches Gehör*), possessed by 'citified' listeners ('Urbaner'), who tolerate only music that is 'elegant' (*zierlich*), but without knowledge;
4. a 'musical ear', possessed by 'noble' listeners ('Auditores Nobiles'), who support the judgement of their ears with rational knowledge.

It is understandable that composers seem seldom to have sought to adopt Printz's *stylus siberianus*, if one may term it that (though some of the more extreme country styles used in pastorellas may have been meant to exemplify something of the sort). It was, rather, the opposition of 'country' and 'town' styles, implicit in his second and third categories, which must normally – whether consciously or not – have supplied the basis for the use of the *stylus rusticanus* by composers.

Early in its history, the *stylus rusticanus* was often used to create comic effects, even for use in church. Indeed, its comic use survived beyond the end of the Second World War in repertories of pastorella-derived folksongs in Austria and South Tirol.[14] Ex. 6.2 (pp. 144–55), which is rather old-fashioned (the copy is dated 22 December 1762), is a pastorella by Johann Georg Zechner (1716–78), who worked at the abbey of Göttweig near Krems in Lower Austria before being ordained priest.[15] The fairly extensive collection of pastorellas at Göttweig[16] uses a

---

[14] For examples, see A. Quellmalz, ed., *Südtiroler Volkslieder*, iii (Kassel and Basel, 1976).

[15] Further on Zechner and his connections with Göttweig (besides the standard reference works), see F. W. Riedel, 'Beiträge zur Geschichte der Musikpflege an der Stadtpfarrkirche St. Veit zu Krems', *950 Jahre Pfarre Krems: Festschrift* (Krems a.d. Donau, 1964), pp. 322–4.

[16] Details of the collection, including lists of performance dates recorded in the copies, can be found in Chew, 'The Christmas Pastorella' i, Appendix 1 and passim.

moderate version of the *stylus rusticanus*; nevertheless, comic effects in narrative compositions remained within its range. The example is very similar, incidentally, to a published Czech vernacular pastorella by Tomáš Norbert Koutník (fl. 1750), which adds a pastoral alphorn to the ensemble.[17]

The first short movement of this piece, given complete in Ex. 6.2, presents, in quasi-dramatic form, the song of the Bethlehem angels ('Gloria in excelsis Deo'; Latin is the language of heaven, and is sung by soprano and alto *putti*). This is interspersed from bar 21 onwards with dialect interruptions from three shepherds in a tenor–tenor–bass ensemble:

Was ist das für ein Gschrey?	What kind of a din is that?
Kleine Büeberl nach der Rey	Little boys in a row
Singen so zart und fein!	are singing sweetly and beautifully!
Gwiß müssens Engerl seyn?	Can they really be angels?
Gwiß müssens Engerl seyn!	They really *are* angels!

An aria in a more 'elevated' style follows: an older angel calls on the shepherds to make their pilgrimage to Bethlehem; then the shepherds express their resolve to obey, in a markedly rustic final andante chorus. The beginnings of these, shown in the example, illustrate the range of styles in the piece.

In the first movement, the 'comic' depends on the quick dialogue between angels and shepherds, and in the gaps this reveals in the shepherds' grasp of the situation; the audience has, of course, an angel's-eye view of the proceedings. Comic effects are most marked in miniature-cantata pastorellas in the early repertory, of which Zechner's piece is a classic example; such pieces present a narrative sequence of a selection of the events of Christmas Eve – the appearance of the angels, the awakening of the shepherds, their resolve to depart for Bethlehem, and their arrival and self-oblation at the crib. (Austrian shepherds did not visit a manger.)

Dialogue of this type – one of the longest-lasting characteristics of the pastorella, used later also in strophic pieces[18] – depends essentially on the *stylus rusticanus*, and requires a 'pastoral' discrepancy to be set up between the naïveté of the characters and the knowingness of the audience. Equally – and this too is part of the pastoral constellation of ideas – the 'simple' reaction of the shepherds is presented as universally human, and thus supplies an essential yardstick for judging the response of the audience. Thus the real basis of the rustic style in this brand of pastoral is moral, and in this respect pastoral has much in common with dramatic comedy at its highest.

Between about 1750 and 1850, the pastorella repertory expanded very rapidly, and scores of local composers composed hundreds of pastorellas, in a

---

[17] Printed in J. Berkovec (ed.), *České vánoční pastorely*, Musica antiqua bohemica, xxiii (Prague, 1955).
[18] Nineteenth-century examples are preserved in private manuscript collections of secular songs (e.g. in the Museum Carolino-Augusteum in Salzburg) and there are still examples in the folksongs collected in the twentieth century in South Tirol (see n. 14 above).

Ex. 6.2 J. G. Zechner, Pastorella in C 'Gloria in excelsis – Was ist das für ein Gschrey?'

No. 1 Chorus, 'Gloria - Was ist das'

152 GEOFFREY CHEW

153

No. 2. Aria (Angel, Alto), 'Ihr Hirten laufet all'

No. 3. Chorus [Pastorum], 'Laßt Schaf' und Lämmer stehen'

stream which did not abate until well into the nineteenth century at the earliest. Their composers include, in the realm of Austria narrowly considered, Joseph Haydn (1732–1809), Michael Haydn (1737–1806), Dittersdorf (1739–99), Holzbauer (1711–83), Zechner (1716–78), Hofmann (1738–93) and Vanhal (1739–1813), among many others.[19] At the same time, a comic *buffo* style of Italian derivation came to be favoured in Austrian opera, largely owing to the work of Goldoni and the Italian composers who first set his librettos.[20] These two developments juxtapose two different conceptions of the comic, often in the works of the same composers. In the rest of this chapter, some aspects of the redefinition of the comic and the pastoral which occurred at this time will first be outlined. The results of this redefinition will then be considered, first in terms of pastorellas and then in terms of Mozart's late comic operas.

Pastoral works depend on the sharing of common assumptions by composers, poets, authors or dramatists and their audiences, concerning two principal aspects of such works, which are closely related to each other. These are traditionally termed 'verisimilitude' and 'decorum'. Verisimilitude means credibility, and decorum appropriateness, in the models used to express the pastoral ideal. If the shepherds of a pastoral idyll stray too far from real life, they will lack verisimilitude; if, on the other hand, they fail to express sufficient courtliness, they will lack decorum. And notions of both verisimilitude and decorum change in far-reaching ways from period to period; if we find Renaissance pastoral vapid, for example, it is most likely because our ideas of decorum and verisimilitude are not those of the sixteenth century. Goldoni in 1754, in the preface to his libretto *De gustibus non est disputandum*, complained (no doubt thinking of vulgarities deriving from the *commedia dell'arte*) of the imperfections of Italian comic opera, of its lack of decorum and of the impossibility of pleasing all audiences. This preface pleads for the reform of opera buffa through the paying of careful attention to 'the action, the characters, the plot and the truth, as one should do in a good comedy' ('alla condotta, ai caratteri, all'intreccio, alla verità, come in una Commedia buona dovrebbe farsi'); although the details are left disappointingly vague, the general requirement to maintain an elevated tone is very clear ('I have attempted to write [this comedy] in a way which will correspond to the merit and good taste of the person who honoured me by commanding me to write it') ('Ho procurato di scriverlo in una maniera che corrisponder potesse al merito ed al buon gusto di chi mi ha onorato di comandarmi di scrivere'), and is borne out by the librettos which Goldoni himself wrote and published.

[19] Manuscript sources are widespread in the major national archives and libraries as well as those of local churches and monasteries; for partial bibliographical coverage, see in particular the sources listed above in n. 2.
[20] On Goldoni's influence in this area see, in particular, D. Heartz, 'The Creation of the Buffo Finale in Italian Opera', *Proceedings of the Royal Musical Association*, civ (1977–8), pp. 67–78.

Whatever the nature of aristocratic 'merit and good taste' in Venice may have been these new Italian trends became criteria in Central Europe for judging not only *drammi per musica* but also many other types of music, including church music; and the *stylus rusticanus* was irreconcilable with Italianate taste. It had once been favoured on account of its educational potential, but could now be despised by those of good taste as a vulgar *porcheria tedesca*. The degree to which this view of the *stylus rusticanus* came eventually to be accepted by all who aspired to taste can be judged by the verdict of Johann Michael Binder, the sacristan of Maria-Taferl, who in 1818 apologetically submitted some pastorellas (*Krippelgsangl*) from a manuscript collection dated 1735 in response to a request from the Gesellschaft der Musikfreunde in Vienna for folksongs from all parts of Austria:[21]

Da eben die Rede von Kirchenliedern ist, so kann der Unterzeichnete nicht umhin, etwas von den alten, ehemahls gewöhnlichen Weihnachtliedern /:vulgo Krippelgsangl:/ zu sagen. Diese Lieder, ein Gemisch vom Geistlichen und Niedrigkomischen, wie die spanischen Autos Sacramentales, waren öfters das non plus altra aller Knittelverse und pöbelhaften Ausdrücke, und . . . waren meistens für eine Baßstimme gesetzt, und von mancherley Albernheiten begleitet.

Since *Kirchenlieder* are being mentioned, the undersigned cannot help saying something about the old *Weihnachtslieder* (in the vernacular, *Krippelgsangl*), which were formerly common. These songs, a mixture of the spiritual and of comic vulgarity, like the Spanish *autos sacramentales*, frequently represented the *ne plus ultra* of every kind of doggerel and vulgarity in expression, and were . . . usually set for a bass voice, and accompanied by many kinds of foolishness.

The Maria-Taferl pastorellas to which he is referring, still preserved in the Sonnleithner collection of the Gesellschaft der Musikfreunde,[22] are very representative of their period. Binder was quite wrong to suggest, as he does later, that the pastorella had disappeared by his time; but the change in taste to which he refers had already caused considerable changes in the tradition. A middle course was steered by some institutions, roughly from the middle of the eighteenth century: this brought modifications to the tradition, in establishments where pastorellas were still required, rather than simple acceptance or rejection of it. One of the forms of such accommodation to 'Italian' standards required the most markedly folk-like elements of the *stylus rusticanus* to be eliminated or attenuated, or, most typically, made Classical by being placed in well-defined, stereotyped positions within pieces, within regular sonata-form

---

[21] Original: Vienna, Gesellschaft der Musikfreunde, Sonnleithner-Sammlung, Niederösterreich XI/37; Binder's comments are printed (with slight modifications) in K. M. Klier, ed., *Schatz österreichischer Weihnachtslieder aus den ältesten Quellen mit den Weisen herausgegeben* (Klosterneuburg, n.d. [c. 1939]), i, Nos. 35–7 (pp. 45–7).

[22] Cf. W. Deutsch and G. Hofer, eds., *Die Volksmusiksammlung der Gesellschaft der Musikfreunde in Wien: Sonnleithner-Sammlung*, Schriften zur Volksmusik, ii (Vienna, 1969–71).

Ex. 6.3 J. Krottendorfer, Pastorella ex E♭ 'Losts nur grad auf, was das ist für ä Mär'

160 GEOFFREY CHEW

No. 2. Recitative (Angel, Soprano), 'Höret, ihr Hirten'

No. 3. Aria (Angel, Soprano), 'Lasset euch in Wahrheit sagen'

No. 4. Recitative (Tenor/Bass), 'Verweilt keine Zeit'

No. 5. Chorus, 'So laufen wir nach Bethlehem'

Ex. 6.4 F. Schneider, Pastorella in A 'Parvulus filius natus est nobis'

structures. Three examples will be given here, each presenting a slightly different solution to the problem.

At Göttweig, the assorted manifestations of the *stylus rusticanus*, including bird-calls and toy instruments, in pastorellas of the 1740s, 1750s and early 1760s gave place in the second half of the 1760s to two compositions by minor Viennese court musicians, Matthias Schlöger (d. 1766) and Josef Krottendorfer (1741–98), and these two pastorellas then dominated the Christmas repertory at Göttweig for almost half a century (performances are recorded until 1811). Krottendorfer's pastorella, copied in 1768, may serve as an example of the new toned-down *stylus rusticanus* (Ex. 6. 3, pp. 158–69).[23]

This composition is traditional in being narrative and multi-movement, with a vernacular, indeed dialect text (for example, 'habs nie ä so ghört', 'I have never heard anything like that before'); but the quick comic dialogue is now absent, and the allusions establishing the *stylus rusticanus* are limited to some conventional pastoral effects in the final chorus, besides the short pedal point at the end of No. 1, the first chorus (bb. 15–17).

Even this combination of multi-movement structure and vernacular text seems to have been too much for some churches. The point may be illustrated first by reference to one of the vocal pastorellas of Franz Schneider (1737–1812) at the Benedictine abbey of Melk (Ex. 6.4, pp. 170–5).[24]

This pastorella supplies a typical transformation of the *stylus rusticanus* into the 'tuneful' style common in certain mid-century Austrian church music. The text is a Latin paraphrase of the introit for the third mass of Christmas Day; a homophonic four-part chorus in effect fills in the full-orchestra sections in a single-movement organ concerto. The *stylus rusticanus* is restricted to the short broken-chord arpeggiations after principal cadences articulating tonic and dominant; thus it is not allowed in any way to cut across the clear projection of a sonata or concerto structure, with which it would have seriously interfered if it had been used more traditionally. In this way the *stylus rusticanus*, too, contributes to the stylistic differentiation within movements (such as the distinctions in style between thematic groups) typical of the mature Classical style; in effect, it becomes the trademark of a 'second-subject' or 'closing' group in exposition or recapitulation.

Ex. 6.5 is one of a pair of settings both of the same Latin text from the Christmas Proper ('Tui sunt caeli', the offertory from the third mass of Christmas Day) from the cathedral of Sv. Vít in Prague, by Johann Anton Kozeluch (1738–1814), the *Kapellmeister* there in the 1770s.[25] He distinguishes

---

[23] Source: Benedictine abbey of Göttweig, MS Krottendorfer 30. Schlöger's pastorella (MS Schlöger 1) was copied in 1766.

[24] Source: MS at Melk.

[25] The source for the pair of offertories: Prague, Cathedral Chapter Archive (Archiv metropolitní kapituly), MSS 699–700. On Kozeluch himself, see Rudolf Fikrle, *Jan Ev. Ant. Koželuh: život, dílo a osobnost svatovítského kapelníka* (Prague, 1946).

Ex. 6.5 J. A. Kozeluch, *Offertorium pastorale* in G 'Tui sunt caeli'

THE AUSTRIAN PASTORELLA AND THE *STYLUS RUSTICANUS*   179

the two settings, both symphonically conceived and evidently copied at the same time, as 'Offertorium serium' and 'Offertorium pastorale' respectively; the 'pastoral' piece is the more homophonic, with occasional short fanfare-motifs, comparable to the pedal-points in Ex. 6.4 although played down even more radically than they are. Thus this piece drastically attenuates the old *stylus rusticanus*. And it accordingly illustrates Kozeluch's own pronouncements on church music, reported by Dlabacž in his contemporary lexicon of Bohemian and Moravian musicians,[26] where Kozeluch complained in quasi-Goldonian terms about the corrupt taste displayed in Catholic church music in Austria, Bavaria and Bohemia; he would undoubtedly have criticized Schneider's style for its frivolity, as he criticized the comparable tuneful style of the church music (including pastorellas) of his friend and Prague contemporary F. X. Brixi (1732–71). (Dlabacž reports a conversation between Brixi and Kozeluch: to a complaint by Brixi that Kozeluch's mass settings were making churches sound like theatres, Kozeluch retorted that Brixi's mass settings were making churches sound like taverns – and he adds that though they were both young hotheads at the time, neither took offence. This anecdote puts the issue of decorum in church music in a nutshell.)

The working-out of these stylistic issues is seen at the highest level, however, in comic opera, both in Italian and in the vernacular. It might seem self-evident that composers of opera, writing for metropolitan audiences, should have avoided using the *stylus rusticanus* in comic operas, whatever its pastoral potential; and Mozart, unlike Haydn, is generally believed to have been unusually unwilling to use it.[27] Yet pastoral is everywhere to be found in his operas, and everywhere depends on distinctions of style. Almost all the arias in Act 4 of *Le nozze di Figaro*, for example, are versions of Italian pastoral current since Corelli and Alessandro Scarlatti; indeed, Wye Allanbrook has pointed out the basic dependence of *Figaro* in general, and this act in particular, on pastoral.[28] Thus a version of the siciliano, traditionally used for 'painful' pastoral, is used for Barbarina's short aria 'L'ho perduta' which opens the act; the minuet, representing a 'moderately elegant' pastoral, is used for Marcellina's 'Il capro e la capretta', whose text is explicitly pastoral; and the classic F major and 6/8 metre of Susanna's aria 'Deh vieni non tardar' and of traditional Italian pastoral provides a 'lower-class' light amorous pastoral.

Together these references contribute to the construction of what Polonius called the 'pastoral-comical', meeting the demands of verisimilitude and decorum now appropriate to the genre: these characters (and the others who have arias in Act 4, Basilio and Figaro) are all distanced from the audience

---

[26] G. J. Dlabacž, *Allgemeines historisches Künstler-Lexikon für Böhmen und zum Theil auch für Mähren und Schlesien* (Prague, 1815), s.v. 'Kozeluch'.
[27] Cf. G. Chew, 'The Night-Watchman's Song Quoted by Haydn and its Implications', *Haydn-Studien*, iii (1974), pp. 106–24.
[28] W. J. Allanbrook, *Rhythmic Gesture in Mozart*: Le nozze di Figaro *and* Don Giovanni (Chicago, 1983).

through the use of pastoral allusions in text and music, as they are from each other by the darkness in the garden and by the disguises they wear. For this reason they are able to express generalized, larger-than-life pastoral sentiments concerning love and human relationships to the audience and to each other. These arias make the last act a great paean to the universality of love, and show how far *Figaro* is from being a realistic opera; it is those who search for realism, perhaps, who consider the Act 4 arias (particularly those of Marcellina and Basilio) redundant to the action.

Of all these arias, Susanna's 'Deh vieni' would have been the most likely to make use of the *stylus rusticanus*, since this is the 'lowest-class' aria – musically speaking, whatever its appropriateness to Susanna herself – in the act. (This may explain its being dropped in favour of the big *rondò* 'Al desio di chi t'adora', a number which balances the others more evenly, in the 1789 Viennese revival of *Figaro*.) A glance at the post-cadential figuration in 'Deh vieni', however, shows that the process of attenuating the rustic style, evident in the pastorellas of the second half of the century which I have quoted, has now continued up to vanishing point; if there had been references to that style, they would most likely have been evident as broken-chord effects, for example, in passages like bars 18–20 of the aria.

On the other hand, there is obvious use of the rustic style in the German-language comic idiom of *Die Zauberflöte*, and the many correspondences of the musical language of this opera with that of the pastorella have never been noted. Papageno's 'Der Vogelfänger bin ich ja' in Act 1 matches many typical strophic *ariae pastorellae* of a generation earlier, in tempo and time (Andante, 2/4), in key (G major), in comic tone, in instrumentation, in its strophic structure with introductory ritornello, and in its most characteristic feature, the little pastoral motif Papageno plays on his 'Faunen-Flötchen' after the principal cadence. The numbers for Monostatos represent another 'dialect' of the *stylus rusticanus*, and some of his numbers recall Epiphany pastorellas in which the Three Kings are characterized with 'Turkish' music. There are obvious similarities between the handling of the music for the Three Ladies and that customarily used for the Three Kings in Epiphany pastorellas, as Ex. 6.6 will illustrate (pp. 185–90).

Similarly, Mozart's use of the magic flute and the magic bells is very comparable with the use of bells and toy instruments in certain pastorellas half a century earlier, best illustrated perhaps by their analogous use in the so-called Toy Symphony and in other pieces by Leopold Mozart.

A more extended and well-differentiated use of the *stylus rusticanus* (and by the same token a close resemblance to the structure of a multi-movement pastorella) is exhibited in Scene 17 of *Zauberflöte*, which is part of the finale to Act 1 (pp. 154–62 of the full score in the *Neue Mozart-Ausgabe*; all page numbers in the following discussion refer to this edition).

Ex. 6.6
(a) Mozart, *Die Zauberflöte*, Act 1, Scene 1

(b) F. X. Brixi, *Offertorium de Epiphania Domini* in D 'Reges de Saba'

Papageno and Pamina are seeking Tamino, and are unexpectedly overtaken by Monostatos. The scene begins with the close of the previous duet between Pamina and Papageno; Papageno's rustic style has governed the music for both characters. The interruption brings a sudden change to a faster tempo (Allegro) and a more markedly rustic style (broken-chord fanfares, all parts in unison), with brief comic interjections from Monostatos ('Ha! hab' ich euch noch erwischt!') ('Aha, I've caught you'). The progressive simplification of the texture which ensues, until halfway through p. 161, recalls a typical transition to a final chorus in a pastorella. At Papageno's invocation of the bells (bottom of p. 156), the texture reverts to unisons (including the arpeggiations of the tonic chord characteristic of the rustic style). These arpeggiations continue, with a duple-time *Ländler*, both in the music of the bells (as a rustic dance tune for Monostatos and the slaves), and in the moral rhyming couplets sung by Pamina and Papageno once the danger is past, which should probably remain in the same fast tempo. All this is very close to the songs shepherds usually sing in front of the crib.

In the new section which follows (p. 161), the *stylus rusticanus* is still strongly evident, and a new pastorella cycle is effectively set in motion. Papageno hears the sounds of Sarastro's triumphal procession, which are incomprehensible to him although Pamina is self-possessed. The parallel between Papageno and a Bethlehem shepherd reacting to the Bethlehem angels' song is striking, and the musical treatment is that of a pastorella, with Pamina explaining as only an angel could. Papageno's opening gambit, 'Was soll dies bedeuten?' ('What does this mean?'), p. 161, was so well-known as a shepherd's stock response to the angels' song, that it instantly evokes the *stylus rusticanus*; Ex. 6.7 gives one of numerous examples (German as well as Czech) that contain this phrase, from a pastorella ascribed doubtfully to Joseph Haydn:[29]

Q.: Schau eini, o du liebe Gott,	Q.: Have a look! Good Lord,
Was soll denn das bedeuten?	What can this mean?
A.: Er leid't da ja die größti Not,	A.: He's badly provided for,
Das seynd verkehrti Zeiten!	Times are obviously bad!

Pamina's expression of reassurance to Papageno is, as expected, sharply contrasted with Papageno's own line. The unaccompanied unisons of Papageno's music, and the comic chromaticism of 'O wär' ich eine Maus' ('If only I were a mouse'), which follow, are further established clichés of the *stylus rusticanus*. Accordingly, the situations in these sections are all established as pastoral-comical, both on the basis of the text alone and by text and music working together, and examples could easily be multiplied.

---

[29] Joseph Haydn (?), 'Der Tag, der ist so freudenreich', Hob.XXIIId: G2; modern edition in Chew, 'The Christmas Pastorella', ii.

Ex. 6.7 'Jos. Heyden', Pastorella in G 'Der Tag, der ist so freudenreich'

It may seem paradoxical that the *stylus rusticanus* should survive at all in opera, when it was strongly questioned even in church music. The paradox may be resolved by returning to a consideration of verisimilitude and decorum, matters which depend on genre, and which in turn help to define it. For both Italian *opere buffe* and church music, Italian standards were appropriate. But for German Singspiel, nothing required the changing of old habits, a fact that goes far to explain the curiously mixed impression that *Die Zauberflöte* tends to leave on the modern listener.

The history and characteristics of the pastorella, and of the *stylus rusticanus* which formed so important a part of it, help to explain Austrian music in the second half of the eighteenth century in a number of significant ways. First, they illustrate changing taste in church music in a perhaps uniquely clear manner. In addition, they show how native late-Baroque comic techniques offered compositional models which remained viable and attractive in certain contexts as late as the 1790s, even to Mozart, even in opera, even in Vienna. Moreover, the rustic style supplies a useful criterion for distinguishing various styles of 'pastoral, comical and pastoral-comical' in opera as well as church music. And this in turn helps to supply a secure basis for the distinctions of genre which must lie at the centre of any informed comment on the Austrian repertory as a whole, and about which too little is still known.

PART III

Opera and drama

7

The applausus musicus, or Singgedicht: a neglected genre of eighteenth-century musical theatre

ROBERT N. FREEMAN

On 23 January 1765 the second marriage of Joseph, newly crowned King of the Romans, and Josepha of Bavaria, notoriously one of Europe's most ugly princesses, took place in Vienna. Having been politically arranged by Prince Kaunitz with the wild dream of achieving 'the union with Austria of the entire complex of Bavarian lands',[1] this particular marriage was destined to be brief and unhappy. Habsburg weddings, nevertheless, constituted important state events and inevitably generated a great number of art works. Gluck alone, for example, was commissioned to provide three major compositions for this occasion: the serious opera *Telemaco*, his pantomime *Semiramis* and, as the court's surprise wedding present, *Il Parnaso confuso*, a one-act azione or serenata teatrale.

Individuals and institutions wishing to establish new contacts with the monarchy or those interested in maintaining traditional ties took part in the festivities to the extent these could be afforded. It probably did not surprise anyone, therefore, that the venerable Benedictine abbey of Melk would play a prominent role in the celebrations, or that it was chosen as the final overnight station for members of the combined Bavarian and, after they had been received by Joseph near Lambach on 20 January, Austrian courts on their way to attend the ceremonies in Vienna. Located along the old highway connecting the imperial capital with the west, Melk had been one of the favourite honeymoon havens for the Habsburgs at least since the time Joseph's great-grandparents, Emperor Leopold I and Eleonore Magdalena, had made a visit there on the return from their nuptial ceremonies in Passau in 1676.[2] Five years after Joseph's own wedding, his sister Marie Antoinette was to stay at the abbey following her marriage by proxy in Vienna to Louis of France, bringing with her a retinue of 260, the greatest number of overnight visitors in Melk's eighteenth-century history.[3] The reasons

---

[1] D. Beales, *Joseph II: I: In the shadow of Maria Theresa 1741–1780* (Cambridge, 1987), p. 389.
[2] I. F. Keiblinger, *Geschichte des Benediktinerstiftes Melk in Niederösterreich, seiner Besitzungen und Umgebungen* (Vienna, 1851) i, p. 907 (note 2).
[3] Concerning the music for this visit see the present author's 'Marie Antoinettes Hochzeitsbesuch im Stifte Melk – 1770' in *Stift Melk, Geschichte und Gegenwart*, i (1980), pp. 172–84.

for this attraction to the abbey, of course, had to do not so much with its convenient location, its tradition of Benedictine hospitality and the picturesqueness of the vicinity as with the desire on the part of the Habsburgs to reaffirm in a symbolic manner the continuity of the imperial line by making contact at these critical moments with the institution that stood guard over the remains of a dozen of their medieval predecessors, the Babenbergs.

For the visit of Joseph and Josepha (21–2 January 1765), arrangements were made for the abbey's organist, Johann Georg Albrechtsberger, to compose a vocal-orchestral setting of a German text supplied by the house poet Beda Schuster. The autograph score, perhaps later presented to the court as a gift, survives in the music collection of the Austrian National Library in Vienna and carries the title *Singgedicht*.[4] The manuscript reveals a work richly scored for six vocal parts, string orchestra, pairs of flutes, oboes, horns, clarini, timpani and a continuo section consisting of bass instruments and harpsichord, with bassoon and cello serving both continuo and obbligato functions. It is laid out in one large part or act containing seven numbers, each preceded by recitative: an arioso, four arias (one of which is an ambitious rage aria encompassing no fewer than 540 bars), a duet and a concluding 'Chorus'. The whole is introduced by a three-movement Sinfonia.

Scholars who have examined this source and who have attempted to describe it in the past have been at odds as to how to classify it: Oskar Kapp in the foreword to his volume of Albrechtsberger's instrumental music published in the Austrian *Denkmäler* in 1909 considered it to be a cantata; Edmund Kummer, the late Melk archivist and historian, referred to it as an operetta in an article concerning the visit of the court published in 1952; and most recently, Dorothea Schröder, in her valuable study of Albrechtsberger's sacred vocal music, believed it to be a 'secular oratorio'.[5] The *Singgedicht*, then, not only raises some interesting questions as to its classification, pertinent terminology and manner of performance (staged or concert), but also, and perhaps more important, it poses the question as to whether or not it stands alone as a unique entity, tied exclusively to this particular occasion. Is it a work representing part of some larger, ongoing tradition?

By drawing upon a newly completed reconstruction of eighteenth-century theatrical practice at Melk[6] and a number of recent studies dealing with specific

---

[4] Vienna, Österreichische Nationalbibliothek, Musiksammlung, Sm 16451.
[5] O. Kapp, *Johann Georg Albrechtsberger, Instrumentalwerke. Denkmäler der Tonkunst in Österreich*, xxxiii (Vienna, 1909), 'Einleitung', p. x; E. Kummer, 'Eine Übernachtung des kaiserlichen Hofes im Stifte Melk (21.1.–22.1.1765)', *Jahresbericht des öffentlichen Stiftsgymnasiums der Benediktiner zu Melk a.d.D.*, xcv (1952–3), p. 7 et passim; D. Schröder, *Die geistlichen Vokalkompositionen Johann Georg Albrechtsbergers*, Hamburger Beiträge zur Musikwissenschaft, xxxiv (Hamburg, 1987), i, pp. 209f.
[6] See R. N. Freeman, *The Practice of Music at Melk Abbey Based upon the Documents, 1681–1826* (Vienna, 1989), Ch. 4 and Appendix B.

repertories or examples of the type at Melk and elsewhere,[7] I will attempt to clarify these questions. It will be proposed and demonstrated that a distinct genre and repertory for the *Singgedicht* and its Latin equivalent, the applausus musicus, existed, that it had a life spanning the middle of the century, that it evolved out of a convergence of an older, indigenous monastic tradition with an Italian model transplanted to Vienna, and that it experienced an abrupt decline beginning in the middle of the 1770s.

The copious documents preserved at Melk pertaining to the preparations, rehearsals and performance of Albrechtsberger's *Singgedicht*[8] serve as a point of departure. The work is referred to in these sources in consistently precise terms, a precision rarely encountered in the eighteenth century. One finds the following forms: a 'brevis applausus metro germanico', that is a brief applausus in German verse; an 'applausus'; an 'applausus germanicus'; and finally an 'applausus musicus cuius titulus Singgedicht'. The number of adjectives and qualifiers seems to suggest that the applausus in the vernacular was something novel or unusual.

The only known copies of the printed textbook for Albrechtsberger's *Singgedicht* are preserved at Melk and Seitenstetten,[9] provincial locations that may account for their having been overlooked by previous investigators (see Plate 7.1). The textual sources contain stage directions that supplement the few that are given in the score. The entrance of Fama, the allegorical figure for Justice, is announced by an off-stage fanfare, a favourite theatrical device at Melk, while another character, Saturnus or Time, humorously remarks, 'what a peculiar sound . . .'[10] Later there is another instruction indicating that a portrait of the royal couple – Joseph and Josepha – is to appear descending from the clouds.[11] One document refers to the work as an 'Operete' and another suggests it was given in 'theatro',[12] which at Melk meant that it was to be performed either on a temporary stage or in a standing theatre. These same sources show small payments to a sculptor, indicating that at least some statuary was used as props in this particular production.

---

[7] Such as R. Angermüller, 'Amor subditorum: ein Applausus von Michael Haydn für den letzten Fürstpropst von Berchtesgaden im Musikalienarchiv von St. Peter', in A. Kolb, ed., *Festschrift St. Peter zu Salzburg 582–1982* (Salzburg, [1982]), pp. 766–75; J. Senigl, 'Johann Michael Haydn und das Salzburger Universitätstheater', *Musicologica Austriaca*, ix (1989), pp. 63–73; K. Schumacher, 'Bemerkungen zu den Applausus-Kantaten von Johann Michael Haydn', in *Das Benediktinerstift St. Peter in Salzburg zur Zeit Mozart* (Salzburg, 1991), pp. 149–54; H. Walter, 'Über zwei Applausus-Kantaten von Johann Georg Albrechtsberger', in K. Schlager, ed., *Festschrift Hubert Unverricht zum 65. Geburtstage* (Tutzing, 1992), pp. 291–303. F. W. Riedel, 'Joseph Haydns "Applausus" und die Tradition des musikalischen Schultheaters in Österreich', in G. Winkler, ed., *Joseph Haydn und die Oper seiner Zeit* (Eisenstadt, 1992), pp. 88–106.
[8] See the documents cited in Freeman, *The Practice*, Appendix B, OW 36 and Appendix C.
[9] Melk, SA, 15. Gymnasium, Karton 2; Seitenstetten, Stiftsbibliothek, Misc. VII/2.
[10] *Singgedicht*, textbook, [p. 4]: 'Hier stözt die Fama noch unter der Seen in die Trompete'; 'Was für ein ungewöhnter Schall . . .'
[11] *Ibid.*, [p. 7]: 'Hier wird das Bildnis des allerhöchsten Brautpaares aus den Wolken herabgelassen.'
[12] Freeman, *The Practice*, Appendix C, doc. nos. 7654 and 76518.

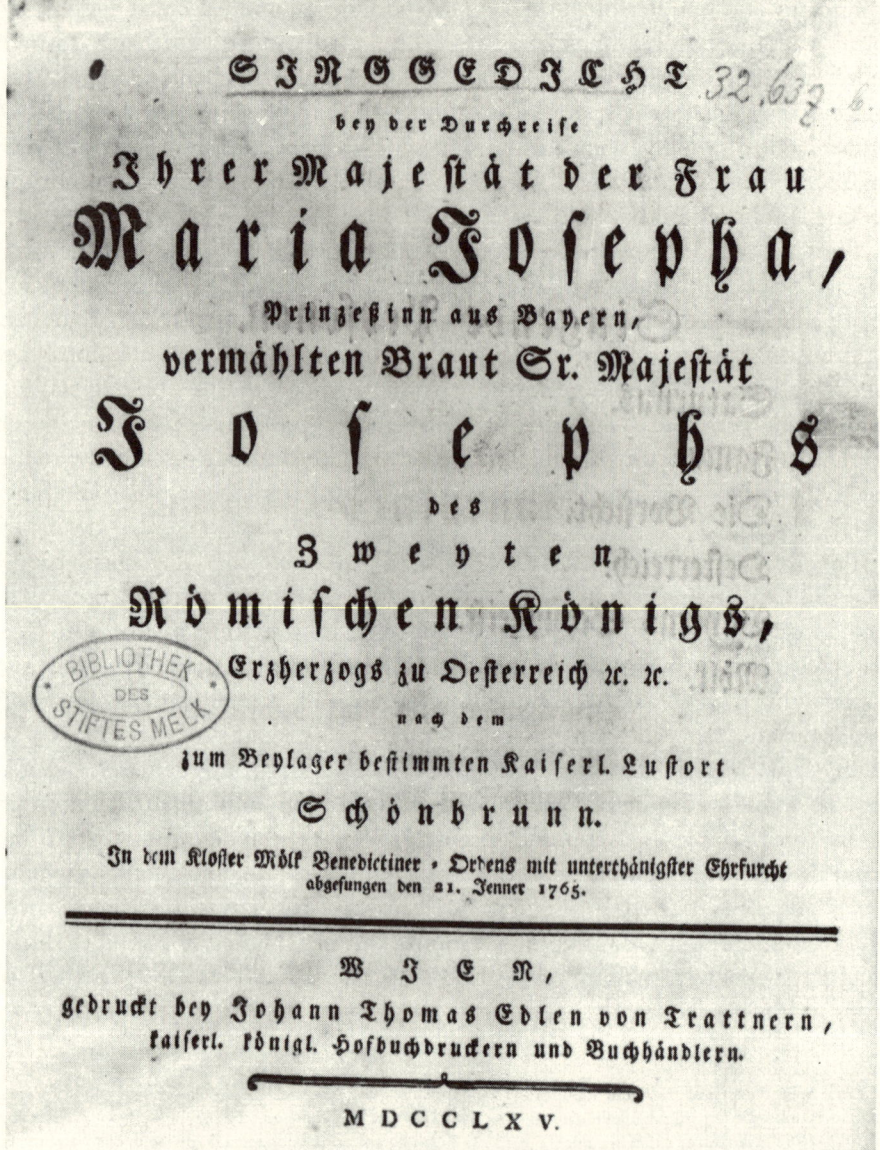

Plate 7.1 Title-page of the textbook to Albrechtsberger's *Singgedicht*, Vienna, 1765 (Melk, SA 15. Gymnasium, Karton 2)

Just nine months before the performance of the *Singgedicht* two other large-scale productions were given at Melk on the occasion of Archduke Joseph's visits there during his trip to and from his coronation as King of the Romans in Frankfurt. The compositions, which have been attributed to the Viennese composer-lutenist Karl Kohaut (1726–84) on the basis of documentary evidence[13] are in Latin, but in all other respects they are very similar to the *Singgedicht*. Once more the sources are complete, with extant textbooks and scores carrying terms such as 'plausus', 'adplausus musicus' or 'applausus mellicensis' on their title-pages or on their handsome eighteenth-century covers. Two other applausus that were composed by Albrechtsberger and performed at Melk in 1763 on the occasions of the election and investment of Abbot Urban Hauer are now lost, but their scores were known to the Haydn biographer Carl Ferdinand Pohl, who, as Horst Walter recently discovered,[14] sketched their outlines in 1867 using textual and musical incipits and scorings. Pohl's notes serve to confirm the basic nomenclature and characteristics of the applausus model that will be described below.

From here the applausus can be traced back several decades at Melk through a number of works on whose title-pages the term appears. The earliest example of the use of the expression in connection with a stage production at the abbey dates from 1736. In that year a work in German entitled *Martis und Irene Verbindung* was performed in celebration of yet another marriage, that of Maria Theresia and Francis of Lorraine. The wedding had taken place in Vienna in February, but the first performance at Melk had to be postponed until later in the year on account of a serious illness that befell the ruling abbot, Berthold Dietmayr. Since 1960, when a manuscript libretto for *Irene* was first described,[15] it has been known that the work resulted from a collaboration between Franz Tuma, who was responsible for providing music for the relatively brief prologue, and the Melk organist Joseph Weiss, who provided music for the main body of the work. The texts for both sections were very likely composed by Father Martin Kropf, professor of rhetoric of the cloister school, who was described in 1736 as 'Herr Comicus', the usual phrase used to refer to the house poet or librettist.

The significance of this work as the only known dramatic attempt by Tuma and its important place in the eighteenth-century theatrical repertory at the Austrian cloisters – it is perhaps the earliest example of an independently performed stage work in German at an Upper or Lower Austrian monastery – have been discussed briefly elsewhere.[16] For our purposes, however, *Irene* is particularly relevant because, as will be shown, its prologue may stand very near the beginning of the 'applausus' tradition.

[13] *Ibid.*, doc. nos. 7645 and 7647; one of the two applausus scores survives in Albrechtsberger's hand, and for this and other reasons, such as the concertante treatment of the continuo instruments (bassoon and cello), which is found also in the *Singgedicht* and is typical of Albrechtsberger's orchestral writing from the mid 1760s to early 1770s, and the fact that Kohaut was primarily a composer of instrumental music, I believe this composition to be largely or entirely the work of Albrechtsberger rather than Kohaut.

[14] See his 'Über zwei Applausus-Kantaten', pp. 291ff.

[15] R. Feuchtmüller, ed., *Jakob Prandtauer und sein Kunstkreis* (Vienna, 1960), pp. 245–6; the text is preserved at Melk, Stiftsarchiv, 15. Gymnasium, Karton 2, and its title-page is reproduced in Freeman, *The Practice*, p. 270, Fig. 36.

[16] See Freeman, 'The Fux Tradition and the Mystery of the Music Archive at Melk Abbey', in H. White, ed., *Johann Joseph Fux and the Music of the Austro-Italian Baroque* (Aldershot, 1992), pp. 25ff, where newly discovered musical fragments to the prologue are described.

The prologue's 'plot' is simple: Austria, Melk and the river Melk lament the recent illness of the Abbot in recitatives and four arias. Midway, at the fourth aria, Fama or Justice enters announcing Dietmayr's miraculous recovery, and, after another recitative and trio, the prologue ends with a final da capo 'Schlußchor' of thanksgiving directed to the Abbot in the manner of an operatic *licenza*. Only four roles are called for, a conservative number when compared to the large cast of the main portion of the work by Weiss that follows. This has over a dozen characters of its own as well as a separate plot dealing allegorically with the recent War of Polish Succession and the marriage of Francis and Maria Theresia. Two characters from the prologue, Justice and Austria, reappear at the end of the main drama, thus providing a degree of unity between the two plays. Although there is only a single stage instruction contained in the prologue, its presence is important because it indicates at least a modicum of scenery and acting. Perhaps in such custom-made, in-house productions some of the stage activity was improvised. At any rate Austria is directed to render her first recitative 'lying very sadly on her throne . . . in a half-broken voice'.[17]

Tuma's prologue has several features in common with the examples of applausus performed later at Melk, especially with Albrechtsberger's *Singgedicht*. The prologue contains six vocal items, a total close to the seven in Albrechtsberger's work, and like those in the *Singgedicht* these pieces were substantial (as far as can be determined from the musical fragments that survive). Tuma's third number, the duet 'So verändert sich das Glück!', for alto and bass, consists of over one hundred bars. Both compositions have a purposeful arrangement of ensembles building towards a climactic finale. The limited number of roles is similar, with stock allegorical types such as Justice, Austria and Melk appearing in both Tuma's prologue and Albrechtsberger's *Singgedicht*. One difference, however, reminds us that thirty years separate these two works. A variety of formal designs – strophic, ABA' in addition to da capo types – is found in Tuma. For example, a strophic pattern with ritornello is clearly indicated in the alto part to the duet mentioned above,[18] but in Albrechtsberger's later work the da capo aria predominates to the extent that all other categories are excluded. Nothing can be said of Tuma's orchestration, unfortunately, since none of the instrumental parts survives. It is, then, not without significance that the prologue is referred to as an 'applausus' in the text itself.[19]

The term 'applausus musicus' seems viable, therefore, to the extent that it was applied fairly consistently to certain works of a pronounced occasional character produced at Melk between 1736 and 1772. Based upon common features contained in the compositions discussed so far, together with those of another

---

[17] *Irene*, Prologue [fol. 2]: 'Ganz traurig auf ihren Thron setzend und . . . fangt an mit halbgebrochener Stimme zu reden'.
[18] See the reproduction in Freeman, 'The Fux Tradition', p. 29, Plate 5.
[19] *Irene*, Prologue [fol. 6]: 'Schlußchor dieses Applausus'.

half-dozen texts and scores that survive from this period, a tentative definition for the genre can be put forward. The applausus was a Latin operetta or semi-dramatic cantata in one act or part containing six or seven numbers, for which the texts and often also the music were composed by local artists. Works of a similar character rendered in German could be entitled *Singgedichte*. The plots were simple, the casts small with four to six persons, and places were treated allegorically. They were produced on a temporary stage or in a theatre with props and therefore probably also costumes, but acting took place only in the form of an occasional posture or gesture. Characteristic of the applausus was its lavish orchestration and climactic ordering of its movements, invariably terminating in a large, weighty choral or ensemble finale.[20] Maximilian Stadler, who attended performances of several of these works, already noted the extraordinary finale to one of Kohaut's applausus of 1764, scored for SSAAB soloists, chorus and eighteen instrumental lines all written out independently (see Plate 7.2).[21] Carl Paradeiser's seven-voiced concluding 'Coro' to his *Hirten-Gedicht, Seladon*, performed in 1772 'placed him among the great, thoroughly grounded masters' of his day.[22]

There is substantial evidence to indicate that the applausus was not a musical category confined to Melk alone, but was one cultivated more widely in Austria. A critical role in its dissemination, in Lower Austria at least, may have been played by Georg Joseph Donberger (1709–68), a student of Antonio Caldara (Vice-Kapellmeister at the imperial court) and music director for the Augustinians at Herzogenburg after 1733.[23] In this latter capacity Donberger very likely composed the music for *Fiducia in Deum per arma iustitiae virtutis Dei*, a work performed at Melk on 3 July 1743 in celebration of the first visit of Empress Maria Theresia to that abbey.[24] The music is lost, but a MS copy of the text survives uncatalogued in the abbey library at Göttweig.[25] This source indicates that *Fiducia* may have represented some kind of intermediate stage for the applausus. It is larger than the later applausus with fifteen musical items distributed among three 'partes', each consisting of four to six numbers.[26] Two of the parts conclude with choruses. Altogether there are nine roles drawn from Greek mythology or allegorically representing geographical territories (e.g. Upper and Lower Austria), but no more than three or four roles appear in each

[20] A somewhat different definition of applausus is given by Schumacher, 'Bemerkungen', p. 153, who at the same time argues against establishing an independent category for it, distinguishable from a congratulatory cantata.
[21] K. Wagner, ed., *Abbé Maximilian Stadler, seine Materialien zur Geschichte der Musik unter den österreichischen Regenten* (Kassel, [1974]), p. 106.
[22] Ibid., p. 151; see also 'Bericht über den Musikzustand des löbl. Stiftes Mölk in alter und neuer Zeit', *Allgemeine musikalische Zeitung* (Vienna), ii (1818), p. [358].
[23] R. Hug, 'Georg Donberger. Leben und Werk' (Ph.D. diss., Mainz University, in progress) (including thematic catalogue).
[24] Ibid., them. cat. XVIII,10.
[25] I am grateful to R. Hug, who graciously sent me a copy of the text.
[26] I could identify only one other applausus arranged in three parts: Michael Haydn's late (1782) *Sanctificatio Jubilaei*.

Plate 7.2 'Spes Josephe', finale to K. Kohaut's *Securitas Germaniae Josepho II.*, Melk, 1764 (Vienna, Österreichische Nationalbibliothek, Musiksammlung, Sm18041 (copy by J. G. Albrechtsberger))

part. Although it is not referred to as an applausus in any contemporary source, the effect of the whole of *Fiducia* seems to approximate to a cycle of three applausus works. It is appropriately designated with the plural 'Cantate' in the principal thematic catalogue at Göttweig,[27] where it is listed anonymously.

The thematic *Catalogus Selectiorum Musicalium* at Herzogenburg, which was begun in 1751 during Donberger's administration as music director there, has a section devoted to 'Applausus Music[i]': listing incipits for thirteen works – one anonymous, four by 'Finckh', presumably Franz Xavier Fink (d. 1760), who was a 'Bassetlisten' employed at Herzogenburg contemporaneously with Donberger,[28] and eight by Donberger himself.[29] Unfortunately, only one of these works, Donberger's 'Ad plausus ad gaudia', survives with music in copies at Göttweig (acquired 1739), Brno (cloister Rjahred) and Prague, locations where the work was known either as an offertory or a motet.[30] Indeed the 'Ad plausus' has little in common with the 'mature' Melk applausus: it lacks the dramatic element and has no designated roles as such; the scoring does not exceed that of the 'solemn' or festive church orchestra of the period (church trio plus trumpets and timpani); and its layout – chorus, recitative–aria (= duet), chorus – hardly even approaches the chamber cantata-like design of Donberger's other offertories and motets. Perhaps this work and some of the others listed in the Herzogenburg catalogue with small scorings (such as nos. 7 and 11) came to be included among the applausus because of their text incipits. At any rate, from the information contained in this celebrated catalogue possibly as many as a dozen more works dating from before 1768, the year of Donberger's death, can be added to the applausus repertory.

Another highly regarded figure in Lower Austrian music who also contributed fairly early on to this genre was Johann Georg Zechner (1716–78), the influential composer active at Göttweig, Krems and Stein. Friedrich Wilhelm Riedel has identified at least two works by Zechner entitled applausus musicus dating from 1749 and 1753, both performed scenically at Göttweig in honour of Abbot Odilo Piazol.[31] Like so many of the works that will be mentioned here, only the texts for these applausus survive. Similarly, the music is lost for the first work of this type performed at Seitenstetten in 1752, an 'Applausus' intended for the name-day of Abbot Dominik Gussmann with music provided by the former organist at Seitenstetten and Regens chori for the Augustinians in St. Pölten, Johann Adam Scheibl (1710–73), on a text by Roman Digl.[32]

---

[27] Cf. F. W. Riedel, *Der Göttweiger thematische Katalog von 1830*, Studien zur Landes- und Sozialgeschichte der Musik, ii/3 (Munich, 1979), i, 1747.
[28] Freeman, *The Practice*, Appendix C, doc. no. 7437.
[29] Herzogenburg, Musikarchiv (Brook no. 582), fols. 196ff.
[30] Hug, them. cat., V,1.
[31] F. W. Riedel, 'Die Libretto-Sammlung im Benediktinerstift Göttweig', *Fontis Artis Musicae*, xiii (1966/7), p. 107, nos. 7–8. Riedel, 'Joseph Haydns "Applausus"', pp. 92–104.
[32] J. Haider, *Die Geschichte des Theaterwesens im Benediktinerstift Seitenstetten in Barock und Aufklärung*, Theatergeschichte Österreichs, iv/1 (Vienna, 1973), p. 117.

Beyond Lower Austria, at religious houses and educational institutions throughout the Austrian dominions where something of the theatrical operations is known, we find applausus musici introduced around this same time. In 1737, only a year after the Tuma–Weiss production of *Irene* was performed in Melk, the term was used in connection with a published text originating in St. Paul in Lavanttal, Carinthia, and now located in the Stiftsbibliothek of the abbey of St Peter, Salzburg.[33] Klaus Schumacher states categorically that this Carinthian source represents the first use of the term (in Austria?),[34] but he must have in mind the confines of the archives at St Peter's. Elsewhere the expression goes back much further, most notably in Vienna where 'applausus musicus' is found on the title-page of a textbook to a likely theatrical production with music (now lost) composed by the Kapellmeister at the Jesuit College, Johann Bernhard Staudt, and performed there in 1696.[35] To what extent this work was associated with the contemporary *Ludi caesarei* or with some kind of prototype for the later applausus remains to be determined since, by itself, the use of the term in a title gives little indication of what is to follows.

At the Benedictine abbey of St Peter in Salzburg fifteen productions given between 1737 and 1797 may have been related to this type as can be verified on the basis of surviving texts, documentary references and in one or two cases autograph scores, including one by Leopold Mozart and several by Michael Haydn.[36] The earliest recorded production of such a work at the influential Benedictine university theatre in Salzburg occurred in 1759 with the performance of J. E. Eberlin's *Phoebus sacratior coelo*.[37] Probably through the powerful influence of Salzburg the applausus musicus came to Upper Austrian cloister theatres, although at a considerably later date. The earliest references that can be traced at Lambach and at the very active and well-documented theatre in Kremsmünster both date from 1771.[38]

The most familiar work relating to this repertory is, of course, the applausus composed by Joseph Haydn in 1768 for Abbot Rayner Kollmann of the Cistercian abbey of Zwettl. Today this work is better known for the

---

[33] Schumacher, 'Bemerkungen', p. 153.
[34] *Ibid.*
[35] Riedel, 'Die Libretto-Sammlung', p. 109, no. 45; the occasion marked the conferring of doctorate degrees upon three Benedictines including a future Abbot (1714–49) of Göttweig, Gottfried Bessel.
[36] Schumacher, 'Bemerkungen', pp. 149 and 153; Angermüller, 'Amor subditorum'; I am not convinced, however, that all of the nine works listed by Schumacher, 'Bemerkungen', p. 149 should properly be included in the applausus category. Haydn's *Rebekka als Braut*, written in 1766 for Nonnberg, for example, is typical of a kind of Biblical Singspiel performed in Austrian cloisters. Robert Kimmerling's *Rebekka, die Braut Isaaks*, produced at Melk in 1770, is another example; Senigl also loosely groups seemingly diverse works under the portmanteau term *Applausus-Kantaten*; see her article, 'Johann Michael Haydn', p. 63.
[37] H. Boberski, *Das Theater der Benediktiner an der alten Universität Salzburg* (1617–1778), Theatergeschichte Österreichs, vi/2 (Vienna, 1978), p. 298, no. 583.
[38] *Jacob pater optimus* probably composed by Josef Langthaller and Georg Pasterwitz's *Erchenbertus I*; see F. Fuhrich, *Theatergeschichte Oberösterreichs im 18. Jahrhundert*, Theatergeschichte Österreichs, i/2 (Vienna, 1968), p. 312 and A. Kellner, *Musikgeschichte des Stiftes Kremsmünster* (Kassel, 1956), pp. 452–3.

accompanying letter sent by the composer, one of the most valuable documents of eighteenth-century performance practice.[39] Less well known perhaps is the fact that Haydn's applausus was just one in a series of such works composed anonymously and performed for Abbot Kollmann at the rate of about one every three or four years up until 1775.[40] The occasional nature of Haydn's example, its Latin text, the large dimensions of the individual numbers, limited number and types of roles, etc. all fit well into the applausus tradition as defined here. The distribution of ensembles with a quartet and duet placed at or near the beginning, however, may point more to Haydn's operas composed around this time; *L'infedeltà delusa* of 1773 with its opening ensemble comes to mind.

With an exception of a brief entry in *The New Grove Dictionary of Opera*[41] one will not find the term 'applausus musicus' defined in any music dictionary or encyclopedia, although as has been seen here, a small body of literature has grown up around it in recent years. Since no previous attempt has been made to describe its historical evolution as a form, only a hypothetical line of development can be proposed at this time.

The applausus musicus may have grown out of a convergence of two older traditions: the first and most immediate model could have been the prologue–epilogue that encased the acts of the so-called *Ludi caesarei* or cloister dramas cultivated from the beginning of the seventeenth century at Jesuit and Benedictine educational institutions in Vienna and elsewhere in Austria. Mozart's *Apollo et Hyacinthus*, K38, performed as the prologue and intermezzos for the school drama *Clementia croesi* in the Salzburg university theatre in 1767, is a late example. As we have seen, the applausus had many features in common with the old prologue–epilogue, including the mythological and allegorical characters and the *licenza*-like function of the final chorus, which corresponded to the epilogue. The Austrian theatre historian Fritz Fuhrich has shown quite convincingly how the 'parallel plot' of the prologue–epilogue at Kremsmünster gradually grew more independent from the main plot of the late Baroque cloister drama so that by 1760 there was no inner connection between the two.[42] It would have been merely the next logical step to have the prologue–epilogue produced separately as the applausus musicus. Viewed in this way, someone like Georg Donberger would have been in an excellent position to have effected such a separation. While still a student in Vienna, he provided the Jesuit College with at least one *Ludi caesarei* in 1727, then probably

---

[39] Both the applausus and applausus letter edited by H. Wien and the late I. Becker-Glauch have been published in *Joseph Haydn Werke*, xxvii/2 (Munich–Duisburg, 1969). For a convenient English translation see H. C. Robbins Landon, *Haydn: Chronicle and Works. Haydn at Eszterháza, 1766–1790* (London, 1978), pp. 146–8. Riedel, 'Joseph Haydns "Applausus"', pp. 92–104.
[40] H. Özelt, 'Geschichte der Sängerknaben im Stifte Zwettl', *Jahresbericht des Bundes-Gymnasiums und Realgymnasiums Krems* (1959–60), pp. 11–29.
[41] (New York, 1992), i, pp. 154f.
[42] Fuhrich, *Theatergeschichte Oberösterreichs*, pp. 112ff.

composed the experimental applausus cycle *Fiducia* for Melk in 1743 and, finally, at Herzogenburg seems to have gone on to become one of the most prolific composers of independent, single-part applausus.[43] Likewise from this same perspective Franz Tuma's prologue to *Irene* of 1736 can be viewed as representing an intermediate stage in this development, an applausus not yet detached from its principal play but containing most of the features that were to become characteristic of the genre.

The other model for the applausus may have been the Italian *serenate teatrali* which were introduced into the musical repertory of the Viennese court by Draghi and Minato as early as 1663–4[44] and later continued to flourish in the hands of Fux, Caldara and others who, like Caldara, had composed them in Italy prior to their arrival in Vienna. From the serenata the applausus could have acquired its elaborate orchestration, its one-off nature (including temporary staging), its quasi-dramatic character and special kind of non-action gesturing. If the Habsburg court's surprise wedding gift for Joseph and Josepha in 1765 was to be Gluck's *Il Parnaso confuso*, then perhaps Melk felt obliged to imitate and anticipate this with its own special brand of serenata: the applausus musicus in German.

The applausus, therefore, were essentially derivatives of older, Baroque genres. By the 1760s they must have already been considered anachronistic, and their emphatic occasional nature caused them to disseminate very little except as contrafacta. The many arrangements of numbers from Haydn's applausus as church music,[45] Mozart's adaptation of a duet from *Apollo et Hyacinthus* as a slow movement for one of his symphonies (K43) and Albrechtsberger's apparent lifting of a final chorus from one of his own applausus of 1763 for a setting of the offertorium *Justus ut palma florebit* in 1778,[46] illustrate this point very well. The applausus existed usually only in one set of parts and perhaps in a gift copy of a score, and they were, therefore, particularly vulnerable to loss. The Melk scores referred to here are, therefore, indeed rarities. Because so much of this music has vanished, our new generic term in a sense represents a 'phantom' repertory. Mostly, one is left with surviving texts, documents and catalogue references.

In the wake of the dramatic events that unfolded in the last decades of the eighteenth century and the relentless attacks on the wealth and influence of

---

[43] Hug, 'Georg Donberger', conjectures interestingly that the origins of the applausus might be sought in Donberger's festive offertories, the so-called 'liturgical' applausus such as the 'ad plausus ad gaudia' described on p. 205. As evidence he points to their cantata-like designs and to a work composed around 1730 by the Austrian-born Kapellmeister in Passau, Benedict Aufschnaiter (1665–1742), where the two genres are equated in the title, 'applausus vel offertorium solemne'; see G. Haberkamp, ed., *Die Musikhandschriften der Benediktiner-Abtei Ottobeuren, Thematischer Katalog*, Kataloge Bayerischer Musiksammlungen, xii (Munich, 1986), p. 29, no. 0013.

[44] H. Seifert, *Die Oper am Wiener Kaiserhof im 17. Jahrhundert*, Wiener Veröffentlichungen zur Musikgeschichte, ed. O. Wessely, xxv (Tutzing, 1985), p. 50.

[45] *Joseph Haydn Werke*, xxvii/2, 'Vorwort', pp. viiif.; Kritischer Bericht, pp. 16ff.

[46] Walter, 'Über zwei Applausus-Kantaten', p. 291.

religious institutions in Austria, a great number of monastic and provincial musical traditions fell by the wayside, resulting in a commensurate number of what might be called 'dead-end' musical genres. Various forms that were closely bound to monastic culture disappeared rather quickly. They ranged from the small cantilenae – the solo motet-like German arias which had been composed by the hundreds for Christmas and Easter, for sacramental and Marian celebrations – to the great choral-orchestral settings of Vespers and Litanies. To these casualties of the Enlightenment we may now add one more, the applausus musicus.

8

The operas of Antonio Salieri as a reflection of Viennese opera, 1770–1800

JOHN A. RICE

Our view of Viennese opera in the last third of the eighteenth century has, not surprisingly, been strongly influenced by our knowledge of two of the greatest composers of the period, Gluck and Mozart. But Gluck wrote his last Viennese opera in 1770; and Mozart was active in Vienna for a single decade only, 1781 to 1791. The works of neither composer can thus provide us with a clear picture of the evolution of Viennese opera during the crucial period of more than thirty years that separates Gluck's *Paride ed Elena* from Beethoven's *Fidelio*. Even when we consider the works of Gluck and Mozart together, the 1770s and the 1790s remain largely unknown.

The operas of Antonio Salieri (1750–1825) offer us an opportunity to fill the gaps and to correct some of the distortions resulting from our preoccupation with Gluck and Mozart. Salieri's importance as an artistic and historical figure has been obscured by fascination with his supposed rivalry with Mozart. Yet Salieri was active as an opera composer in Vienna from 1770 to 1804, before and after Mozart's Viennese decade as well as during it. He wrote many more operas for the Viennese court theatres than either Gluck or Mozart, and over a longer period. His operas reflect the changes in Viennese opera during that period more fully than do the operas of Gluck and Mozart.

One of the most remarkable aspects of Salieri's career is that he, an Italian musician, stayed in the employ of a single court during his entire adult life. For all the popularity of Italian opera at the courts of northern Europe, most Italian composers stayed at these courts for relatively short periods. Many of the best Italian opera composers, including Galuppi (1706–85), Traetta (1727–79), Paisiello (1740–1816) and Sarti (1729–1802), occupied positions of musical leadership at the Russian court. All of them were famous musicians when they arrived in Russia; and only one of them, Sarti, stayed in Russia more than seven years. Salieri, on the other hand, arrived in Vienna as a sixteen-year-old orphan; he won the friendship of leading musicians and the patronage of Emperor Joseph II; he married a Viennese, raised a family in Vienna; he retired, died and was buried there.

The permanence of Salieri's place in Viennese musical life is perhaps related to the fact that he was not just any Italian – he was a Venetian, born in Legnago, on the Venetian *terraferma*, in 1750. Venice had long enjoyed a special operatic relationship with Vienna. Marc'Antonio Ziani (c. 1653–1715), Kapellmeister under Leopold I and Charles VI, was Venetian; so was Antonio Caldara (c. 1670–1736), who spent the last twenty-three years of his life at the Habsburg court as Vice-Kapellmeister under Johann Joseph Fux. Venetian librettists – Metastasio's predecessor Apostolo Zeno (1668–1750), Lorenzo da Ponte (1749–1838), Caterino Mazzolà (1745–1806) and Giovanni Bertati (1735–c. 1815) – found employment in Vienna.

Another sign of the operatic ties between Vienna and Venice was the extraordinary popularity of librettos by the Venetian Carlo Goldoni, and the use of his plays as the source of librettos in Vienna. Da Ponte's libretto *Il burbero di buon cuore*, based on Goldoni's play *Le bourru bienfaisant* and set to music by Vicente Martín y Soler in 1786, was one of the last in a series of Goldonian comic operas written for the Viennese court theatres that included Florian Gassmann's *Il viaggiatore ridicolo* (1766), *L'amore artigiano* (1767), *La notte critica* (1768), *Le pescatrici* (1771) and *Il filosofo inamorato* (1771); Salieri's *La locandiera* (1773, based on Goldoni's play of the same title), *La calamita de' cuori* (1774) and the Viennese version of *Il talismano* (1788); and Mozart's *La finta semplice* (1768).

Il burbero di buon cuore, like many of Goldoni's dramas, is set in Venice. It is one of many theatrical works – ballets and plays as well as operas – in which Viennese audiences could see the scenic splendours, the people and customs of Venice represented in the court theatres of Vienna: the ballets *Les fêtes vénitiennes* (first performed in Vienna in 1750), *Les masques de St. Marc à Venise* (1754) and *Les gondoliers de Venise* (1755); Goldoni's plays *La vedova scaltra* (1751), *I due gemelli veneziani* (which actually takes place in Verona, on the Venetian *terraferma*, 1751), *L'avvocato veneziano* (1757); Gassmann's *La contessina* (1770), Salieri's *La fiera di Venezia* (1772) and Paisiello's only Viennese opera, *Il re Teodoro in Venezia* (1784).

Operatic ties between Venice and Vienna may have partly had to do with geography: Venice was the Italian operatic centre closest to Vienna (significantly closer than Milan or Florence, which were both much closer to Vienna, from a political point of view, than Venice was). Another link in the chain connecting Venice and Vienna was the Austrian ambassador in Venice from 1764: none other than Count Giacomo Durazzo, who had supervised Viennese opera during the flourishing years of the early 1760s; he continued to deal with opera in Venice, serving there as an informal agent for the Viennese court opera. We know from Michael Kelly's *Reminiscences* that when Joseph II formed an opera buffa troupe in 1783, Durazzo engaged singers for the troupe in Venice.

Salieri's position in Vienna was but one product of the special relationship between Viennese opera and Venetian opera; indeed, one might say that Salieri personified that relationship, to the extent that by the end of his life he might have found it hard to decide if he was himself Viennese or Venetian.

One can see signs of the Venice–Vienna connection in Salieri's operas. One of his most successful early operas was *La fiera di Venezia*, which takes place in Venice during the Ascension Fair, with its carnival-like festivities. *La fiera di Venezia*, first performed in January 1772, is a carnival opera, and it sought to represent on the Viennese stage the gaiety of the Venetian *fiera*. The climax of the opera is a masked ball, for which the libretto calls for a band of musicians on stage, although the score contains no music specifically designated for performance on stage. Salieri's overture anticipates the ball by presenting, as the second and third movments, a minuet and a *forlana* from the ballroom scene. Salieri's elegant thirty-two-bar minuet, and the dramatic situation of which it is a part, may well have been in Mozart's mind when he wrote his ballroom scene in *Don Giovanni*, with its thirty-two-bar minuet. We know that Mozart knew Salieri's ballroom scene because he used a melody from it (another thirty-two-bar minuet that accompanies the ensemble 'Mio caro Adone') for a set of keyboard variations, K173c, probably composed in the autumn of 1773.

Another example of the Venice–Vienna connection is the *commedia dell'arte* scene in Salieri's *Axur re d'Ormus*, a scene written by Da Ponte in Venetian dialect and culminating in the canon, 'All'erta zovenotti'. *Axur*, first performed on 8 January 1788, is another carnival opera, and this amusing scene another example of Viennese interest in representing Venetian revelry on its stage (Ex. 8.1).

The *commedia dell'arte* canon in *Axur*, incidentally, is by no means the only vocal canon in Salieri's Viennese operas. There is a nine-part canon in *La cifra* (1789) and two canons in *Falstaff* (1799). The duet 'La stessa, la stessissima' (*Falstaff*, Act 1), on which Beethoven wrote piano variations (WoO 73, 1799), is canonic in the vocal parts. Near the end of *Falstaff* Mr and Mrs Ford celebrate their reconciliation in a gentle, amorous canon, 'Te sol amo'. Although canons were not limited to Viennese opera, they seem to have been particularly popular with composers there; there are, for example, several canons in the Viennese operas of Martín y Soler. The canons near the the end of *Così fan tutte* and near the beginning of *Fidelio* were far from isolated examples of this technique in Viennese opera. Salieri's use of canon is one of many ways in which his operas represent Viennese opera in general.[1]

The predominance of opera buffa in Salieri's Viennese output is typical of Viennese opera during the last third of the eighteenth century. Almost all his Viennese operas were to some degree comic operas. This reflects the hegemony of opera buffa in Vienna, a result largely of the Viennese aristocracy's preference for Italian opera over German, and Joseph II's preference for comic over serious opera.

---

[1] See D. Link, 'The Viennese Operatic Canon and Mozart's "Così fan tutte"', *Mitteilungen der Internationalen Stiftung Mozarteum*, xxxviii (1990), pp. 111–21.

THE OPERAS OF ANTONIO SALIERI

Ex. 8.1 *Axur, re d'Ormus*, 'All'erta zovenotti'

Italian comic opera had not always been an important genre in Vienna. It was only in 1763, near the end of Durazzo's theatrical reign, that opera buffa began to establish a regular place in the repertory. During the years that followed, Salieri's teacher Gassmann (1729–74) helped Viennese audiences develop a taste for the best in opera buffa by writing several fine comic operas himself and by supervising the production of many operas imported from Italy. From the mid 1760s to the end of the eighteenth century Viennese composers contributed to a tradition of Viennese opera buffa, composing comic operas in Italian but conceived specifically for Viennese singers, theatres and audiences. Salieri's career as an operatic composer, which began in 1770 with *Le donne letterate*, coincided almost exactly with the life of this tradition. His *Angiolina, ossia Il matrimonio per sussurro* (1800) and *La bella selvaggia* (1802) are among the last comic operas in Italian written for performance in Vienna by a composer resident in Vienna. *La bella selvaggia* arrived too late: it remained unperformed. Salieri's successors – Weigl, Beethoven, Gyrowetz, Schubert (many of whom were also his students) – were henceforth expected to write operas in German.

In spite of its preference for comedy over tragedy, Viennese opera betrayed a certain fascination with opera seria, a fascination exemplified by the tendency of the court theatre management to hire singers such as the tenor Domenico Mombelli and the sopranos Nancy Storace (Mozart's first Susanna) and Adriana Ferrarese (the first Fiordiligi), who had experience in opera seria as well as opera buffa. Mombelli and Ferrarese had rarely sung in opera buffa in Italy before coming to Vienna; and yet in Vienna they rarely if ever had the chance to sing opera seria.

Salieri's operas reveal this paradoxical – and typically Viennese – interest in opera seria singers, and nowhere more clearly than in *Prima la musica poi le parole*, on a libretto by Giambattista Casti. This is yet another carnival opera, first performed in February 1786. The opera seria *virtuosa* Eleonora, a role created by Nancy Storace, shows a librettist and a music director how she can imitate the style of the *musico* Luigi Marchesi by singing a *scena* in the serious style. Instead of using their own words and their own music, Casti and Salieri lifted the entire *scena* from Giuseppe Sarti's opera seria *Giulio Sabino*, first performed in Venice during Carnival 1781, and performed in Vienna in 1785 (the Venice–Vienna connection again). This music, although it is an essential part of Salieri's *Prima la musica*, was in fact written by Sarti, not Salieri, for an opera seria, not an opera buffa, and for a male, not a female soprano. This is an extreme example of the way in which Viennese fascination with opera seria, combined with a rejection of the genre, contributed to the richness of Viennese comic opera in the 1780s.

Viennese opera was characterized by an extraordinary cosmopolitanism, a confluence of Italian, German, French and Bohemian musical cultures that reflects the cosmopolitanism of the Habsburg territories. No composer exemplified

Viennese cosmopolitanism better than Salieri. He wrote operas in three languages: Italian, German and French. (Mozart and Haydn wrote no operas in French; Gluck no operas in German.) He received commissions from Italy, France and Germany as well as Vienna. (The adult Mozart, in comparison, was limited in his operatic activities to Munich, Vienna and Prague.)

Salieri's cosmopolitanism is reflected, on a comic level, in multilingual scenes in at least two of his Viennese operas, one early and one late. In *La fiera di Venezia* an Italian woman tries to pass herself off first as the wife of a French merchant, singing a song in French, and later as a German baroness, resulting in the trio 'So wie bey den deutschen Tänzen', in which German and Italian are sung simultaneously. In *Falstaff*, an opera buffa composed almost thirty years later, Mrs Ford tricks Falstaff by pretending to be a young German woman; a long dialogue follows in which German and Italian are comically mixed:

MRS FORD: Guten Morgen, mein Herr!
FALSTAFF: (Una tedesca!) Guten Morgen, mein Frau!
MRS FORD: Bitt' um Vergebung! Ich noch nicht Frau: Ich Jungfer.
FALSTAFF: Oh, gratulieren! E was wollen von mich, schöne Jungfretta?
MRS FORD: Sie sind ein loser Mann!
Sie haben, kleiner Schelm, zugleich zwei Herzen
So – mir nichts dir nichts – weggefischt.
FALSTAFF: Mein Jungfer, ich sag in confidenz:
Von deutsch nit haben viel Intelligenz:
Vor das ich dir preghieren,
Nostra lingua du will mit mich parlieren.
MRS FORD: Mein Herr! Io poco posso vostra lingua parlar.

The scene culminates in Mrs Ford's aria 'O die Männer kenn' ich schon'.

Salieri's cosmopolitanism enhanced the cosmopolitanism of Viennese opera in general. This point can be best demonstrated by considering the influence of French opera on Salieri's Viennese operas of the 1780s. Salieri could not have written an opera like *Les Danaïdes* (1784) in Vienna or Italy. The violence and horror of the libretto, and of Salieri's score, with its emphasis on the minor mode, its free-flowing alternation of arioso, aria, ensemble, accompanied recitative and chorus, its orchestra enriched with trombones, could only have been produced on the Parisian stage. The beginning of the overture, with its sepulchral D minor sonorities, orchestrated with trombones, looks back to the beginning of Gluck's *Alceste* (Ex. 8.2). At the same time its dynamic contrasts, syncopations and alternating tonic–dominant harmony anticipate Mozart's overture to *Don Giovanni*. Even closer to *Don Giovanni* is a passage later in the overture, where a gentle major-mode melody is followed by a savage diminished seventh chord, fortissimo: almost exactly the same sonority as that which accompanies the entrance of the Commendatore near the end of *Don Giovanni*.

Ex. 8.2 *Les Danaïdes*, overture

Les Danaïdes was not performed in Vienna; but Salieri brought its musical language back to Vienna with him. Lorenzo da Ponte noticed the effect of Salieri's experience in Paris on the first opera that he completed in Vienna after returning from the triumph of *Les Danaïdes*. Trying to explain the failure of the composer's *Il ricco d'un giorno*, Da Ponte wrote:

Il libro era positivamente cattivo, e non molto migliore la musica: ché Salieri, tornato da Parigi coll'orecchio pieno di Gluck, di Lais, di *Danaidi* e di stridi da spiritati, scrisse una musica interamente francese, e le belle melodie e popolari, onde soleva essere fertilissimo, sepolte le aveva nella Senna.[2]

The libretto was positively awful, and the music not much better. Salieri, having returned from Paris with his ears full of Gluck, of Lais [one of the singers who created a role in *Les Danaïdes*], of Danaids, of the screams of the possessed, wrote music in an entirely French style, and the beautiful, popular melodies of which he had been so fertile: these he had drowned in the Seine.

About a year and a half after the premiere of *Les Danaïdes*, Salieri presented *La grotta di Trofonio* in Vienna, with a libretto by Casti. *La grotta* is an opera buffa whose plot is set in motion by the activities of a magician, Trofonio, in whose cave people's personalities are strangely altered. Salieri chose to emphasize the threatening, mysterious aspects of Trofonio's magic. He introduced the

[2] L. da Ponte, *Memorie*, ed. C. Pagnini (Milan, 1960), p. 100.

magician to the sound of dark, slow music in D minor. A stark opening unison is followed by a chilling passage, orchestrated with trumpets, in which repeated syncopated notes alternate between *piano* and *fortissimo*, much like the beginning of *Les Danaïdes*. To draw the attention of his audience to the darker side of the opera, Salieri quoted this minor-mode music at the beginning of the overture, where it is heard in C minor (Ex. 8.3).

Ex. 8.3 *La grotta di Trofonio*, overture

It is difficult to think of an opera buffa overture written earlier than this one that begins with a slow introduction, let alone one that begins in the minor mode. Is this any way to open a witty comic opera? Probably the horror and the dramatic power of *Les Danaïdes* were still in Salieri's mind when he wrote *La grotta di Trofonio*. Through *La grotta* and other Viennese works, Salieri introduced aspects of French opera into Viennese opera buffa, and encouraged other composers, such as Mozart, to do the same.

Among Salieri's Viennese operas, the one that represents most clearly his incorporation of French elements is *Axur, re d'Ormus*. This *dramma tragicomico* is neither an opera buffa nor an opera seria: an Italian adaptation of Salieri's third and last opera for Paris, *Tarare* (1787). Da Ponte reshaped Beaumarchais's libretto (based on the story 'Sadak and Kalasrade' in James Ridley's pseudo-oriental *Tales of the Genii*) and Salieri set Da Ponte's poetry to music that only occasionally borrows from the score of *Tarare*. Yet much of the character of the French opera is still there: flexibility of form, with many short arias and arioso passages; frequent recourse to the minor mode, frequent use of accompanied recitative, integration of chorus into an often continuous musical fabric.

Salieri achieved this continuity by means of many striking musical devices. Near the beginning of *Axur* a love duet between the hero Atar and his beloved Aspasia is rudely interrupted by an offstage chorus, crying out "Ah!" on a sustained diminished seventh chord as King Axur's troops attack Atar's residence. Just before the end of the opera there is another military attack, this one against Axur and in support of Atar; the music here was taken directly from *Tarare*. A fine trio in E♭ for Axur, Atar and Aspasia, 'Barbaro, il mio coraggio', reaches a cadence in C minor. Suddenly Axur's slaves cry for help, interrupting the cadence with an A♭ major triad, as soldiers rush in to rescue Atar and Aspasia; the dramatic action surges forward (Ex. 8.4). Another example of the flexibility of form that characterizes Salieri's *Axur* (and again borrowed from *Tarare*) is near the end of Act 3 (Act 2 in Salieri's revised version of *Axur*, which combines the original Acts 1 and 2 into a single act), where a quartet of male principals in E♭, 'Non partir, la scelta è ingiusta', leads directly into a transition passage that ends on the dominant of C; a chorus in C major, 'O tu che tutto puoi', concludes the act.

Ex. 8.4 *Axur, re d'Ormus*, 'Barbaro, il mio coraggio'

Such passages anticipate certain aspects of Mozart's late operatic style as exemplifed in *La clemenza di Tito* and *Die Zauberflöte*. Mozart's use, in the finale

Ex. 8.5 *Axur, re d'Ormus*, 'Qual piacer la nostr'anima ingombra'

of the first act of *La clemenza di Tito*, of an offstage chorus singing "Ah" on a diminished seventh harmony recalls Salieri's offstage chorus in Act 1 of *Axur*. The sudden arrival of the three ladies near the beginning of *Die Zauberflöte*, where Tamino's C minor cadence leads directly to an A♭ major triad, looks back to the interruption of the C minor cadence near the end of *Axur*, also with an A♭ major chord. A transition passage in *La clemenza di Tito*, linking Vitellia's F major rondo, 'Non più di fiori', with the following G major chorus, 'Che del ciel, che degli dei', reminds one of the transition passage with which Salieri linked the male quartet and the concluding chorus in the finale of Act 3 of *Axur*.

These similarities are not cited as evidence that Mozart learnt from particular passages in Salieri's operas (although it is certainly possible that he did); rather they serve to illustrate the point that Mozart's late operas were not the only Viennese operas of the late 1780s and early 1790s to bring chorus, ensembles and solo passages together for dramatic effect. The similarities show that some of the most dramatic moments in Mozart's late operas are not unique in concept: their uniqueness lies in the perfection of Mozart's execution. If it is true that *tragédie lyrique* contributed to the increasing musical flexibility and dramatic range of Viennese opera during the 1780s, then Salieri, with his close ties to French opera, must be considered a crucial link between the two operatic cultures.

Some aspects of Salieri's art do not have much in common with Mozart's music. The final C major chorus of *Axur*, celebrating the coronation of Atar as King of Hormuz, is approached by way of an accompanied recitative for the tenor Atar in much the same way as the final C major ensemble with chorus of Mozart's *La clemenza di Tito* is preceded by an accompanied recitative for the tenor Tito. But with its sustained high notes, its declamatory style and its somewhat disjointed construction, Salieri's chorus 'Qual piacer la nostr'anima ingombra' sounds more Beethovenian than Mozartian: a reminder that *Axur* formed part of the operatic culture that produced *Fidelio* as well as *La clemenza di Tito* and *Die Zauberflöte* (Ex. 8.5).

9

Lorenzo da Ponte's Viennese librettos

KONRAD KÜSTER

How does the action of a late eighteenth-century opera proceed? In most cases one may presume that the process will be a straightforwardly linear one, with the action gradually unfolding independently of an arbitrary division into acts. Such a structure can be found in all kinds of operas of the time: in Mozart's early opera buffa *La finta giardiniera* as well as in his late opera seria *La clemenza di Tito*. It is most apparent in his Singspiel *Die Entführung aus dem Serail*; in that opera the abduction does not take place at all, but the attempt is made only in the last of its three acts, the two preceding ones functioning as some kind of preparation for it.

But for the dramatic structure of Mozart's three operas to librettos by Lorenzo da Ponte we find a totally different design. The focal points in the action of *Don Giovanni*, for example, are as follows. The *dissoluto*, Don Giovanni, fails to violate Donna Anna and kills her father in a duel; her fiancé Don Ottavio swears vengeance. He attempts revenge at the ball during which Giovanni tries to seduce Zerlina but, in the finale of the first act, he fails. In the second-act sextet he is ready to stab Giovanni, but the person he thinks to be the *dissoluto* is in fact Leporello in disguise. Finally the Commendatore himself, acting as a *deus ex machina*, sends Giovanni to Hell. To secure a *lieto fine* the remaining actors have to point the moral of the drama. Thus, the plot of *Don Giovanni* seems to be built on one relatively short process which occurs three times in all: Giovanni is to be punished, but it is only the third attempt that is successful. Until then the drama seems to move in a circle, and this circular plot is integrated into a linear process in which Giovanni attempts to escape the revenge. Linearity is what we expect from a plot, and it is this linearity that transforms the circular plot into what may be termed a spiral construction, something rather unusual in the dramatic tradition.

Mozart's other two Da Ponte operas exemplify a similar type of dramatic construction. The four acts of *Le nozze di Figaro* concern the attempts of Susanna and Figaro to obtain Almaviva's consent for their marriage. At the first two attempts Almaviva is able to maintain his opposition; at the third attempt this is no longer possible, but even then he succeeds in delaying the marriage from the end of Act 3 to the end of Act 4. In *Così fan tutte* Ferrando and Guilelmo[1] try three times to win their bet with Don Alfonso. In the first act they twice attempt, as a pair, to win over the sisters and believe that they have already won the bet; in the second act they each try to seduce one of the sisters, and at this third attempt they lose the bet. Therefore in all three Mozart–Da Ponte operas the circular and linear elements are integrated. The two major differences between them are, first, that *Figaro* seems to be built on four circular elements, the other two operas on a threefold action; and, second, that while the focal points of the action in *Figaro* and *Don Giovanni* lie in big ensembles (finales and sextet), the resolution in the second finale of *Così* is not part of a threefold construction that ends with the two duets Dorabella–Guilelmo and Fiordiligi–Ferrando. Three questions arise, then. Is the principle of spiral construction traceable in other Da Ponte operas as well? How did Da Ponte discover this technique, and how did he develop it during his Vienna years?

Lorenzo da Ponte came to Vienna in 1781; in 1783 he was appointed poet to the newly founded Italian company at the Burgtheater despite not having previously written any dramatic texts; his only recommendation was a letter written by Caterino Mazzolà, the Dresden court poet. After serving the imperial court in Vienna for eight years, Da Ponte was dismissed shortly after the death of Emperor Joseph II and went eventually to London. During those eight years he was responsible for the librettos of nineteen operas in all, five for Antonio Salieri (1750–1825), three for Vicente Martín y Soler (1754–1806), three for Mozart and one each for Giuseppe Gazzaniga (1743–1818), Pietro Guglielmi (1728–1804), Francesco Piticchio (fl. 1760–1800), Vincenzo Righini (1756–1812), Stephen Storace (1762–96) and Joseph Weigl (1766–1846); two further works were pasticcios. In some cases Da Ponte was responsible only for adapting new words to music already composed for another version of the opera by the same composer. This is true of four of the Salieri operas, of the opera by Guglielmi and perhaps also of Piticchio's *Il Bertoldo*.[2] Therefore only

---

[1] On the original spelling of 'Guilelmo', see A. Tyson, *Mozart: Studies of the Autograph Sources* (Cambridge, Massachusetts, and London, 1987), pp. 185–6.

[2] For a broad survey of the Salieri operas, see V. Braunbehrens, *Salieri: ein Musiker im Schatten Mozarts* (Munich, 1989); more detailed information is contained in R. Angermüller, *Antonio Salieri: sein Leben und seine weltlichen Werke unter besonderer Berücksichtigung seiner 'großen' Opern* (Munich, 1971–4). Da Ponte had to integrate material from earlier operas written by Salieri into *Axur, re d'Ormus* (from *Tarare*, libretto by Beaumarchais; Paris, Opéra, 1787), *La cifra* (from *La dama pastorella*, libretto by Giuseppe Petrosellini; Rome, Teatro Valle, 1780) and *Il talismano* (by Carlo Goldoni; Milan, Teatro Cannobiana, 1779; composed only partly by Salieri). Robert Eitner (*Biographisch-bibliographisches Quellen-Lexikon*, viii (Leipzig, 1903), p. 396) reports that the original score of *Il pastor fido* bears the date 'Rome, 22 December 1779', while the first Viennese performance of the opera took place on 11 February 1789. This is not mentioned by Angermüller and Braunbehrens, but Eitner's information is in any case suspect, since the score (at least in its present state) bears no date. Guglielmi's *La Quakera spiritosa* was written for Naples in 1783 (cf. E. Zanetti, 'Guglielmi, Pietro', in *MGG*, v, col. 1057). Da Ponte himself reported that parts of his text to Piticchio's *Il Bertoldo* were modelled on music already composed by Piticchio to words by Brunati; see *Lorenzo Da Ponte: memorie, libretti mozartiani*, ed. G. Armani (Milan, 1976; 3rd edn, 1988), p. 125.

eleven operas remain, three by Martín, three by Mozart and one each by Gazzaniga, Righini, Salieri, Storace and Weigl. For these operas Da Ponte not only wrote the words but conceived the plot as well (though in some cases this was based on another dramatic work).

As one might expect, there is nothing exceptional about Da Ponte's first three Vienna librettos. The first of them, Salieri's *Il ricco d'un giorno*, has a conventional plot.[3] Emilia is to be married to the miser Strettonio, who is favoured by Emilia's father Berto; but Emilia loves Strettonio's spendthrift brother Giacinto. It would be possible to create a spiral construction from this story, with Giacinto succeeding only 'after various complications'. But apparently this was not Da Ponte's aim, and perhaps he was not even aware of its possibilities. He designed the opera in three acts. In the first he creates the confusion that results from the existence of two lovers. In the second both brothers court Emilia, and Giacinto, whom Emilia pretended to reject for some time because of his extravagance, is finally successful. The only purpose of the third act is to prepare the final love duet between Emilia and Giacinto.

The dramatic conception is not the only conventional thing about *Il ricco d'un giorno*. To begin the second act with a chorus instead of an action ensemble or recitative, to have a very short third act and to do without a real finale at the end of the opera all seem *vieux jeu* in comparison with Mozart's Da Ponte operas. These unfashionable elements dominate Da Ponte's next libretto as well – that for Martín's *Il burbero di buon cuore*.[4] This is a two-act opera, but the plot is not very different from that of *Il ricco d'un giorno*. The dispositon of roles is not exactly the same. Dorval, who is to marry Angelica, is not nearly as unpleasant a figure as Strettonio, but he and Angelica have not yet met when the opera begins; also, Angelica has not one but two opponents: her uncle, who wishes her to marry Dorval, and her brother, who is determined to send her to a cloister. Act 1 ends with the first encounter between Angelica and Dorval, who takes pity on her situation and from then on agrees to support her desire to marry the otherwise totally unimportant Valerio (he appears only at the beginning and end of each act).

The constellation of roles is here somewhat more complicated and in certain respects more interesting, but even in this opera there is no finale at the end of Act 2, but merely a simple *vaudeville*. Da Ponte, who reports in his memoirs the characteristics needed to construct a *buffa* finale,[5] seems once more to have surrendered in the face of the technical difficulties involved. His memoirs seem to reflect not only the problems of any librettist at that time, but, in particular, his own problems, encountered in the course of his long search for an appropriate finale structure.

[3] Score in Vienna, Österreichische Nationalbibliothek, 17846.
[4] Libretto in Vienna, Österreichische Nationalbibliothek, 641.432-A.M. (VI, 7).
[5] Da Ponte, *Memorie*, pp. 92–3.

It is not quite clear how much of the plot in the next opera, Gazzaniga's *Il finto cieco*, is actually by Da Ponte.[6] The plot itself is unadventurous, dealing with the same conflicts as in the two preceding works. The only new element is that there are now three lovers for the prima donna, Elisa: the *cieco*, his nephew and a poet allied with the blind uncle.

It emerges, then, that *Le nozze di Figaro* was Da Ponte's first opera in which the two above-mentioned characteristics of the Mozart–Da Ponte operas – straightforward linear action and the moving in circles – are combined. Much of the dramatic process is determined by Beaumarchais's drama, but the possibilities offered by an operatic finale were not to be found in a spoken play. So there are two important ways in which the opera transforms the French material; one of these lies in the placing of ensemble scenes and the other in the number of acts. In the opera the most substantial ensembles occur at the ends of the acts, whereas in Beaumarchais's play only a few actors remain on stage when the curtain falls. This profoundly affects the role of Almaviva, who in the play is absent at the end of each act except the last, while in Da Ponte's libretto he plays an important part at the end of every act. Following the demands of a *buffa* finale, Da Ponte created a polarity between Almaviva and Figaro which is not established by Beaumarchais to the same extent. This enabled Da Ponte to raise the question of the Figaro–Susanna marriage at the end of each act, thus departing from Beaumarchais's intentions not only in the disposition of roles at the end of each act, but also in the number of acts itself. There are five acts in the play, the third ending with the trial that forms only the middle section of Da Ponte's third act. Da Ponte could therefore avoid ending an act with the question of the Figaro–Marcellina marriage (with which Beaumarchais's act had ended), so that each act would lead to a similar climax: the question of the Figaro–Susanna marriage.

The possibility that Mozart was responsible for that alteration to Beaumarchais's dramatic conception is suggested by the tonal structure of the music. At the end of both the first and second acts we find the tonal sequence E♭, B♭, G and C major – in the first act as a sequence of individual movements (nos. 6–10 in the *NMA* score), in the second as the opening sections of the finale (no. 16), subsequently rounded off by steps back from C to E♭. In both cases the sudden entrance of G major after B♭ major is a dramatic jolt, redirecting the tonal progress away from flat keys and towards D major (the tonal centre of the opera); G major marks Figaro's premature entrances with the chorus into situations which are not yet ripe enough to elicit the Count's consent to his marriage with Susanna. In the fourth act the redirection occurs in the part of the Count, who thinks that his wife has been deceiving him. But there is nothing

---

[6] Da Ponte, *Memorie*, p. 105: 'Ho dovuto . . . incastrare in un second'atto de' pezzi fatti vent'anni prima; prender varie scene d'altr'opere, tanto sue che d'altri maestri . . .' Libretto in Vienna, Österreichische Nationalbibliothek, 641.432-A.M. (XII, 4).

complementing this tonal procedure at the end of Act 3. So Mozart seems to have been more determined than Da Ponte to abandon Beaumarchais's original structure; perhaps he did not feel any necessity to match the number of parallel dramatic processes to the number of acts. By understanding the dance scene at the end of Act 3 more as a retarding element than as part of the circular motion of the drama, the idea of a spiral construction is more clearly discernible.[7]

Apparently Da Ponte was very conscious of the structure of his librettos; in more than one case he grasped the theoretical principles behind his practical work. For this reason his second and third operas were not simply reiterations of the somewhat tedious plot of the first, but rather explorations of its possibilities; and for this reason, too, the newly found dramatic structure of *Le nozze di Figaro* is encountered in his subsequent librettos. In the first of them, Righini's *Il Demogorgone, ovvero Il filosofo confuso*,[8] the story again deals with the problem of thwarted marriage plans; the confused philosopher Demogorgone is to be compromised so that he cannot marry Lesbina, who loves the young Ricciardo. It is significant that Da Ponte returned to the simplest form of the plot – one in which the female is affronted by only one undesirable male – so that he could concentrate on his new structural designs; furthermore, he again used the uncle–nephew–maid scheme of Gazzaniga's *Il finto cieco*.[9] Lesbina first tries to defeat Demogorgone on his own terms: she pretends to be a philosopher and develops a new kind of philosophy based only on love. But Demogorgone sees through this and Lesbina fails. This is the content of the first act, and again it is clear that the opera could end at this point were Demogorgone to concede defeat. During Act 2 opposition to the philosopher is stirred again; then Lesbina tries to teach him everything he needs to know to be an affectionate and polite lover. This turns out to be an impossible task, and thus nobody can raise any objection to a marriage between Ricciardo and Lesbina.

This was Da Ponte's first attempt to create a two-act version of the 'circular motion' displayed in the three (or four) dramatic steps of *Le nozze di Figaro*. *Demogorgone* is a pioneering libretto in other ways too. The second act begins neither with recitative nor with a static chorus, but with an ensemble; and the finale contains not only the dénouement as some kind of show-down (which at the beginning of the finale seemed impossible) but also a pointing of the moral to ensure a *lieto fine*.

Unfortunately not every story was equally suitable for adaptation in this way, and the next opera was, from a dramatic viewpoint, a failure. This was Storace's *Gli equivoci*, based on Shakespeare's *The Comedy of Errors*.[10] Shakespeare's play

---

[7] See K. Küster, *Mozart: eine musikalische Biographie* (Stuttgart, 1990), pp. 241–7.
[8] Libretto in Vienna, Österreichische Nationalbibliothek, 641.432-A.M. (VI, 13).
[9] H. Goertz, *Mozarts Dichter Lorenzo Da Ponte: Genie und Abenteurer* (Munich and Mainz, 1988), p. 114.
[10] Libretto in Vienna, Österreichische Nationalbibliothek, 641.432-A.M. (XIV, 11).

tells the story of two pairs of twin brothers, one pair being merchants and the other their servants, who were shipwrecked in childhood; while one of the merchants and his servant were rescued and brought to Ephesus, the others were returned home to Syracuse. The merchant from Syracuse comes with his servant to Ephesus, where they are taken for their Ephesus twins; it is only at the end of the fifth act that the father of the two merchants can clear up this most complicated situation – a situation which can have its full dramatic effect only if, as in Shakespeare's comedy, the two sets of twins do not meet until the last act. But Da Ponte destroyed that idea for the sake of his newly found dramatic scheme. In the opera the twin couples have already met by the end of the first of Da Ponte's two acts, and it would require only the entrance of a *deus ex machina* to finish the opera at that point. All the 'errors' of the second act are thus rendered unbelievable.

Between *Demogorgone* and *Gli equivoci* Da Ponte wrote *Una cosa rara* for Martín y Soler.[11] The story concerns the Spanish queen Isabella, who is hunting in the countryside with her son Giovanni and the great hunter Corrado. They meet the people of a village, and there the standard story of thwarted marriage plans is acted out. After a dramatic exposition of the situation, Act 1 ends with the queen's consent to the marriage of the peasant Lubino to his beloved Lilla. At that point the opera could come to an end, but both the prince and the hunter have fallen in love with Lilla. During a sextet in the middle of Act 2 the prince tries *incognito* to win Lilla's love, and later, in a septet, he and the hunter try to abduct her. They fail in all cases, and the prince then decides to give up Lilla but Corrado continues to pursue her until the queen intervenes to punish him at the end of the opera.

The libretto of this two-act opera is based on the three-act Spanish play *La luna de la sierra* by Luis Vélez de Guevara.[12] As in Da Ponte's libretto, the difficulties in the way of the marriage of Lubino and Lilla are resolved in Act 1; the three attempts by the prince and Corrado to win Lilla's love are spread over the remaining two acts. With these three attempts it is clear that the model for *Cosa rara* is itself constructed on similar lines to Da Ponte's preceding librettos, and the question of the number of acts and the number of dramatic units is raised again, though in a different way from *Figaro*. In *Figaro* the four acts contained three circular dramatic units; in *Cosa rara* only two acts were available for the same number of dramatic units. The dénouement could, however, be postponed. There was no problem about placing dramatic focal points in the middle of Act 2, since they only reflected Vélez's dramatic structure, which also included more than one focal point in each act. But Da Ponte was faced with

---

[11] Libretto in Vienna Österreichische Nationalbibliothek, 641.432-A.M. (X, 3).

[12] Vélez's play is summarized in D. Link, 'The Da Ponte Operas of Vicente Martín y Soler' (Ph.D. diss., University of Toronto, 1991), pp. 92–4. I am most grateful to the author for pointing out the importance of the source to me and for letting me see the text of her dissertation.

an uncommon pattern, and from it he learnt that he was not obliged to place a finale-like number only at the end of an act. Such a number was, of course, appropriate to conclude an act, or a whole opera, because of the compression of its dramatic power; that late eighteenth-century audiences could understand even the two-act *Cosa rara* as a three-act drama is suggested by a Munich source in which what follows the Act 2 sextet is labelled as Act 3.[13] But it is highly unlikely that Martín saw it in this way, since the sextet comprises only eighty-eight bars of music. From all this it is clear that *Cosa rara* is not a typical example of a drama with a spiral construction.

It was apparently Mozart who was responsible for the further development of these ideas in *Don Giovanni*, thus continuing the process found in *Figaro*. Da Ponte had begun his work on the libretto with the scenes he based on the *Don Giovanni* of Gazzaniga performed in Venice in February 1787; they comprise the first half of Act 1 (ending with the quartet no. 9, 'Non ti fidar, o misera') and the second half of Act 2 (beginning with the churchyard scene).[14] The remaining scenes contain all the elements that can be interpreted as premature attempts to punish the *dissoluto*, and possibly Da Ponte was not sure how to conceive the first finale and the sextet to accommodate these attempts.

All this points to the importance of E. J. Dent's observations on the structure of *Don Giovanni*; the only thing obviously wrong was his suggestion that *Don Giovanni* was originally planned as a three-act opera. He wrote about the sextet:

> The situation is most amusing, but totally unnecessary to the drama . . . Nothing but a curtain can follow it. Leporello's explanatory aria is an anticlimax, and any way it tells us nothing that we do not know already. Ottavio's aria, lovely as it is, is a still worse anticlimax . . .[15]

But *Don Giovanni* was not planned as a three-act opera; the suggestion that there were originally to have been three acts is apt for *Cosa rara* at best. So the anticlimax Dent noted in the arias following the sextet was a dramatic ideal actually pursued by both Da Ponte and Mozart, because the sextet proves to be part of the spiral construction of the drama – or, perhaps more superficially, an incipient finale.[16]

When Da Ponte created the text for Mozart's *Don Giovanni* he was working simultaneously on two other librettos, *L'arbore di Diana* for Martín and a reworking of Salieri's Paris opera, *Tarare*, as the Italian *Axur, re d'Ormus*. The last of these is as conventional as Da Ponte's first opera for Salieri; perhaps he

---

[13] Munich, Bayerische Staatsbibliothek, Musikabteilung, St. Th. 27, *Soufflierbuch* for the recitatives. After the scene ending with the sextet (2, 9) the numbering continues with 'III/10', and the third act begins.
[14] See S. Kunze, *Don Giovanni vor Mozart: die Tradition der Don-Giovanni-Opern im italienischen Buffa-Theater des 18. Jahrhunderts* (Munich, 1972), p. 61; see also C. Bitter, *Wandlungen in den Inszenierungsformen des 'Don Giovanni' von 1787 bis 1928: zur Problematik des musikalischen Theaters in Deutschland* (Regensburg, 1961), pp. 46–7, notes 34 and 39.
[15] E. J. Dent: *Mozart's Operas: a Critical Study* (London, 1913; 2nd edn, 1947), p. 168.
[16] See Küster, *Mozart*, pp. 304–5.

had to keep strictly to Salieri's original version. *Don Giovanni* became, as we have seen, the culminating point of the ideas Da Ponte had developed since his last Mozart opera, *Figaro*. But, once more, an opera for Martín provided Da Ponte with the opportunity for fresh development: in *L'arbore di Diana* he constructed a still more elaborate version of the spiral dramatic plot.[17]

Amore wants to teach the chaste goddess Diana the ways of love. He uses some ordinary mortals as tools: the shepherd Endimione, the hunter Silvio and the shepherd Doristo, who is the guardian of Diana's famous magic tree. First of all Amore tries himself to overcome Diana's chastity, but fails; this takes place in a quintet during the first act. Then he employs one of his human companions for the first time, and Endimione wounds Diana in the heart; but when the first act is over Diana does not yet believe that her situation has changed. For the second act Amore has to regroup the characters on stage (as in *Demogorgone* or the second and third acts of *Figaro*). The act culminates in Diana's bath, for which she must remove her cloak; Amore hides Endimione underneath it so that Diana will discover him when she returns. At this point Amore's plan is fulfilled: Endimione and Diana devote themselves to their mutual love. Thus Amore is successful at his third attempt, like Don Giovanni's adversaries or the couple in *Figaro*. To this extent the conception of the opera is similar to that of the other two works. But Da Ponte's thoughts had changed since *Il ricco d'un giorno*, when a love duet, such as that between Diana and Endimione, could form the conclusion of a whole opera. He had learnt how desirable a finale was, and how to deal with its potentialities. So an additional dramatic element was needed in *L'arbore di Diana*, and this was provided by a separate scene, outside the spiral construction, in which the fallen goddess is declared guilty and Amore acts as a *deus ex machina* to resolve the problems. Thus it appears that the circular motion within the dramatic construction becomes totally independent of the finales: the recurring, circular elements can culminate in intimate numbers such as a love duet, while a separate resolution is afforded in an added finale. This foreshadows the construction of *Così fan tutte* in all its details; major differences in the later opera result mainly from doubling the number of pupils in the 'scuola degli amanti' and transferring the action from the mythological to a more cruel, realistic world.[18]

It may be said, then, that the dramatic pattern of *Così fan tutte* results directly from Da Ponte's own development as a dramatist. The typical Da Ponte finale with its show-down and concluding moral in *Demogorgone*, the spiral construction in *Figaro* and the roots of an incipient finale in *Cosa rara*, and finally the

---

[17] Libretto in Vienna, Österreichische Nationalbibliothek, 641.432-A.M. (XV, 8).

[18] For further elements in *L'arbore di Diana* foreshadowing the plot of *Così fan tutte*, see A. Steptoe, *The Mozart–Da Ponte Operas: the Cultural and Musical Background to Le nozze di Figaro, Don Giovanni and Così fan tutte* (Oxford, 1988), pp. 122–3; and D. Link, '*Così fan tutte*: Dorabella and Amore', *Mozart-Jahrbuch 1991*, pp. 888–94.

separation of the dénouement from the finale: these all seem to follow each other in a logical way. But it is precisely in this separation between dénouement and finale that Da Ponte reflects a much older device already used by Apostolo Zeno and Pietro Pariati in their Hamlet opera, *Ambleto*, set by Francesco Gasparini in 1705,[19] in which Gedone makes three attempts to discover the reason for Hamlet's assumed madness; clearly the opera cannot end with the third attempt, but only with a typical *Hamlet* conclusion. It is possible that Da Ponte knew the play, which is preserved in several versions in the Nationalbibliothek, Vienna, including a German translation from 1742.[20]

The operas for Salieri that Da Ponte worked on in 1788–9 add nothing of importance to these observations regarding dramatic structure. Evidently Salieri's thoughts about the structure of an opera differed from those of Da Ponte as exemplified in the latter's work with Martín and Mozart. It is also possible that Salieri maintained his aversion to Da Ponte even at this late stage, so that the poet could not draw on all his knowledge when writing a libretto for the *Hofkapellmeister*.[21] Da Ponte's last Viennese libretto, *La caffettiera bizzarra*, set by Weigl, is likewise poor.[22] In this case Da Ponte's ideas were perhaps constrained by the fact that the opera was written for the visit of King Ferdinand I of Sicily, who was apparently an imbecile and unable to follow operas which contained dramatic complications.[23] So Da Ponte's dramatic experiments had come to an end with Mozart's *Così fan tutte*, in which all the important aspects are present to a high degree: the circular motion, the intimate dénouement, the showdown which begins when the last finale has already run for some time, and a moral as its 'happy ending' – all this in a story which in parts seems to reflect Da Ponte's experience gained from an earlier libretto, Martín's *L'arbore di Diana*.

Neither do the two pasticcios that Da Ponte wrote in 1789 and 1791 (both entitled *L'ape musicale*)[24] reach the dramatic standard of the librettos he wrote for Martín and Mozart. The reason was perhaps that in the pasticcios Da Ponte was obliged to concentrate on the music; he incorporated many arias evidently favoured by the Viennese audience, mostly from operas for which he himself had written the texts. *L'ape musicale* lends itself to this practice very well, since its plot deals with the preparation of an operatic production. Act 1 deals with the preliminaries: the librettist is chosen and the singers come together to let him know their wishes regarding the numbers he will write for each of them. Act 2 deals mainly with the first rehearsal of the opera. These pasticcios are not

---

[19] I am grateful to Malcolm Boyd, Cardiff, for this detail.
[20] Shelfmark 26.050-A.M.
[21] Even in *Falstaff, ossia Le tre* [!] *burle* (Vienna, 1799; two acts!) Salieri and his librettist Carlo Prospero Defranceschi do not follow Da Ponte's model; the second of the three 'burle' does not end in an incipient finale but only in a normal sequence of recitatives and short ensemble movements.
[22] Libretto in Dresden, Sächsische Landesbibliothek, MT 8° 1955 Rara.
[23] Goertz, *Mozarts Dichter*, p. 119.
[24] For a facsimile reproduction of the librettos (four versions: Vienna, 1789; Vienna, 1791; Trieste, 1792; and New York, 1830) see M. M. Siniscalchi, *L'ape musicale di Lorenzo da Ponte* (Rome, 1988).

important for their dramatic structure but rather for the allusions they contain to the state of opera in Vienna at the time. They include comments on the difference between French and Italian opera, on the quality of singers and on the music of different composers, and Da Ponte even criticizes his own writing.[25] He included one number from a Mozart opera in each pasticcio. In the 1789 version it was 'Là ci darem la mano' from *Don Giovanni*. The text, only slightly different from the original one, is sung in Act 1 Scene 7 (no. 12) by two of the most important characters, the librettist Bonario and Farinella, one of the prima donnas:

L'ape musicale (1789)		*Don Giovanni (1787)*	
BONARIO:	Là ci darem la mano,	GIOVANNI:	Là ci darem la mano,
	Là mi dirai di sì;		Là mi dirai di sì;
	Napoli è un po' lontano		Vedi, non è lontano
	Partiam ben mio di qui.		Partiam ben mio da qui.
FARINELLA:	Vorrei, e non vorrei	ZERLINA:	Vorrei, e non vorrei
	Incerto in petto ho il cor,		Mi trema un poco il cor,
	Contenta è ver sarei		Felice, è ver, sarei
	Ma può burlarmi ancor.		Ma può burlarmi ancor.
BONARIO:	Vieni mio bel diletto.	GIOVANNI:	Vieni mio bel diletto!
FARINELLA:	Ho un poco di sospetto.	ZERLINA:	Mi fa pietà Masetto!
BONARIO:	Là cangerem di sorte.	GIOVANNI:	Io cangierò tua sorte!
FARINELLA:	Presto, non son più forte.	ZERLINA:	Presto, non son più forte!
BOTH:	Andiam, andiam mio bene,	BOTH:	Andiam, andiam mio bene,
	A ristorar le pene		A ristorar le pene
	D'un innocente amor.		D'un innocente amor.

For the 1791 version Da Ponte chose the Letter Duet from the third act of *Le nozze di Figaro*;[26] the original text is retained, but it was only in a later version of the pasticcio performed in Trieste in 1792 that the movement began as Mozart had composed it, with the somewhat complicated transition from the *secco* recitative to the duettino (*Figaro*, 3, x):

Recitative, conclusion
COUNTESS: Canzonetta sull'aria . . .

---

[25] The 1789 version includes the following remark on Martín's music (1, 2): 'O bestia di maestro! a una mia pari questa razza di musica! e che versi da far piangere i gatti!' ('O what a stupid *maestro* to write such music for someone like me! And the words would make a cat weep!'). A further instance of comments on the Viennese theatres occurs in Gazzaniga's *Il finto cieco* (see Goertz, *Mozarts Dichter*, p. 114). Music by Mozart is mentioned in the 1791 version of *L'ape musicale* (2/5, Don Capriccio: Zerlina's aria, 'Batti, batti o bel Masetto' from *Don Giovanni*).

[26] Vienna version: 2/5; Trieste version: end of 2/4.

Duettino, no. 21
SUSANNA: . . . sull'aria . . .
COUNTESS: Che soave zeffiretto
[. . .]

In the second Vienna version the movement began directly with the 'canzonetta' itself ('Che soave zeffiretto') and the transition was omitted. Both quotations are commented on by the librettist Bonario afterwards, notwithstanding the formal problems of the transition: 'Oh questo è un capo d'Opera' ('Oh, this is a splendid opera').[27] Apparently Mozart research has not yet taken note of these adaptations.[28]

---

[27] The 1791 version was performed at the Burgtheater, Vienna, on 30 March, 6 April and 9 April; see O. Michtner, *Das alte Burgtheater als Opernbühne: von der Einführung des deutschen Singspiels (1778) bis zum Tod Kaisers Leopolds II. (1792)* (Vienna, 1970), p. 507. The insertion of the duettino reflects Mozart's connections to the Viennese court theatres and his continuing reputation in Vienna at this late stage in his life.

[28] I am indebted to my friend Tim Ingles for his help with the English text of this paper.

10

Viennese amateur or London professional? A reconsideration of Haydn's tragic cantata *Arianna a Naxos*

JULIAN RUSHTON

Although its exact date of composition is unknown, *Arianna a Naxos* (Hob.XXVIb: 2) appeared when Haydn's career as a dramatic composer had been interrupted after *Armida* (1784); the first documentation of its existence is a letter to Marianne von Genzinger dated 9 February 1790.[1] It was probably written late in 1789, and it is the principal vocal and dramatic composition from a period in which Haydn was making increasing contact with society in the imperial capital.[2] On the other hand, its piano accompaniment is a worthy contribution to one of his ripest periods of keyboard composition, which besides two magnificent sonatas (Hob.XVI: 48, 49) and the Capriccio in C major (Hob.XVII: 4) saw Haydn reach a new level of achievement in works for piano trio. Haydn visited Vienna twice in 1789; after his second visit he professed to find conditions at home nearly intolerable.[3] Doubtless what he most missed at Eszterháza was contact with professional colleagues, including Mozart; but his growing circle of friends also included cultivated amateurs. He had been in correspondence with Marianne von Genzinger, wife of Prince Esterházy's doctor, before they met during his second 1789 visit, and he became warmly attracted to this intelligent and charming woman who treated him as a social equal. One of the works which links her to Haydn is *Arianna*; and this kind of social contact also prepared Haydn for his visits to England, in which *Arianna* played a rather different role.

Arianna a Naxos is a dramatic solo cantata, a long-standing genre which usually deals with pastoral or tragic topics. But cantatas normally have continuo support or a full instrumental accompaniment: *Arianna*, exceptionally, has an accompaniment fully notated for solo keyboard (the dynamic and expressive

---

[1] H. C. Robbins Landon, *Haydn: Chronicle and Works. Haydn at Eszterháza, 1766–1790* (London, 1978); henceforward CW, p. 737.

[2] The period included a few insertion arias including the delightful mock-serious 'Infelice sventurata', for Cimarosa's *I due supposti conti*. This piece begins like a *seria* aria, but after the melodramatic reference to the ghost of the singer's 'Papà' it ends protestingly in *buffa* style.

[3] See note 1.

tendencies of the music imply piano rather than harpsichord). It belongs unequivocally to the tragic genre; there is no Bacchus, and the ending suggests that Ariadne has hurled herself from a cliff to her death. Whereas the ethos of opera seria permitted, even encouraged, a happy ending, the cantata, deprived of the realities of staging, and addressed to connoisseurs, will often leave the agony unresolved.[4] The dramatic cantata must not be confused with isolated vocal works whose text is drawn from an opera, like most of Mozart's 'concert arias' and Haydn's later *Scena di Berenice*. These are a different genre, neither part of a larger unit nor self-sufficient since full understanding requires knowledge of the whole opera. The dramatic cantata is free-standing, requiring no more than a little background knowledge of the subject for its appreciation.

Arianna a Naxos has come down to us in two authorized printed editions. The autograph manuscript (entitled 'Cantata a voce sola' and wrongly described as unpublished) reached England by an unknown route and was sold from the collection of Joseph Warren on 28 June 1872, for thirty shillings, the purchaser being one Robinson; it has not been seen since.[5] The first edition was Artaria's (Vienna, August 1790); the second was the composer's own – extant copies bear his signature – and was handled by Bland (London, 1791).[6] Otherwise the history of *Arianna* is enshrined in a few contemporary references which include a number of Haydn's letters and reports in the London press which may have given rise to the notion that it was composed there. It was, however, almost certainly revised for the London edition; several of the different readings must be classified as compositional choices.[7]

We do not know exactly for whom Haydn intended *Arianna*. Carpani's statement that it was written for Mrs Billington may be discounted since Haydn did not encounter her until he reached London; more credible is the report in the *Allgemeine musikalische Zeitung* that it was written for the Venetian singer

---

[4] The suicidal ending to Ariadne's story is anticipated in Edelmann's *Ariane dans l'isle de Naxos* given at the Paris Opéra in 1782. An ever-popular victim, Ariadne also features in Benda's melodrama of 1775 and Reichardt's cantata published in 1780.

[5] Anthony van Hoboken, *Joseph Haydn. Thematisch-bibliographisches Werkverzeichnis*, ii (Mainz, 1971), pp. 296–9, lists editions and manuscript sources. On the sale, see J. Coover, *Music at Auction: Puttick and Simpson (London), 1794–1971* (Detroit Studies in Music Bibliography, Pinewood Warren, 1988), p. 215. It seems likely that the autograph was in London in 1791 at the time of preparation of the second edition; see note 6 below.

[6] The editions are henceforward referred to as 'Artaria' and 'London'. It is alleged that Haydn sold *Arianna* to Bland in 1789, but on 15 November he wrote to Artaria that 'on your account he [Bland] did not receive a single note' (CW: 728). Landon says 'this is, of course, not true' because Bland received the 'Razor' quartet (op. 55 no. 2) and *Arianna*. But no evidence supports inclusion of *Arianna*, which Bland did not publish. On 12 April 1790 Haydn wrote to him concerning three cantatas: one, for Salomon, was never completed; another, 'Miseri noi, misera patria', 'is for the voice of my dear Storace'; and 'The cantata *Ariadne on Naxos*, however, I intend later on to orchestrate for a full band and then I shall send it to you.' There is no reason to infer a prior sale to Bland.

[7] Two modern editions have been consulted, referred to hereafter as HMP (ed. M. Flothuis, Salzburg, 1965), and GHV (ed. M. Helms, Munich, 1990, reprinted from G. Feder, ed.: Joseph Haydn Werke (Cologne, Munich, 1958-), series xxix vol. 2, pp. 2–23. HMP follows Artaria as a principal source; I concur with GHV in regarding the London edition as superior; some differences are noted below.

Bianca Sacchetti.[8] There may have been some confusion with the superficially similar *Scena di Berenice*, written in 1795 for Brigida Banti. The major difference between these marvellous compositions is that *Scena di Berenice* is overtly conceived for a professional singer, its tragic tone enhanced (like Mozart's music for Fiordiligi and Vitellia) by a range of over two octaves, a higher degree of ornamentation, and fast passage-work towards the end.[9] Haydn's letters about *Arianna* concern its performance by amateurs, the first of them 'Pepi', the young daughter of Marianne von Genzinger; conceivably it was composed with her in mind.[10] Ten years later it was sung by 'Mylady Hammelton' in 1800.[11] One of the most intriguing aspects of *Arianna*, its instrumentation, makes it particularly suited to this type of singer, from whom it requires expressive rather than technical virtuosity, diverging in this respect from most of Haydn's vocal music intended for public performance.

Haydn found an audience for professional concert performances of *Arianna* in England, probably to his accompaniment. Somewhat grotesquely, it was performed by a castrato, Gasparo Pacchierotti, and with considerable success.[12] Nevertheless, the range of only a twelfth (b♮–g♭^{2}) also permits amateur performance, and the composition of the English Canzonettas, with their frequently elaborate keyboard parts, is a reminder that in England, too, Haydn was happy to supply music for the cultivated amateur.[13] There is no real passage-work, even in the final Allegro, and the decorative ornamentaion is largely confined to the piano part. The result is a directness of expression which owes something, not surprisingly, to Gluck. Haydn had directed *Orfeo ed Euridice* at Eszterháza, and he knew other Gluck works, as well as operas by another reformer, Traetta, for whose *Ifigenia in Tauride* he wrote an insertion aria in 1786.[14]

---

[8] Hoboken, *Werkverzeichnis*, p. 299; *AmZ*, ii (1799), col. 336; see J. L. Baldauf-Berdes, *Women Musicians of Venice* (Oxford, 1993), pp. 123–4.

[9] There is no reason to connect a surviving ornamented text of *Arianna* directly with Haydn (facsimile of a page from No. 2, *Die Musik in Geschichte und Gegenwart*, vii (Kassel, 1958), p. 570). I am indebted to A. Peter Brown for drawing this to my attention.

[10] See the letters of Haydn to Genzinger of 9 February (note 1) and 14 March 1790 (CW, p. 739).

[11] Letter to Artaria of 3 September 1800, asking for a copy to be sent to Eisenstadt. See Landon, *Haydn: Chronicle and Works. The Years of The Creation: 1796–1800* (London, 1977), p. 557.

[12] For some reason the Porro edition of *Arianna* (Paris, 1792) advertised it as sung in London by 'Maru' (*sic* – presumably Mara) and dedicated to the Queen of England (Hoboken, *Werkverzeichnis*, p. 297). *The World*, on Wednesday 2 March 1791, announced: 'ARIANA à [*sic*] NAXOS, with Accompaniment for a Piano Forte, and sung by Signor PACCHIEROTTI, is this day published, price 5s, to be had of Mr HAYDN, No. 18 Great Pultney-Street, Golden Square, and at Bland's Music Warehouse, No. 45, Holborn' (I am indebted to David Wyn Jones for the full citation). On London performances see also Landon, *Haydn: Chronicle and Works. Haydn in London: 1791–1795*, (London, 1976), pp. 28, 47 and 75.

[13] The piano writing of *Arianna* anticipates in particular the rich A♭ sonority of 'She never told her love' and the dramatic F minor of 'Fidelity'. Haydn is said to have sung some of the Canzonettas himself before the King and Queen (Landon, *Haydn in London*, p. 284).

[14] On Haydn's knowledge of these composers and on the *Ifigenia* aria see A. P. Brown, 'Tommaso Traetta and the Genesis of a Haydn Aria', *Chigiana*, xxxvi (1979) pp. 101–42; D. P. Schroeder, *Haydn and the Enlightenment* (Oxford, 1988), p. 47.

Arianna consists of four sections of approximately equal duration. No. 1 is a meditative recitative (81 bars); No. 2 a slow aria (73 bars); No. 3 a dramatic recitative (97 bars); and No. 4 the second aria (117 bars, most of them at the only sustained fast tempo).[15] No. 1 begins in E♭, the first aria is in B♭, and after the widely modulating second recitative, No. 4 is in F. Unlike the standard concert aria or scena, the cantata embodies dramatic development: Ariadne's luxuriant awakening, her passionate desire for Theseus's return, her search for him, the revelation that he has deserted her, and suicidal despair. Musical unity would hardly be appropriate to such a sequence, and it is not symbolically represented by tonal means; even the ascending series of fifths implied above is imperceptible in practice. But Haydn did achieve a fusion of contrast and coherence matched, among his contemporaries, only in the operas of Mozart. The slow tempo and duple metre of Nos. 1 and 2 make for continuity despite the change of motives and texture. No. 3 marks a developmental contrast before the restoration of common time and a slow tempo in the first section of No. 4. No. 3 begins with an 'echo' of the aria cadence (bb. 154–63); the continuation is marked by a change to triple time, and a faster tempo. The major chord which ends the cantata is a tierce de Picardie, a process twice anticipated during No. 3. The coherence of the scena lies in the close relationship between a consistently patterned text and the matching expressiveness of the music, which sometimes supports, sometimes amplifies, and may even lightly contradict the overt sense of the poem.

NO. 1. ADAGIO SOSTENUTO[16]

Haydn's opening recitative is exceptional for sustaining its considerable length with no change of tempo. The first recitative of *Scena di Berenice* extends to 93 bars: Allegro (53 bars), Adagio (7), Allegro (15), and Adagio (18). Operatic recitatives normally exploit such musical changes, corresponding to shifts in the singer's mood; in *Arianna* Haydn retains a single affect throughout by constant reference to his opening motives, which interact and develop over a clear tonal scheme and with a clear point of thematic reprise (b. 57). It lacks only a concluding ritornello to mimic an aria form (it ends with a somewhat muted cadence in G minor).

The model is the nature or sleep scene of seventeenth-century opera (e.g. 'Plus j'observe ces lieux' in Lully's *Armide*); the clearest precedent is Gluck's

---

[15] This form is mysteriously misconstrued by Karl Geiringer, who says 'the recitative not only precedes, but interrupts, the aria' (a possible description of *Scena di Berenice* where the recitatives are cadentially elided with the aria), and Rosemary Hughes: 'As in Reichardt's *Ariadne*, the conventional divisions into recitative and aria are discarded in favour of an almost continuous recitative broken by only two short arias.' Geiringer, *Haydn: a Creative Life in Music* (London, 1947), 2nd edn 1964, p. 331; Hughes, 'Solo Song' in E. Wellesz and F. W. Sternfeld, eds., *The Age of Enlightenment, New Oxford History of Music*, vii (London, 1973), p. 365.

[16] In some sources, Largo, and/or sostenuto.

Ex. 10.1

recitative for Orpheus, 'Che puro ciel', an instrumental tapestry with occasional interventions from the singer, which Haydn had conducted. Like Rinaldo and Orpheus, Ariadne cannot quite grasp what is happening. She wakes believing Theseus is near; the music is gently voluptuous, its opening full texture contrasted with unaccompanied *sospiri* (b. 4; see Ex. 10.1, A1, A2). The music matches the Mediterranean morning, Ariadne's languorous awakening to consciousness, then her erotically induced agitation. It is motivically taut: the *sospiri* derive from the falling minor third of the second bar, audibly transformed into a tone (c^2–$b\flat^1$) which generates the new figure. This motivic richness is supported by a tonic prolongation. There follows (Ex. 10.1, B, b. 10) a contrast of texture (quaver continuum), but with motives linked by the same rhythmic cells and minor thirds (bracketed in Ex. 10.1) which blossom to cover a tenth (bb. 13–14). But the 'B' material, as in an aria ritornello, remains in the tonic.

What in aria or concerto terminology would be the 'first solo' (bb. 19–31) unfolds as recitative over an expanded restatement of the ritornello with modulation to the dominant. The voice uses minor thirds in response to the instrumental shapes, and engages in its own dialectic between the pitches g^1 and $a\flat^1$ (Ex. 10.2). The 'A' material spawns a new shape at b. 28 (Ex. 10.2, A3), repeated in the minor as Ariadne refers to her enticing dream.

The dominant (from b. 36) brings a new animation; Haydn revels in the opportunity to paint the dawn. But Ariadne's growing impatience overrides the potential cadence. In the 'second solo' (bb. 40–56) the 'dawn music' responds to her mood by moving to C minor; 'sposo adorato, dove guidasti il piè?' is marked by a querulous augmented sixth (b. 46). The intermediate ritornello modulates harshly from C minor to B♭ minor, blending 'A' and 'B' material (Ex. 10.3).

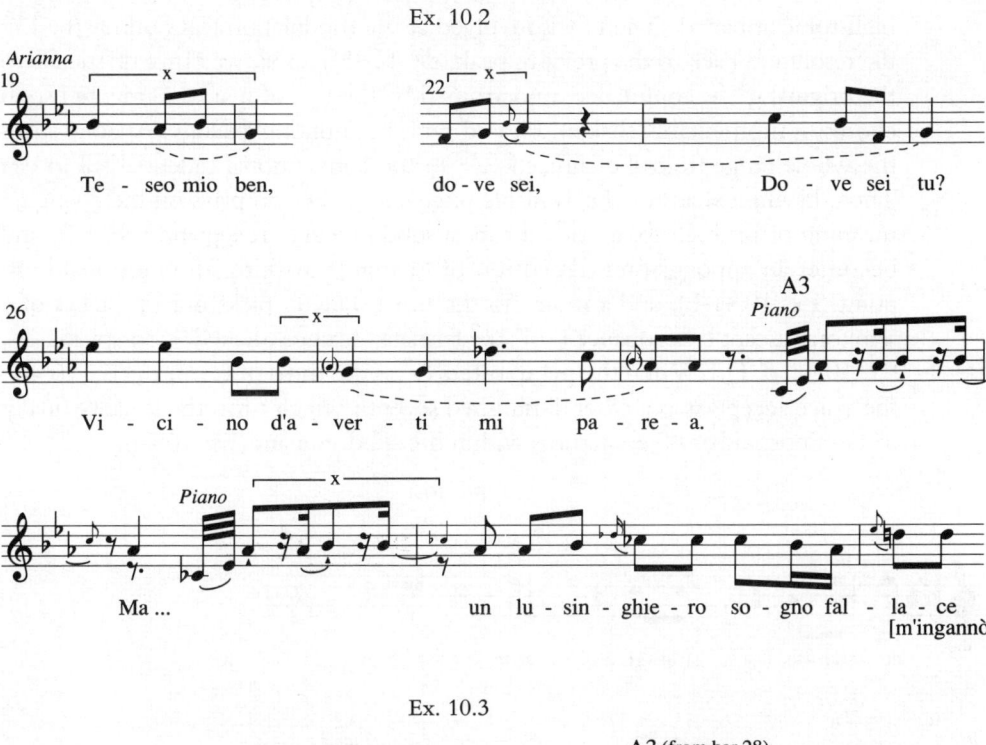

Ex. 10.2

Ex. 10.3

Then in a more lyrical passage ('Ah vieni, o caro . . .') Ariadne varies a familiar hunting topic: she is worthier prey than the wild animals of Naxos. At 'Ah vieni, o caro' the voice attains its highest note, $g\flat^2$ (b. 54), but in confidence, not anxiety, marked by the relaxing harmonic descent through the cycle of fifths to D♭. The reprise (third solo, b. 57) starts in the subdominant and refers only to 'A' material. Ariadne's confidence is shown in her firm return to the tonic, cadencing at 'splenda del nostro amor', followed by the literal reprise of b. 4 (b. 67). But the sighing figure alone remains, apart from a reference to Ex. 10.3 in b. 75 (see Ex. 10.4b). The ascending modulations (E♭, F minor, then by fifths through C to G minor) are commanding rather than desperate: she is in the grip of desire, not fear ('già mi strugge il desio . . . vieni idol mio'), and it is frustration which brings her to the minor mode of the conclusion.

Throughout this recitative Haydn exerts careful control over register in a vocal line spanning only a tenth. Having rung the changes on G and A♭ as melodic goals (see Ex. 10.2), he ascends to a conventional cadence including the high tonic at bar 31. Then f^2 is involved at the modulation to C minor (b. 43); the resolution back to the previous peak, eb^2 (b. 45), is followed by a drastic fall to the original g^1, as confidence, undermined by the first of many augmented sixth chords, is momentarily shaken. Pleased with her hunting analogy, Ariadne spans the whole range from the climactic gb^2 to the conventional cadential fall to eb^1. Then, having exhausted the available pitch-range, Haydn plays on the changing meaning of his high tonic, eb^2. It tops a subdominant arpeggiation (b. 62), and becomes an appoggiatura (repetition of 'stringi'), marking an emotional high point (Ex. 10.4a–b), and a return to the tonic. Haydn picks out the stages of a semitonal ascent by assonance ('sol', db^2 fermata; 'strugge', held $d\natural^2$, 'so-spi-ra', eb^2, Ex. 10.4c, d, f).[17] When the piano offers eb^2 as the third of C minor (Ex.10.4e), the voice accepts it as a cruel diminished seventh which turns the tonality finally to G minor: in bar 80 eb^2 returns within the subdominant (Ex. 10.4g).

Ex. 10.4

[17] The $d\natural^2$ on 'strugge' may also respond in pitch and assonance to the earlier 'stringi'. The 'strugge' phrase comes in five different rhythms in the sources; that of GHV seems on this analysis the best reading expressively and structurally.

NO 2. ARIA, 'DOVE SEI, MIO BEL TESORO'

Although her dream has dissipated, Ariadne still has no inkling that she has been deserted; hence the aria transforms the musical insecurity of the recitative into a firm statement. That, at least, is what the libretto implies; but Haydn contrives to suggest both Ariadne's overt confidence and the fear to which she will not yet admit ('If you don't come I shall die' is not meant literally; it is what classical lovers say). Arias normally imply a single affect, and this one conforms with its decorous reprise and tonic cadence. Nevertheless, Ariadne's complacency is constantly, and at the end definitively, subverted by melodic and harmonic detail.

She begins by listening: a low tonic B♭ precedes the half-bar entry of the ritornello, with the character of a slow gavotte. The chromatic *Eingang* of b. 89 recalls b. 9 in No. 1, but here leads to a half-bar's silence. The voice, instead of a clear continuation to the first loving phrase, breaks into fragments, finally divided by fermate. The first distich ends ambiguously: a half-close into b. 96, on the dominant, acts as a basis for continuation in the dominant, where Haydn finishes the first quatrain (the cadence is not complete in the voice part, closing on the third, not the root). In the restatement of the quatrain, the dominant minor intrudes with an ominous roar in the bass (bb. 107–8). The second distich ('Se non vieni . . .') begins like its first setting (compare b. 98 and b. 110), but a radical modulation brings the (local) relative major, A♭, which unlike the previous F major is authentically cadenced. Rhythmically, textually, indeed texturally, b. 116 should mark the end of the first part of a three-part aria; but the ♭VII lies outside the tonal range of the original tonic (B♭), a shattering blow to the stability of the language.

The second stanza, a prayer of three lines, escapes from this tonal quagmire with difficulty (and some ambiguity in the sources).[18] Haydn devotes only enough time to Ariadne's prayer to raise the tonality by one fifth, to E♭. In her growing anxiety, she soon breaks off to apostrophize Theseus again (in words which fall outside the verse form: 'Dove sei, Teseo, dove sei?').[19] This passage of dominant preparation is a recitative punctuated by instrumental flurries which fade into silence: not even echo replies. The harmonic, thematic and textual reprise lasts only four bars. Instead of repeating 'chi t'invola a questo cor' (bb. 95–6) Haydn moves at once to the second distich, 'Se non vieni' (b. 139), where tonic minor corresponds to the previous dominant minor but without the unnerving modulation to its relative (which would be D♭). Haydn despatches the reprise in little over half the length of the first section (16 bars against 27), the third line now set to an incantatory repetition of a minor third over an expressive shifting bass.

---

[18] In b. 124 Artaria gives the first bass-note as D♭; HMP follows. London has no accidental, and this implied D♮, which moves the tonality more clearly towards E♭, seems preferable.

[19] It is not included in the printed libretto, of which there is a facsimile in GHV: 112.

Ex. 10.5

Haydn's long-term strategy is to preserve, but also subvert, the expectations of an aria. Registrally, the whole aria is subdued, its total range a minor third lower than No. 1 (c^1–$e\flat^2$). The line 'né resisto al mio dolor' was first set in F, with a *galanterie* suited to Mozart's Dorabella (Ex. 10.5a); death is only a conceit. Its second setting contained a real threat, turned aside by teasing *sospiri* (Ex. 10.5b); a delusory security is implied by the cadence: delusory because it is in A♭, not F. But in the end, the vocal line is mournful, insecure; the voice avoids the tonic by descending from the leading-note (Ex. 10.5c), the *sospiri* are slower and no longer teasing, and the last $e\flat^2$ is resolved a ninth lower, again avoiding the root (Ex. 10.5d).

NO. 3. 'MA, A CHI PARLO?'

The aria cadence spills into the second recitative, prolonging the movement to b. 163; this subverts the piano's B♭ cadence, in any case interrupted at bb. 153–4, so that the section ends in G minor, like the opening recitative, but with a tierce de Picardie. The first recitative was a meditation. No. 3, overtly operatic, involves action, with changes of motive according to illustrative or expressive need. At 'Poco da me lontano' comes the only music in 3/4 time and the first acceleration of tempo to Andante (later Più moto). Haydn makes further use of available keyboard registers, and anticipates instrumentally his heroine's verbal articulation of feeling and action. The Andante begins with climbing music, in a closely crunched middle register, at b. 164, as she begins the difficult ascent of the cliff. From the aria's B♭, the music describes a circle of fifths as far as A (b. 187).[20] The view of the sea opens before Ariadne: the circle of fifths begins to descend, from D to F, as wave-figures inexorably ascend (bb. 191ff). For the first time, Haydn uses abrupt tempo changes – Adagio, Allegro, Più allegro – with corresponding harmonic wrenches. An Adagio (b. 206)[21] represents Ariadne's realization: 'Ei qui mi lascia in abbandono . . . tradita io sono'. The cadence in C major is interrupted by ♭VI (b. 213) and turbulent figuration initiates another falling fifth pattern (A♭, C♯, and its subdominant): she calls Theseus, then realizes that her effort is futile. The imminent cadence in C♯ minor is also interrupted by ♭VI (b. 223), a correspondence on the immediate harmonic level which confuses the broad tonal direction still further. To grandly sweeping scales, she calls on the gods to punish Theseus. The fifths, from A (b. 223), descend again to F, reached at the return of common time and the slowest Adagio (b. 240: 𝐂 not 𝄵). At the nadir of despair, the music takes on a hallucinatory quality. An apparently gentle major ninth harmony (b. 241) is contradicted by a minor ninth in b. 242, the termination of a rhapsodic flourish (a potential clarinet cadenza).[22] Yet Ariadne poises the major ninth (d^2) with the utmost pathos ('da chi pietà sperar?', b. 244), only for the piano to set off in F minor in an arioso worthy of a Bach passion, though utterly Haydnesque. The singing bass lures us to a fall of tonality (and spirits) as far as A♭ major (b. 248), then reaches C by the chillingly simple device of moving A♭^{6} down a semitone (bb. 248–9). The cadence which follows is chromatically saturated (Neapolitan sixth, diminished seventh to the dominant) in C minor, contradicted by the tierce de Picardie (thus V of F).

NO. 4. ARIA 'AH, CHE MORIR VORREI . . . MISERA ABBANDONATA'

The two-tempo aria, cantabile followed by presto, befits a heroine at the end of her tether, its Larghetto/Presto implying resignation/anger as the outcome of despair.[23] This slow–fast pattern is by no means uncommon in comic and

---

[20] The A major at b. 174 is clearly the dominant of D.
[21] The Adagio marking in b. 206, and the following Più allegro, are missing in HMP.
[22] Most sources read b♭ in the piano on the last beat of b. 241, the ornament in unison with the voice. Surprising as it first appears, London's d^2, favoured by GHV, is more appealing as a prolongation of the major ninth sonority to which b. 244 returns.
[23] London (hence GHV) has no tempo marking for the first section; Artaria has Larghetto.

serious opera, but Haydn's major key followed by parallel minor is unusual.[24] The piano introduction is almost galant; summoning her inner strength for a supreme farewell, Ariadne reverts to the language natural to herself as a social being. The chromaticism begins decoratively, but the hollow 'horn fifths' (bb. 258–9) may be an ironic reference back to Ariadne's own vision of herself as prey to Theseus the lover.[25]

The voice cannot rival the piano's decorative agility, or the serenity of the introduction. The piano's flattened seventh (b. 256, Ex. 10.6A) was resolved at once, but the voice draws it down the octave (b. 264, Ex. 10.6B) and extends it by the *sforzando* diminished seventh. As this chromatically enriched ii–V–I cadence is interrupted (b. 267), the singing bass recalls the crisis of the preceding recitative. Yet Ariadne is still the daughter of Minos; her reproof to the gods ('Mi serba ingiusto il ciel') planes majestically from f^2 to her low c^1 (bb. 270–1).

The quatrain is repeated, the modulation to the dominant as clear as Ariadne's grasp of her situation, a telling contrast with the first aria. A harsh first move to D minor (b. 271) yields conventionally to C major, but the directness of the modulation conveys fatalism even in its sturdy attachment to V/V (at 'sì fatal momento', b. 275).[26]

Only now does Ariadne give way to despair. The presto, introduced by the piano building a harsh minor ninth, is a cry of anger and self-pity poured out as a perpetual motion in F minor.[27] The first words of this second quatrain ('Misera abbandonata') sum up the whole story, but it is the second distich ('Chi tanto amai s'invola barbaro ed infedel') which is obsessively repeated. In his letter of 14 March 1790 Haydn urged Marianne von Genzinger to ensure that her daughter paid especial attention to these words: 'who loved so much'.[28] Haydn spun out the same nagging repetitions over the larger canvas of *Berenice*, which suggests that the passage had a special significance (Ex. 10.7). But any dramatic setting would have to focus on these words: it is through her excessive love that Ariadne has betrayed her father and fatherland, allowing Theseus to slay the minotaur and end the Athenian tribute to Crete. In the extent of her own treachery lies the horror of her betrayal, for it is also her punishment.

Harmonically, the Presto resolves the cantabile, which ends in the dominant. But it has its own structure, modulating quickly to A♭ and cadencing emphatically there (A♭ is implied by b. 295, the cadence is at b. 315). An outburst of

---

[24] A precedent from 1779 is the three-section aria 'A trionfar' from *La vera costanza*.
[25] They could conceivably signify sexual betrayal, a topical allusion more suited to comedy (e.g. Figaro's 'Aprite un po' quegl'occhi'). But there is no indication that Theseus has betrayed Ariadne sexually.
[26] According to London and GHV this is prepared by a daring, but perfectly logical, minor ninth (b. 274) which is not found in Artaria/HMP.
[27] Haydn had used this agitated F minor style in Rosina's first aria in Act 2 of *La vera costanza* and in the *Ifigenia* aria (see note 14); it returns at the end of *Scena di Berenice*.
[28] Letter of 14 March 1790; see note 10. Was this no more than a composer drawing attention to a critical point in the text, or was it a coded message to the mother?

Ex. 10.6

rage in the piano acts as a ritornello. The disorder of Ariadne's senses is expressed by a reprise of the first quatrain, now functioning as the middle of the Presto (from b. 319). Ariadne is too perturbed for a simple reprise of the second quatrain; when it resumes, it is to an obsessive dominant preparation (b. 332). Thus the overall form is binary, whereas the layout of the text is ternary. This contradiction is not found in the *Berenice* aria which gives the text twice in its entirety within the Allegro, forming a longer and more secure binary structure (the two are compared in Table 10.1). In *Arianna*, decorum is partly restored by a full reprise of the second part, now in F minor, slightly extended with a powerful rhetorical flourish involving two diminished sevenths. The piano coda corresponds to its central ritornello, but closes with two cadences, the last a tierce de Picardie of horrible finality.

Haydn's *Arianna* runs the full gamut of tragic emotions while remaining essentially vocal chamber music. Haydn did contemplate orchestration, as he

Ex. 10.7

wrote to Bland; nevertheless the piano writing is thoroughly idiomatic. The decoration of the opening recitative, the transition within the first aria, the pianistic layout of the Largo to the second aria, the link to the Presto – these are only a few of the places for which orchestration in Haydn's own style is virtually impossible. Of course Haydn would have recomposed them in orchestral format; but that underlines the idiomatic nature of the original.

We should not be surprised that Haydn achieved a fully dramatic form on this intimate scale. The arousing and contradiction of expectation in thematic patterning and harmonic closure, and the often radically transformed reprises, are familiar from his instrumental music, especially the quartets. It has generally been assumed that Haydn's vocal music is more conventional, an assumption which may have been exaggerated, but is not entirely unfounded; operas were written for a wider public, even at Eszterháza, rather than for connoisseurs.[29] In his instrumental works Haydn expanded his musical frame of reference and enhanced his subtlety of communication, while preserving the broad outlines of a familiar form. He could thus offer string quartets to the London public, opp. 71 and 74, and he similarly reconciles *Kenner* and *Liebhaber* in *Arianna a Naxos*, composed for the cultivated amateurs of Vienna and professionally performed in London, by clever transformation of conventional gesture and form by ambiguity and contradiction of the predictable.

[29] The subtlety of Haydn's operas is only now coming to be appreciated; see for instance M. Hunter, 'Text, Music, and Drama in Haydn's Italian Opera Arias', *Journal of Musicology*, vii (1989), pp. 29–57.

Table 10.1 *The F minor arias in Arianna and Scena de Berenice*

	Intro.	A (in F minor)	B (in A♭)	X[a]	B (F minor), Coda
Arianna					
Quatrains		2[b]	rep.	1 2 -------	------------
Bars	8 (on V)	8	8 + 14	13 + 13	8 + 12 5 [elision]
Berenice					
Quatrains		2[b]	3[c] 2	3 -----	-----------
Bars	12	28	27 + 35 [elision]	21	16 + 36 11 [elision]

a. In both arias the reprise of the text starts before the recovery of the tonic.
b. The first quatrain is set in the previous slow tempo of each aria.
c. Actually a quintain.

Landon places *Scena di Berenice* 'among the finest dramatic pieces for soprano of the period . . . it shows Haydn the dramatist at his most striking and persuasive'.[30] Every word of this encomium could be applied to *Arianna*, the more complete work of the two, with no inferred operatic context, and the more powerful for its intimacy. The world into which Haydn locked himself in his late 1780s visits to Vienna produced, in 'Meine Liebe Arianna', a work of the highest originality and perhaps his most completely satisfying work in the tragic mode.[31]

---

[30] H. C. Robbins Landon, 'Haydn's Operas', in Wellesz and Sternfeld, eds., *The Age of Enlightenment* (see note 15), p. 199.

[31] 'Meine Liebe Arianna': letter of 14 March 1790 (see note 10). When this paper was presented in Cardiff, Virginia Rushton and Stephen Price gave performances of 'Infelice sventurata', the Canzonettas mentioned in note 13, and *Arianna*. I am grateful to Virginia for sharing a performer's insight, and to David Wyn Jones for many helpful observations.

PART IV

Pianos and pianism

11

The Viennese fortepiano in the eighteenth century

EVA BADURA-SKODA

The prevailing view that pianos remained unknown in England in the first half of the eighteenth century may well be true. Apparently, the first piano in England arrived in 1752, bought from a certain Father Wood in Rome. More pianos were imported around 1760, and soon were manufactured in London in ever-increasing quantities, especially after 1780; by 1790, England had become one of the leading countries for the manufacture of pianos.

The situation in Vienna, however, was quite different. Recent research suggests that Cristofori's invention of a reliable hammer action was greeted with much more enthusiasm in southern Europe than previously thought. The news of Cristofori's 'harpsichord that plays quietly and strongly' ('arpicembalo che fa il piano e il forte') probably spread quickly in Italy and Austria, also to the Iberian peninsula, Alsace-Lorraine, south Germany and Saxony (where keyboard instruments with a hammer action were built at least from the 1720s onwards). A 'Flügel without quills' ('Flügel ohne Kiele'), which hardly could be anything other than a kind of *Hammerflügel*, was advertised in the *Wiennerisches Diarium* in 1725.[1] An old misconception, based on the writings of Curt Sachs and Rosamond Harding, thus needs correcting. When Harding wrote in 1933 that 'The importance of Cristofori's invention was not realized by his countrymen',[2] she was simply wrong. And when she later, in another context, wrote that pianos were considered cheap instruments bought only by people who could not afford a good harpsichord, she may have been correct with regard to some mid-century square pianos, but certainly wrong if she was referring to Cristofori's sophisticated instruments or the wing-shaped pianos of Silbermann or Ferrini. Here the exact opposite was the case. Harpsichords with quills were

---

[1] See E. Badura-Skoda, 'Zur Frühgeschichte des Hammerklaviers', in *Florilegium Musicologium. Festschrift für Hellmut Federhofer zum 75. Geburtstag*, ed. C.-H. Mahling (Tutzing, 1988), p. 41.
[2] R. E. Harding, *The Piano-Forte. Its History traced to the Great Exhibition 1851* (Cambridge, 1933), pp. 8–9; K. Restle, *Bartolomeo Cristofori und die Anfänge des Hammerclaviers (Münchner Arbeiten zur Musiktheorie und Instrumentenkunde,* i) (Munich, 1991), pp. 247–8.

much easier to build and to maintain than harpsichords with a hammer action; consequently Cristofori's 'cembali con martelli' ('hammer-harpsichords') were more often purchased by royalty, Roman cardinals and wealthy noblemen than by poor musicians.

The wording of the advertisement in the *Wiennerisches Diarium* 1725, mentioned above, suggests that *Hammerflügel* were so well-known in Vienna in 1725 that they did not require further description. A recently discovered inscription on the soundboard of a Viennese harpsichord built in 1697 and converted into a piano in 1703 or 1726 (the inscription is not quite clear)[3] confirms the early acquaintance of musicians in the city with the *Hammerflügel* or hammer harpsichord. We do not know how many pianos were built in the first half of the century in Vienna and it will not concern us here, but recent discoveries suggest that around 1750 probably nearly all of the organ and instrument makers living in the city tried to build an instrument with a hammer action.

Why was this situation not previously perceived correctly? The main reason is a terminological problem which has misled scholars in the past and continues to mislead many today; the modern and, therefore, anachronistic perception of the words cembalo, clavecin and harpsichord has led to many misconceptions. Cristofori had introduced his hammer action into a harpsichord case, which is why he always termed his instrument 'cembalo' (or 'cimbalo'), sometimes adding adjectival phrases such as 'che fa il piano e il forte' ('that plays quietly and strongly'), ' con martelli' ('with hammers'), 'con piano e forte' ('with soft and loud') or 'di martellati' ('capable of striking'). As far as Cristofori was concerned the instrument continued to be a 'cembalo' (usually the sources have 'cimbalo' rather than 'cembalo').[4] Later Italian terms for the instrument were 'nuovo cembalo' ('new harpsichord'), 'cembalo con martellini' ('harpsichord with little hammers'), 'cimbalo a martelli' ('harpsichord with hammers'), 'cimbalo di piano e forte' ('harpsichord with soft and loud'), 'cembali senza penne' ('harpsichords without quills'), 'cembalo straordinario' ('extraordinary harpsichord') or simply 'cembalo'. The use of the term 'piano e forte' as a substantive begins to make its appearance in Italian documents only towards the end of the eighteenth century. As late as 1850 an instruction manual was published in Naples on the subject of replacing the leather of 'i martelli dei cembali' (clearly meaning the hammers of pianos). Thus, it is hardly surprising that German and Austrian composers of Mozart's time, whenever they used

---

[3] A. Huber, 'Der Österreichische Klavierbau im 18. Jahrhundert' and 'Das "Clavier" im 18. Jahrhundert', in *Die Klangwelt Mozarts, eine Ausstellung des Kunsthistorischen Museums, Wien 1991* (Vienna, 1991), p. 64.

[4] Cristofori was responsible for the musical instruments at the Florentine court. In an inventory compiled in 1700 he described his newly invented instrument as 'Arpicimbalo di nuova invenzione che fa il piano e il forte' ('Large harpsichord newly invented that plays quietly and strongly'). In a later inventory, compiled by Cristofori in 1716, only 'cimbali' are mentioned, of which several are listed; none is precisely defined by an additional descriptive phrase – clear proof that for Cristofori, at least, the novel 'cembalo con martelli' ('hammer-harpsichord', as in later English documents) continued to be a 'cimbalo' or cembalo.

Italian terminology in their scores, continued to use the word 'cembalo' when designating the fortepiano. Mozart did this in his piano concertos, and Beethoven, for instance, in the second movement of the piano sonata in A, op. 101, where one finds in the autograph the successive markings of 'sul una corda', 'poco a poco tutte le corde' and, in bar 21 of the second movement, 'tutto il cembalo ma piano' (incidentally, the original edition (S. A. Steiner and Company) of op. 101 appeared under the general heading 'Musée des clavecinistes'). Even Schubert, when he was a pupil of Salieri, made use of the Italian terminology in the single movement in B flat for piano trio (D28), first writing 'Cembalo' over the appropriate system before changing it to 'Pianoforte'.

The term 'piano' or 'pianoforte' – the modern name for 'cembalo con martelli' ('hammer-harpsichord') – was completely unknown in the first three decades of the eighteenth century. According to a passage in the fifth volume of Zedler's *Universal-Lexicon*,[5] which appeared in Leipzig in 1733, the noun 'Pianofort(e)' was invented by Gottfried Silbermann in 1732. But it was not used until Frederick the Great of Prussia developed an enthusiasm for Silbermann's pianos in the 1740s. Afterwards, German instrument builders introduced the new term slowly into the musical life of London and Paris. In south Germany, away from Berlin, it also took more than a decade before the adjectival formation 'piano e forte' was used as a noun. In Vienna, I have traced the first use of the word 'fortepiano' to an account book from March 1763 in the Hofkammer Archiv. The term 'Fortipiano' is mentioned here, and then a second time in May 1763, in connection with concert fees given to Johann Baptist Schmid for playing in the Burgtheater.[6]

In France, the terms 'clavecin à maillets' ('harpsichord with hammers') or simply 'clavecin' were applied for a long time to the piano; even in the nineteenth century the words 'clavecinists' and 'pianists' were still interchangeable. In Germany, before the terms 'Kielflügel' and 'Hammerflügel' came into use for distinguishing between a harpsichord with quills and one with hammers, expressions such as 'Flügel mit und ohne Kiele' ('wing-shaped instruments with or without quills') were a way of making the same distinction. As late as 1802 Heinrich Christoph Koch stated in his dictionary: 'The real form of the fortepiano is wing-shaped, and for this reason it is often termed Flügel ('Die eigentliche Form des Fortepiano ist die des Flügels, daher es auch oft ein Flügel genannt wird').[7] Thus, it is dangerous and misleading consistently to translate the German word 'Flügel', common in documents and treatises throughout the eighteenth century, as 'harpsichord', without acknowledging the alternative contemporary sense of 'harpsichord with hammers'. Readers of the treatises of

---

[5] At the end of the article 'Cembal d'amour', v (1733), col. 1803.
[6] E. Badura-Skoda, 'Prolegomena to a History of the Viennese Fortepiano', *Journal of the Israel Musicological Society*, ii (1980), pp. 78–9. I am indebted to Dexter Edge for informing me of the second reference.
[7] H. Koch, 'Fortepiano', *Musikalisches Lexicon* (Frankfurt, 1802), p. 592.

C. P. E. Bach and Quantz should be especially cautioned not to jump to the conclusion that the terminology found in Berlin in the 1750s was in use elsewhere, and that in Austria, in particular, the word 'Flügel' always meant harpsichord. This assumption has led to a very misleading picture of acceptance and distribution of the piano in eighteenth-century Austria. However, I agree with the general view that around 1750 the harpsichord with quills may still have been the most important keyboard instrument with strings.

It is interesting to note that in the middle of the eighteenth century people remained so fond of the sound of the harpsichord with quills (the *Kielflügel*), that they wished to retain its brilliant sound in the new *Hammerflügel*. One stop found on Gottfried Silbermann's pianos lowers small ivory or metal plates onto the strings, thereby producing a bright, harpsichord-like sound. Another solution that combined the advantages of harpsichords with hammers and harpsichords with quills was a compound instrument with more than one manual, one activating quills, the other a hammer action. Such instruments were sold in Leipzig in the 1730s and 1740s, and continued to be built in southern Germany after 1750 by, for instance, Franz Jacob Späth in Regensburg and Johann Andreas Stein in Augsburg. These interesting instruments deserve greater attention because they were far more common in the second half of the eighteenth century than has hitherto been realized.[8] In J. A. Hiller's *Wöchentliche Nachrichten und Anmerkungen die Musik betreffend*, published in Leipzig in 1766,[9] we read that an instrument maker named Barthold Fritz from Braunschweig has made 'a great number of wing-shaped instruments with quills and hammers' ('eine große Anzahl Flügel mit Federn und Hämmern zugleich').

Although compound harpsichords with hammers and quills were built mainly by German makers, some were manufactured in England too. Rosamond Harding has mentioned quite a number of them. In 1759 an instrument maker named Weltmann received in London a patent for a harpsichord which had not only quills but also, according to his description, 'a kind of jack which instead of plucking the strings strikes these from below'.[10] John Joseph Merlin received a patent in London in 1774 'for his newly invented kind of compound harpsichord in which, besides the jacks with quills, a set of hammers, of the nature of those used in the kinds of harpsichords called piano forte are introduced in such manner that either may be played separately or both together at the pleasure; and for adding the aforesaid hammers to an harpsichord of the common kind already made, so as to render it such a compound harpsichord'.[11] It is likely that J. C.

---

[8] See E. Badura-Skoda, 'Komponierte J. S. Bach "Hammerklavier-Konzerte"?', *Bach Jahrbuch*, lxxvii (1991), p. 170.

[9] p. 47.

[10] Harding, *Piano-Forte*, p. 48. In the same year Weltmann submitted a similar compound instrument to the Académie Royale des Sciences in Paris.

[11] E. F. Rimbault, *The Pianoforte, its Origin, Progress and Construction* (London, 1860), p. 150, as quoted in Restle, *Cristofori*, pp. 302–3.

Bach played two concerts in 1774 on this or a similar compound instrument built by Merlin, since the *Morning Chronicle* of 5 May and 22 May 1774 reported that Bach played 'a new concerto upon Mr. Merlin's lately invented harpsichord'. In later years Merlin built 'The patent Piano-Forte Harpsichord with Kettledrums'. One of Merlin's compound instruments, dated 1780, is owned by the Deutsches Museum in Munich; this instrument is also notable because it has a mechanism that somehow notates the music being played. Another one may have been owned by Dr Charles Burney. In 1777 Robert Stodart, also residing in London, received a patent for another kind of compound instrument combining a harpsichord and a pianoforte.[12] Finally, Harding mentions that in 1792 the piano maker John Geib also received a patent for a compound instrument.

In Germany, Switzerland and France compound instruments are documented from 1731 onwards. Few are extant. One compound instrument was built in Berlin in 1758 'under the direction of the Prussian King' and later given to Count Taxis who took it with him to Italy, where Burney saw it in 1771;[13] a second instrument, built by Johann Ludwig Hellen of Berne and originally dated 1775 but repaired in 1779 in Frankfurt, is now in Berlin (the Musikinstrumenten-Sammlung des Staatlichen Instituts für Musikforschung); and a third, by Joachim Swanen, is preserved in Paris at the Conservatoire des Arts et des Métiers. Many more such instruments must have been manufactured.

As mentioned above Johann Andreas Stein, famous because of his connection with the Mozart family, built various compound instruments. He had learnt his craft with his father, then with Gottfried Silbermann's nephew, Johann Andreas Silbermann, in Strasbourg and, finally, with Franz Jacob Späth in Regensburg. Stein seems to have been a good businessman. The following announcement appeared in Hiller's *Wöchentliche Nachrichten* in July 1769.

Nachricht von Verbesserung des Pianofortinstruments
Ein mit Rabenkielen befiederter und gut mensurirter Flügel hat sich schon von langen Zeiten her, als das brauchbarste Instrument zum Accompagniren, zu Handstücken und Concerten bewiesen. Was man ihm etwan vorwerfen könnte, ist, daß man, wenn nicht eine doppelte Claviatur vorhanden ist, das forte und piano nicht anders als durch Vermehrung oder Verminderung der Stimmen, auf eine sehr unvollkommene Weise, auszudrücken vermag.

Das Instrument, das den Nahmen des Fortepiano führt, so wie es bisher nur Silbermann verfertigt hat, und zu welcher Classe man eine Menge da und dort, theils nachgemachter, theils selbst erfundener Instrumente nicht zählen muß, ist für die meisten Liebhaber ungemein reizend, zumal wenn es gedämpft gebraucht wird . . .

Ein geschickter Orgel- und Instrumentmacher, der zugleich Organist an der evangelischen Barfüßerkirche in Augsburg, Herr Johann Andreas Stein, hat an der

---

[12] R. Harding mentions that the earliest drawing of the so-called English Grand action is to be found in the patent description for this compound instrument; *Piano-Forte*, pp. 57–8.
[13] C. Burney, *The Present State of Music in France and Italy* (London, 1771), p. 181.

Verbesserung der Mängel, die sich bey dem Pianoforte finden, seit zehn Jahren gearbeitet, und ein Instrument zu Stande gebracht, da von Kennern sehr gelobt und bewundert wird . . .

Der etwas stumpfe Ton des Fortepiano brachte besagten Herrn Stein auf die Gedanken, ihm einen scharfen Zug zuzugesellen, und gewissermaaßen den Flügel mit dem Fortepiano zu verbinden. Diese Verbindung aber bestehet weiter in nichts, als daß beyde auf einem Claviere gekoppelt werden können; denn jedes hat seinen besondern Körper und Saiten. Es ist dieses Werk demnach nicht von der Gattung derjenigen, wo die Hämmer und Docken einerley Saiten mit einander gemein haben, und eine abscheuliche Musik hervor bringen, weil der Anschlag der Hämmer eine ganz andere Mensur, und andere Saiten verlangt, als die Docken. Es befinden sich also zwey Instrumente in einem beysammen und sind in der Mitte durch einen Boden von einander abgesondert. Das obere Instrument ist ein gewöhnlicher vierchörigter Flügel wovon drey Saiten in 8 füßigen Einklange stehn, die 4te aber einen ganz gelinden 16 Fußton anspricht; das mittlere und obere Clavier sind diesem Flügel zugeeignet . . . Das untere Instrument ist das Pianoforte . . . Der Deckel, welcher dieselben schließt, stellt sich, bey der Eröffnung, in eine solche abhangende flache Linie, daß er mit unserm Ohre zu rechtem Winkel steht, wodurch die aufprallenden Tonstrahlen so gut in unser Ohr geführt werden, als wenn das Instrument oben wäre. Das dritte oder unterste Clavier ist ihm zugeeignet, und so leicht zu spielen, daß eine jede Hand bequem darauf fortkommt . . .[14]

News about the improvement of the pianoforte instrument
A quilled and well-designed harpsichord has for a long time been considered the best instrument for accompaniment and for concerts. However, what one notes, especially if an instrument has only one keyboard, is that it is capable only of expressing forte and piano imperfectly, by changing the texture and by increasing or decreasing the parts.

The instrument, which has been named Fortepiano and which only Silbermann has been able to construct on such a high level of perfection, belongs to a separate class and should not be placed into the same category as the great number of instruments of the new kind which are either [badly] copied or self-manufactured; it affords special delight to most amateurs, particularly if it is played with dampers . . .

A talented organ and instrument builder, who is also organist at the Protestant Barfüßerkirche in Augsburg, Herr Johann Andreas Stein, has worked for about ten years to find remedies for the shortcomings which are so common in pianofortes . . .

The slightly dull sound of the fortepiano gave him the idea of combining the brilliant sound of the harpsichord with the flexible but soft sound of the pianoforte. This combination consists of nothing else than the coupling of the sound of the harpsichord with that of the fortepiano in such a way that they can be played on one instrument. Each of the two combined instruments has its own mechanism and its own strings. Therefore, this compound instrument does not belong to that category of instruments where hammers and quills touch the same strings and thereby create an ugly sound, because the touch of the hammers requires not only another point of contact than the quills but also different strings. Therefore, there are two instruments built into one frame, separated in the middle by a base-board. The upper instrument is

---

[14] J. A. Hiller, *Anhang zu dem dritten Jahrgange der Wöchentlichen Nachrichten und Anmerkungen die Musik betreffend* (Leipzig, 24 July 1769), p. 32, p. 40.

a common harpsichord with four strings for each note, of which three are 8 ft stops, the fourth, however, is a soft 16 ft stop; the middle and upper manual belongs to this harpsichord . . . The lower instrument is the pianoforte . . . The lid can be opened from below in such a way that the sound of the pianoforte can reach us just as well as if the instrument had been built as the upper one. The lowest manual is connected with the piano and is so easy to play that each hand can use it comfortably . . .

The editor – probably Hiller himself – promised a continuation of the report but none appeared. This compound instrument is not identical with the harpsichord-piano, which Stein named *Politoniclavichord*. According to a description in the *Augsburger Intelligenzblatt* of 5 October 1769, the latter was contained in a large rectangular case with a keyboard at each end, similar to the harpsichord-piano that Stein called *Vis-à-vis Flügel*, a compound instrument which Stein brought to Vienna in 1777 for a demonstration at the imperial court.[15] In Mozart's well-known letter of 17 October 1777, recounting his visit to the Stein workshop in Augsburg, the composer does not mention any compound instruments, a fact for which various explanations are possible: perhaps Stein had sold all the previously built examples or, quite simply, the instrument did not catch Mozart's attention since he himself had ceased to be interested in harpsichords and, therefore, in any instrument that sought to perpetuate its qualities. From Mozart's keyboard sonatas it is patently clear that he regarded the harpsichord as an old-fashioned instrument in the 1770s, unsuitable for the interpretation of his keyboard works. As well as specific dynamic markings the general highly expressive nature of his music shows this attitude clearly.[16]

The more we learn about the history of the fortepiano in the second half of the century, the more it becomes obvious that *Hammerflügel*, *Pyramidenflügel* and *Tafelklaviere* were instruments more widely used in southern Germany and Austria in the 1760s and 1770s than hitherto acknowledged. The specific question whether the child Mozart played a compound harpsichord-piano can probably also be answered in the affirmative.[17] In Vienna prior to the 1770s *Hammerflügel* or fortepianos were certainly in use and liked by the younger generation of musicians. In 1772 Charles Burney heard a girl playing one in the Wagenseil household. It seems that during the third quarter of the century piano construction enjoyed a kind of boom in German-speaking countries (including Alsace-Lorraine). Some important technical improvements in the manufacture and mechanism of the square pianos and smaller instruments were

---

[15] This instrument may be the one kept in the Museo Civico, Verona. Another *Vis-à-vis Flügel* by Stein is preserved at the conservatory in Naples.

[16] There are still some commentators who insist that Mozart intended his early sonatas to be played on the harpsichord, ignoring, *inter alia*, the evidence of dynamic markings in the autographs. The evidence that Mozart preferred the fortepiano is overwhelming.

[17] In a forthcoming article for *Mozart-Jahrbuch* I shall try to prove that such an instrument was available to the composer in Salzburg in the 1760s, but not in Vienna when he visited that city in 1763.

made in that period. Unfortunately, there is no extant evidence from diaries or books written in Vienna. The treatises of Quantz and C. P. E. Bach, however, had spoken about the piano in a way that assumes knowledge of the instrument on the part of the readers. Though in 1753 C. P. E. Bach had insisted that the clavichord, especially for study purposes, was still preferable to the piano, 'whose touch is difficult and requires thorough study' ('dessen Tractirung besonders und nicht ohne Schwierigkeit ausstudiert werden muß'), by 1762 he was giving parity to the piano, clavichord and harpsichord. Johann Andreas Stein seems already to have been working enthusiastically on improvements of piano actions prior to 1758.

The desire to vary and enrich the sound of stringed keyboard instruments led to the invention of many more stops on the fortepiano than had been available on the harpsichord. In southern Germany, Bohemia and Vienna, especially, fortepianos were built with a considerable number of devices for altering the sound. The well-known instrument maker, Franz Jakob Späth (Spath), whose pianos Mozart had liked best before encountering those of Stein,[18] proudly announced in 1770 in Hiller's *Wöchentliche Nachrichten* that he had manufactured a compound instrument allowing fifty possibilities of sound changes; on another occasion he had delivered an instrument to Cologne that had more than thirty ways of altering the sound.[19]

What kind of stops existed on fortepianos from the time of Haydn and Mozart? The instruments of Cristofori were already equipped with an *una corda* device that moved the keyboard so that one string rather than two was struck by the hammer. (Later, this stop was sometimes called 'Guitarre'.) When three strings existed rather than two, a *due corde* stop, a moderator and a *una corda* were provided, allowing several shades of *piano* and *pianissimo*. We have already mentioned the stop found on many Silbermann pianos that imitated the sound of the harpsichord by placing metal or ivory plates on the strings. This stop is found on many German instruments, sometimes under the name 'Cembalo Register'.

The mechanism to lift the dampers was probably the invention of Gottfried Silbermann. On his pianos the dampers could be lifted separately for the treble and bass registers by means of two hand stops. This became the most common stop and, of course, remained fundamental to the sonority of the piano in its later history. Cheaper square pianos sometimes had no dampers at all,[20] but since no Viennese piano of this kind exists this characteristic need not concern us here. Until about 1780 only hand stops were found on Viennese pianos. (Mozart's own fortepiano by Anton Walter is probably one of the earliest

---

[18] See Mozart's famous letter from Augsburg to his father (17 October 1777) in which he describes Stein's fortepianos.
[19] Hiller, *Wöchentliche Nachrichten*, (30 April, 1770), p. 142.
[20] See L. Libin, 'Early pianos without dampers', in *Atti del XIV. Congresso della Società Internazionale di Musicologia, Bologna 1987* (Turin, 1990), ii, p. 287.

Viennese instruments to have knee levers for lifting the dampers, as well as the customary hand stops.) Pedals were probably not known in Vienna before 1800; also split damping – the separate lifting of dampers in the treble and bass registers – is not common on Viennese instruments. The probable reason for this was that other stops, such as *una corda*, a *pp* stop, ' moderator' (a rail covered with cloth that softened the sound) and almost always a bassoon stop, were given greater priority by Viennese manufacturers. Kenneth Mobbs owns a Viennese piano by Johann Heichele,[21] built early in the nineteenth century, which has five knee levers. This instrument is a remarkable exception to the rule that only two or occasionally three knee levers are found on Viennese pianos.

Other devices found on Viennese pianos include lute stops and Turkish band (or Janissary) stops, the latter imitating the sound of drums, cymbals and bells. Although I have never seen an eighteenth-century Viennese instrument with a Turkish music stop, many Viennese pianos from very early in the nineteenth century have one. Recently, it has been doubted that Mozart came across such a piano,[22] but I find it difficult to believe that these stops did not exist in Vienna in 1783. Many years ago Alfred Einstein suggested that the 'Alla Turca' finale of the piano sonata in A (K331) was intended to be played on such an instrument. Alan Tyson's view that the sonata was composed in Vienna in 1783, the centenary of the Turkish siege, rather than five years earlier in Paris, makes it even more likely in this instance that Mozart was inspired by a fortepiano with a Turkish music stop, activated by a hand stop.

As noted above, the first public concerts featuring a fortepiano in Vienna were given at the Burgtheater in 1763. The year marked the end of the Seven Years War (or Third Silesian War) between Prussia and Austria. Naturally, the war years (the 1740s and 1750s) had allowed little commercial or cultural contact between Berlin and Vienna and the terms 'Piano-Forte' and 'Forte-Piano', which had become common in Berlin in the mid-century, were apparently not known in Vienna in those years. It is rather surprising, therefore, that the term 'Fortipiano' occurs in a Viennese document as early as 1763.[23] It is likely, however, that fortepianos existed in significant numbers in Vienna in the 1750s, a hypothesis confirmed by keyboard music of the period by Wagenseil (1715–77), Birck (1718–63) and Steffan (1726–97) that contains stylistic features, especially dynamic markings, suggesting the use of the more modern instrument.[24] During the 1760s even more pianos, square as well as in the form of a *Flügel*, were probably available in Vienna for interested keyboard

---

[21] K. Mobbs, 'Stops and other special effects on the early piano', *Early Music*, xii (1984), p. 474.
[22] S. Rampe, 'Mozarts Clavierwerke. Klangwelt und Aufführungspraxis', in *Die Klangwelt Mozarts, eine Ausstellung des Kunsthistorischen Museums, Wien 1991* (Vienna, 1991), p. 90.
[23] Published in facsimile in E. Badura-Skoda, 'Prolegomena. . .', p. 79.
[24] A. Peter Brown rightly points to Birck's *Trattenimenti per Clavicembalo* as music probably written for the hammer harpsichord. A. P. Brown, *Joseph Haydn's Keyboard Music* (Bloomington, Indiana, 1986), p. 141.

players. One elegantly decorated square piano, apparently from the estate of a noble family, was recently purchased by the Kunsthistorisches Museum, Vienna. Thus, Joseph Haydn (1732–1809) may have become acquainted with the piano early in his life in Vienna. Since the publication of the second volume of Robbins Landon's biography of Haydn we know that the composer played a fortepiano in front of the Prince and some guests at Eszterháza in 1773.[25] Haydn's early acquaintance with the piano is less remarkable than it seems when one remembers that Esterházy documents from the mid century will almost certainly use the word 'Flügel' for 'Kielflügel' as well as 'Hammerflügel'.

Haydn's letters from the 1780s reveal clearly that he expected his sonatas to sound best on a piano. He favoured fortepianos made by the Schantz brothers, preferring them to the instruments of Walter that Mozart valued so highly. Compared with the instruments of Schantz and Walter those by Johann Andreas Stein had a thinner, more silvery tone, the case being rather elongated and the strings very thin; these characteristics are true also of instruments manufactured by Matthias Andreas and Nanette Stein. A sentence in Schönfeld's *Jahrbuch der Tonkunst von Wien und Prag* suggests wrongly that Schantz's pianos were built in a similar way to those of Stein: 'They are in reality virtually an imitation of the fortepiano of [J. A.] Stein in Augsburg' ('Sie sind eigentlich eine bis zur Kopie gebrachte Nachahmung der Fortepiano des Künstlers Stein zu Augsburg').[26] This oft-quoted sentence is highly misleading since the instruments show significant differences in the detail of their construction. For instance, the pianos of Stein and Walter do not have a divided bridge as found in the pianos of Schantz, and there are differences in the action too. Obviously the writer of this passage in Schönfeld's *Jahrbuch* (not necessarily Schönfeld himself) wished to help Nanette Stein and her brother become better known in Vienna as makers of pianos as excellent as those of Schantz.

The purpose of this survey has been to draw attention to the fact that fortepianos existed in Vienna in the first half of the eighteenth century, became more numerous in the 1750s and were readily available from the 1760s onwards. Tracing them in documents, however, will be difficult because they were not yet termed 'fortepiano'. I have also tried to demonstrate that compound instruments were far more common in the second, third and fourth quarters of the eighteenth century than hitherto appreciated; advertisements published in Leipzig's newspapers from the 1730s to the 1770s suggest this, as do surviving instruments by Johann Andreas Stein. Lastly, I wanted to draw attention to the range of stops found in early Viennese pianos.

---

[25] See the report of G. F. Rotenstein cited in H. C. Robbins Landon, *Haydn: Chronicle and Works. Haydn at Eszterháza* (London, 1978), p. 343. This report alone shows that Horst Walter and Georg Feder were incorrect in their view that Haydn did not have a fortepiano before 1780.

[26] J. F. Schönfeld, *Jahrbuch der Tonkunst von Wien und Prag* (Vienna, 1796). Modern facsimile with afterword and index by O. Biba (Munich and Salzburg, 1976), p. 89.

12

The Beethoven–Wölfl piano duel

TIA DENORA

By 1799, Thayer tells us, 'it was now no longer the case that Beethoven was without a rival as pianoforte virtuoso. He had a competitor fully worthy of his powers; one who divided about equally with him the suffrages of the leaders in the Vienna musical circles. In fact the excellencies peculiar to the two were such and so different, that it depended upon the taste of the auditor to which he accorded the praise of superiority.'[1]

The new rival was Joseph Wölfl. Beethoven and Wölfl met in March 1799 at the home of Baron Raimund Wetzlar, where they took part in a piano duel. This contest has not yet been considered extensively by Beethoven scholars as a topic in its own right. Yet it represents much more than an interesting excursion into the colourful backwaters of late eighteenth-century musical life in Vienna. It should, I think, be counted as an important and under-examined 'moment' – a point where some of the characteristic aspects of eighteenth-century aesthetic controversy coalesce. Consideration of this moment, moreover, provides an entrée into the otherwise elusive topic of the interrelation of social networks and networks of musical taste during this period. We are currently learning more about the variety of quasi-public concert locations in Vienna,[2] though the study of musical life as it occurred in the salons and private households often necessitates the use of oblique forms of evidence and of speculation.

From the beginning of his account of the Beethoven–Wölfl duel, Thayer clearly politicizes the contest. He does so, however, in ways that are conspicuously absent from his description, four chapters earlier, of Beethoven's encounter, c. 1793, with the Abbé Joseph Gelinek. In politicizing the contest, Thayer does not over-dramatize. Rather, he seems to be reflecting accurately

---

[1] E. Forbes, rev. and ed., *Thayer's Life of Beethoven* (Princeton, 1967), i, p. 204.
[2] For detailed consideration of concert life and music reception during the 1780s and/or 1790s see N. Zaslaw, *Mozart's Symphonies: Context, Performance Practice, Reception* (Oxford, 1989); M. S. Morrow, *Concert Life in Haydn's Vienna* (Stuyvesant, 1989); and D. Edge, 'Review article: Morrow, *Concert Life in Haydn's Vienna*', *Haydn Yearbook*, xvii (1992), pp. 108–66.

the descriptive categories found in extant contemporary accounts of the event. The Kapellmeister of the Theater auf der Wieden, Ignaz von Seyfried, for example, offered the following description.³

Schon hatte Beethoven durch mehrere Compositionen Aufsehen erregt und galt in Wien für einen Clavierspieler ersten Ranges, als ihm in den letzten Jahren des verflossenen Jahrhunderts ein ebenbürtiger Rival erwuchs. Da erneuerte sich gewissermaßen die alte Pariser Fehde der Gluckisten und Piccinisten, und die zahlreichen Kunstfreunde der Kaiserstadt zerfielen in zwei Parteien.

Beethoven had already attracted attention to himself by several compositions and was rated a first-class pianist in Vienna when he was confronted by a rival in the closing years of the last century. Thereupon there was, in a way, a revival of the old Parisian feud of the Gluckists and Piccinists, and the many friends of art in the Imperial City arrayed themselves in two parties.

By 1799 Beethoven was established within aristocratic circles as a pianist-composer and his piano and chamber works were appearing in published form: op. 10 had been published the year before, as were op. 9, op. 11. WoO 72 and op. 66. At the point of the Beethoven–Wölfl duel, Beethoven's style, as depicted by his contemporaries, emerged for the first time as something distinctive, a way of proceeding *in opposition to* other approaches and, in particular, as we shall see below, to a more dilettante ideology. Seyfried speaks, for example, of the Gluckists and Piccinists, a Parisian aesthetic controversy that was to be invoked to describe differences of opinion concerning Beethoven's works from this period on. As we shall see, it prefigured the ways in which Beethoven's style was later debated. Simultaneously, the Beethoven–Wölfl comparison helped to clarify further Beethoven's artistic identity within the Viennese musical world.

THE SOCIAL ROLE OF THE PIANO DUEL

In Vienna during the eighteenth century music was a socially loaded endeavour. Because the music world was, in comparison to our own, small and interpersonal, musical matters were often magnified and attention concentrated. Musical patronage and social hierarchy reciprocally created each other; the consumption and sponsorship of music (at least in socially conspicuous forms) was embarked upon for a variety of musical and social reasons, inextricably mixed. Through these activities, individuals and groups could constitute and signify their standing with respect to others: they could imitate, attempt to align themselves with, compete with, or attempt to impress those individuals whom

---

³ As quoted in A. W. Thayer, *Ludwig van Beethovens Leben* (Berlin, 1866), ii, p. 27. Translation from Forbes, *Thayer's Life*, i, p. 206.

they regarded as standing above, alongside or below them in terms of prestige. It is within this context that we need to understand the role of the piano contest.

At their most basic, the piano contests we know of were like sporting events. They provided not only 'good music', but also the drama of combat. Simultaneously, it was a forum in which rival musical styles (both compositional and pianistic) could be compared. One of the most detailed descriptions of a piano duel comes from Mozart, who, in a letter to his father, reported his contest with Clementi at the imperial court in December 1781.[4]

der kayser that (nach dem wir uns genug Complimenten machten) den ausspruch, daß Er zu spiellen anfangen sollte . . . er præludirte, und spiellte eine Sonata – dann sagte der kayser zu mir allons drauf los. ich præludirte auch und spiellte variazionen. Dann gab die Grosfürstin Sonaten von Paesiello her . . . daraus musste ich die allegro und er die Andante und Rondò spiellen. dann nammen wir ein thema daraus, und führten es auf 2 Piano forte aus.

after we had stood on ceremony long enough, the Emperor declared that Clementi ought to begin . . . He improvised and then played a sonata. The Emperor then turned to me: 'Allons, fire away'. I improvised and played variations. The Grand Duchess produced some sonatas by Paisiello . . . of which I had to play the Allegros and Clementi the Andantes and Rondos. We then selected a theme from them and developed it on two pianofortes . . .

The Emperor 'declare[s]' that Clementi ought to begin, he turns to Mozart and says, 'fire away' (a modern equivalent might be 'take it away' or 'go for it'), the two musicians take it in turn to play separate movements of Paisiello sonatas, and then each develop a theme (i.e. improvise).

Mozart's contest occurred in 1781. While the organization of musical life changed considerably over the next two decades, the piano duel – both its format and its role as a kind of musical sporting event – seems to have remained stable, if we are to judge by descriptions of Beethoven's own pianistic encounters. For example, we find that Seyfried's description of the Beethoven–Wölfl contest eighteen years later refers to the 'combats of the two athletes', which 'offered an indescribable artistic treat to the numerous and thoroughly select gathering' ('Dort verschaffte der höchst interessante Wettstreit beider Athleten nicht selten der zahlreichen, durchaus gewählten Versammlung einen unbeschreiblichen Kunstgenuß'). Like Mozart and Clementi, Beethoven and Wölfl also took it in turns to demonstrate their improvisatory skills. 'Sometimes', Seyfried tells us, 'they would seat themselves at two pianofortes and improvise alternately on themes which they gave each other' ('bald seßten sich beide an zwei Pianoforte, improvisirten wechselweise über gegenseitig sich angegebene Themas').[5]

---

[4] Letter of 23 January 1782. *Mozart, Briefe und Aufzeichnungen. Gesamtausgabe* (Kassel, 1962–75), iii p. 193. Translation from E. Anderson, trans. and ed., *The Letters of Mozart and his Family*, 3rd. edn (London, 1985), p. 793.

[5] Thayer, *Ludwig van Beethoven*, ii, p. 27. Translation from Forbes, *Thayer's Life*, i, p. 206.

This athletic imagery can be found also in reports of other piano duels involving Beethoven. For example, Czerny reports that Gelinek said of his forthcoming match with Beethoven, 'We're going to thrash him' ('Den wollen wir zusammenhauen').[6] Similarly, Tomaschek, describing the Beethoven–Steibelt duel of 1800, observed that Steibelt was 'knocked in the head by the pianist Beethoven'. Of the same event Ferdinand Ries referred to how Steibelt had 'felt sure of his victory' ('und glaubte sich seines Sieges gewiß') the first time Beethoven and he competed, but the second time Steibelt 'left the room before Beethoven finished, and would never again meet him and, indeed, made it a condition that Beethoven should not be invited before accepting an offer' ('daß Steibelt den Saal verließ, ehe Beethoven aufgehört hatte, nie mehr mit ihm zusammenkommen wollte, ja es sogar zur Bedingung machte, daß Beethoven nicht eingeladen werde, wenn man ihn haben wolle').[7]

Taking account of the social position of the virtuoso through to the 1790s – and, more broadly, of the social position of the occupational musician as servant – it seems reasonable to suggest that competing virtuosos occupied a place not unlike that of, for example, tennis players, wrestlers, boxers or even racehorses, in the sense that they were virtuoso practitioners pitted against each other in controlled contexts for the purpose of entertaining spectators. In this respect, then, the piano duel was not qualitatively different from other forms of entertainment.

At the same time, the piano contest was more than a sporting event. As I consider below in further detail, it was also a forum for aesthetic and stylistic debate. We know, for instance, that Mozart described Clementi as having 'not a farthing's worth of taste or feeling . . .' ('Keinen Kreutzer geschmack noch empfindung')[8] and, in Dittersdorf's autobiography, we find a reconstruction of the author's meeting with Emperor Joseph, where Dittersdorf portrays himself and the Emperor as being in agreement that Clementi is 'merely art' whereas Mozart combines 'art with *taste*' ('In Clementis Spiel herrscht bloss Kunst, in Mozarts aber Kunst und Geschmack').[9]

Thus the piano contest was a place where pianistic athletes were tested, where reputations were raised and lowered, where musical fashions were put on display, and where different types of taste could be compared and pitted against each other. But beyond this, it was also a place where the identities of patrons could be asserted, reaffirmed and undercut. It must not be forgotten that the musical combatants were by no means 'free agents' on the musical playing field. Like professional athletes today, they had backers who would naturally be interested in seeing their representatives 'win'.

[6] H. C. Robbins Landon, *Beethoven: sein Leben und seine Welt in zeitgenössischen Bildern und Texten* (Zurich, 1970), p. 237.
[7] Landon, *Beethoven: sein Leben*, p. 246.
[8] *Mozart: Briefe*, p. 192. Translation from Anderson, *The Letters of Mozart*, p. 793.
[9] N. Miller, ed., *Karl Ditters von Dittersdorfs Lebensbeschreibung*, Lebensläufe, Biographien, Erinnerungen, Briefe, xii (Munich, 1967), p. 227.

If we consider the cluster of issues implicated in the Clementi–Mozart duel in further detail, it seems that the contest would have been coloured by, among other things, an international dimension. Mozart was clearly playing for Vienna, the Monarchy and 'enlightened' Josephinist reform. Because the duel was organised as part of the festivities to honour visiting foreign nobility (the Russian Grand Duke Paul, later Tsar Paul II, and Maria Feodorovna, who was born Princess of Württemberg), the competition served as a forum for the display of the respective merits of 'home-grown' and foreign talent. Indeed, the Emperor refers to Clementi as '*La santa chiesa Catholica . . .* because Clementi is a Roman' ('*La santa chiesa Catholica* sagte er, weil Clementi ein Römer ist').[10] In this case, the competition was a friendly one, featuring two quite different but equally matched players, representatives of two culturally divergent but equally matched European powers.

Like certain sporting or artistically competitive events today, the piano contest could place a variety of issues at stake. It is thus important to enquire into just how lines of competition and stakes were drawn in any given musical contest. How, for example, might there have been social distribution of support for one or the other contestant and, to the extent that the spectators may have constituted 'opposing sides', what sorts of things may have been at stake?

In Beethoven's three known piano duels – the first, with Gelinek c. 1793, the second with Wölfl in 1799, and the third with Steibelt in 1800 – lines were not drawn between European powers as they were in the Mozart–Clementi case. What, then, was at stake in Beethoven's duel with Wölfl, apart from the personal reputation of each musician?

THE RESPECTIVE CAREERS OF WÖLFL AND BEETHOVEN

The contest took place at the home of Baron Raimund Wetzlar in 1799. Wetzlar was the elder son of Karl Abraham Wetzlar. Karl Abraham was a wealthy Jew, originally from Offenbach, who came to Vienna in the 1760s as a court agent. At a time when Jews were barred from business life the elder Wetzlar appears to have received a special permit to conduct business in Vienna. After converting to Catholicism in 1777 he began to acquire residential property. He was ennobled in 1788. By the middle 1790s the Wetzlar sons were fully assimilated into upper-middle-class/second-society Viennese life. They would have been similar, in position, to the newly ennobled banker Spielman and the publisher Trattner (who also invested in real estate). Raimund Wetzlar had earlier been Mozart's friend and patron (and godfather to Mozart's first child, Raimund Leopold, who died in his first year).

In a number of respects Wölfl seems to have been far better matched to Beethoven than either Gelinek or, later, Steibelt. First, he was about Beethoven's

[10] *Mozart: Briefe*, p. 193.

age. He was born on 24 December 1773 in Salzburg. He appeared publicly as a violinist around 1780, and began a career as a chorister at Salzburg Cathedral in 1783, remaining until 1786. He had received his first musical training from Leopold Mozart and Michael Haydn, travelling, on his father's advice, to Vienna in 1790 in order to study with Mozart. (Whether he actually studied with Mozart is not clear, though he *was* a friend of Mozart.) From 1791 to 1795 he worked as a house composer for Count Oginsky in Warsaw and as a piano teacher of young Polish noblemen (including the son of the banker Tepper von Ferguson). He then returned to Vienna and worked as a composer and pianist. In 1798 he married the singer Therese Klemm. After his contest with Beethoven in 1799 he left Vienna to tour Brno, Prague, Dresden, Leipzig, Berlin and Hamburg. He arrived in Paris in 1801, where he remained until 1805. He finally settled in London and died on 21 May 1812.

Wölfl's public Viennese career during the 1790s surpassed Beethoven's. Four stage works were produced in as many years: *Der Höllenberg* (1795), *Das schöne Milchmädchen* (1797), *Der Kopf ohne Mann* (1798) and *Liebe macht kurzen Prozess* (1798). He also published prolifically. During his Viennese years his output consisted of a *Grand concerto militaire*, nine string quartets, three piano trios, eight piano sonatas, three sonatas for violin and piano, and twelve songs. Mary Sue Morrow's Viennese 'Public Concert Calendar'[11] shows that his music appeared on the programme of at least three public concerts: first, at the Burgtheater, when Josepha Auernhammer performed one of his piano concertos, second at the Kärntnertortheater, along with works by Haydn and Süssmayr, and third, at a concert of the Tonkünstler-Societät.

Wölfl's entry in Schönfeld's *Jahrbuch der Tonkunst von Wien und Prag*, though much briefer and far less grandiloquent than Beethoven's, is still highly complimentary.

Ein wahrhaft geschickter Fortepianospieler, welchem eine Fertigkeit eigen ist, die man nicht sobald antreffen wird; er liest alles, was ihm vorkömmt, mit einer unglaublichen Richtigkeit, und zeigt sich izt als Schriftsetzer nicht ohne Staunen, denn seine Oper, Der Höllenberg genannt, zog ihm viel Ehre zu.[12]

A truly skilful piano player, with a particular accomplishment that is unprecedented. He reads everything put in front of him with unbelievable accuracy and shows himself admirably through his compositions. His opera *Der Höllenberg* has brought him much honour.

In short, by March 1799, Wölfl was fairly well established in Vienna. Indeed, taking his operas into consideration, he seems to have enjoyed more of a public career than Beethoven, who had not yet produced a large-scale work

---

[11] Morrow, *Concert Life*, pp. 237–364.
[12] J. F. Schönfeld, *Jahrbuch der Tonkunst von Wien und Prag*, facsimile ed. O. Biba (Munich, 1976), p. 67.

and whose performing career had taken place so far primarily in the salons. On the other hand, Beethoven had far stronger links with aristocrats, and, increasingly, the resource of being known as Haydn's protégé. We can begin to appreciate, therefore, what was at stake, personally, for each. For Wölfl, a triumph over Beethoven could have led to further support from Vienna's old aristocrats and, thus, enhanced prestige. For Beethoven, a triumph over Wölfl would have provided a means to a broader public, and to the public of music consumption outside the salons.

VIENNESE RECEPTION OF BEETHOVEN AND WÖLFL

Wölfl was not only well matched to Beethoven in terms of age and pianistic skill; he was also recognized as stylistically very different from Beethoven. The differences between the two pianists tended to heighten the significance of their competition. For example, in his memoirs, Tomaschek described Wölfl's 'unparalleled cleanliness and precision . . .' and praised him for being able to 'overcome difficulties which, for other pianists, would be impossibilities'. He remarked also on Wölfl's 'somewhat weak but pleasant touch' and 'the quiet composure of his body'.[13]

Nicht lange darauf [März 1799] kam Wölffl nach Prag. Sein durch mehrere Zeitschriften verbreiteter Ruf eines außerordentlichen Klavierspielers machte alle Musikfreunde dieser Stadt auf seine Kunstleistung neugierig. Wer ihn sehen oder sprechen wollte, mußte ihn bei der blauen Weintraube suchen, wo er sich tagelang auf den Billard tummelte . . . Das Konzert fand im Theater statt, wo Zuhörer sich zahlreich versammelten. Wölffl spielte von seiner Composition ein Conzert mit beispielloser Reinheit und Präcision, wie es bei so ungeheuerer Spannung seiner Hände wohl niemand anders herausbringen dürfte. Dann spielte er die Mozart'sche Phantasie in F minor, welche für vier Hände in der Breitkopf'schen Herausgabe erschien, allein so wie sie gedruckt ist, ohne irgend einen Ton auszulassen . . . Wie gesagt, er spielte dieses Tonstück ohne allen Mißgriff. Zuletzt phantasirte er, worin er das Thema aus dem Sonntagskind: "Wenns Lieserl macht" eingewebt, und dann beschloß er mit einigen sehr schönen und sehr brillanten Variationen das Conzert. Ein reichlicher Beifall wurde dem in seiner Art einzigen Virtuosen zu Theil. – Ein Klavierspieler, der sechs Fuß in der Länge mißt, dessen Finger, ungeheuer lang, eine Spannung von einer Terzdecime ohne alle Anstrengung ausführen, der noch dazu so mager ist, daß an ihm alles, wie an einer Vogelscheuche, klappert, der mit der unglaublichsten Leichtigkeit, mit einem zwar schwachen, jedoch einem netten Anschlag alle Schwierigkeiten, für andere Klavierspieler Unmöglichkeiten, vollführt, ohne die ruhige Haltung seines Körpers dabei zu verlieren, der oft ganze Stellen in mäßig bewegtem Tempo mit einem und demselben Finger, wie in dem Andante der Mozartschen Phantasie die lange in Sechzehnteln fortgehende Stelle im Tenor zu binden weiß – ein solcher Klavierspieler ist wohl einzig in seiner Art zu nennen.

[13] Landon, *Beethoven: sein Leben*, pp. 231–2. Translation from Landon, *Beethoven: A Documentary Study* (London, 1970), pp. 104–5.

Not long afterwards [March 1799], Wölffl came to Prague. His fame as an extraordinary pianist, which had been spread abroad through various newspapers, made all the music-lovers in the city curious as to his artistic ability. Whosoever wished so see him or speak to him had to look for him at the Blaue Weintraube, where he was busy all day long around the billiard-table . . . The concert took place in a theatre where a large audience was assembled. Wölffl played a Concerto of his own composition with unparalleled cleanliness and precision, which – on account of the immense stretch of his hands – no one else could perform. Then he played Mozart's Fantasia in F minor published in Breitkopf's edition for four hands, exactly as it is printed without leaving out a single note . . . As I said, he played this piece of music without any mishaps. Finally he improvised, weaving in the theme 'Wenn Lieserl macht', and brought the concert to an end with several very beautiful and brilliant variations. A hearty applause was granted to this (in his own way) unique virtuoso. He is a pianist, six feet tall, whose fingers, monstrously long, can encompass a thirteenth without any strain and moreover, so thin that all his clothes flap on him like a scarecrow. Yet he overcomes difficulties which, for other pianists, would be impossibilities, with a somewhat weak but pleasant touch, and does not lose the quiet composure of his body. He often plays whole sections in a moderately fast tempo with only one finger, as in the Andante of the Mozart Fantasia, where he binds together the section in which the tenor voice goes on for a long time in semiquavers. Such a pianist can certainly be regarded as unique in his own way.

This description differs considerably from the qualities Tomaschek perceived in Beethoven, whose pianism he described as characterized by 'brilliance and power' but which he suggested 'not infrequently' jolted the unsuspecting listener 'violently out of his state of joyful transports' ('. . . ich bewunderte zwar sein kräftiges und glänzendes Spiel . . . Nicht selten wird der unbefangene Zuhörer durch sie gewaltsam aus seiner überseligen Stimmung herausgehoben').[14]

It seems fair to say, therefore, that to debate the respective 'skills' of these two musicians was simultaneously and inevitably to debate aesthetics. To force their quite differently oriented efforts into a single context of winner and loser meant that the aesthetic that flattered each was placed at stake. Ignaz Seyfried's account of the duel makes this clear.

Seyfried would have witnessed the duel when he was twenty-three years old: at the time Beethoven was twenty-nine and Wölfl twenty-seven. Seyfried's account was published, however, thirty years later in the preface to Schindler's biography of Beethoven. Seyfried's retrospective accounts of Beethoven are often problematic, as many scholars have observed. But in this case there are grounds for accepting him as a reliable witness. First, Seyfried came from a minor aristocratic background; he would have been able to move freely either in or on the fringes of the aristocratic worlds in which Beethoven moved. Second, he was a musician himself – one of the Kapellmeisters at the Theater

---

[14] Landon, *Beethoven: sein Leben*, pp. 230–1. Translation from Landon, *Beethoven: A Documentary Study*, p. 104.

auf der Wieden after March 1797 (which meant he would have had contact with Wölfl as well, when the latter's operas were performed there). Third, and most relevant to this case, Seyfried's account of how Beethoven and Wölfl were received tends to parallel that offered in the other extant description of the Beethoven–Wölfl duel.

Having described the rival parties (see p. 260 above), Seyfried goes on to elaborate on the differences that characterized the pianism of Beethoven and Wölfl.[15]

An der Spitze von Beethovens Verehrern stand der liebenswürdige Fürst von Lichnowsky; zu Wölffls eifrigsten Protectoren gehörte der vielseitig gebildete Freiherr Raymund von Wetzlar . . . Dort verschaffte der höchst interessante Wettstreit beider Athleten nicht selten der zahlreichen, durchaus gewählten Versammlung einen unbeschreiblichen Kunstgenuß; jeder trug seine jüngsten Geistesproducte vor; bald ließ der eine oder der andere den momentanen Eingebungen seiner glühenden Phantasie freien ungezügelten Lauf; bald setzten sich beide an zwei Pianoforte, improvisirten wechselweise über gegenseitig sich angegebene Themas und schufen also gar manches vierhändige Capriccio, welches, hätte es im Augenblicke der Geburt zu Papier gebracht werden können, sicherlich der Vergänglichkeit getrotzt haben würde – An mechanischer Geschicklichkeit dürfte es schwer, vielleicht unmöglich gewesen sein, einem der Kämpfer vorzugsweise die Siegespalme zu verleihen: ja, Wölffl'n hatte die gütige Natur noch mütterlicher bedacht, indem sie ihn mit einer Riesenhand ausstattete, die ebenso leicht Decimen als andere Menschenkinder Octaven spannte, und es ihm möglich machte, fortlaufende doppelgriffige Passagen in den genannten Intervallen mit Blitzesschnelligkeit auszuführen – Im Phantasiren verleugnete Beethoven schon damals nicht seinen mehr zum unheimlich Düster sich hinneigenden Charakter . . . Es war die geheimnißreiche Sanscritsprache, deren Hieroglyphen nur der Eingeweihte zu lösen ermächtigt ist! – Wölffl hingegen, in Mozarts Schule gebildet, blieb immerdar sich gleich; nie flach, aber stets klar, und eben deswegen der Mehrzahl zugänglicher; die Kunst diente ihm blos als Mittel zum Zwecke, in keinem Falle als Prunk- und Schaustück trockenen Gelehrtthuens; stets wußte er Antheil zu erregen, und diesen unwandelbar an den Reihengang seiner wohlgeordneten Ideen zu bannen – Wer Hummel'n gehört, wird auch verstehen, was damit gesagt sein will.

At the head of Beethoven's admirers stood the amiable Prince Lichnowsky; among the most zealous patrons of Wölfl was the broadly cultured Baron Raymond von Wetzlar . . . There the interesting combats of the two athletes not infrequently offered an indescribable artistic treat to the numerous and thoroughly select gathering. Each brought forward the latest product of his mind. Now one and then the other gave free rein to his glowing fancy; sometimes they would seat themselves at two pianofortes and improvise alternately on themes which they gave each other, and thus created many a four-hand Capriccio which if it could have been put upon paper at the moment would surely have bidden defiance to time. It would have been difficult, perhaps impossible, to award the palm of victory to either one of the gladiators in respect of technical skill.

[15] As quoted in Thayer, *Beethovens Leben*, ii, pp. 27–8. Translation from Forbes, *Thayer's Life*, i, pp. 206–7.

> Nature had been a particularly kind mother to Wölffl in bestowing upon him a gigantic hand which could span a tenth as easily as other hands compass an octave, and permitted him to play passages of double notes in these intervals with the rapidity of lightning. In his improvisations even then Beethoven did not deny his tendency toward the mysterious and gloomy . . . It was the mystical Sanscrit language whose hieroglyphs can be read only by the initiated. Wölffl, on the contrary, trained in the school of Mozart, was always equable; never superficial but always clear and thus more accessible to the multitude. He used art only as a means to an end, never to exhibit his acquirements. He always enlisted the interest of his hearers and inevitably compelled them to follow the progression of his well-ordered ideas. Whoever has heard Hummel will know what is meant by this . . .

Here, the controversy is characterized as revolving around three axes. First, Beethoven's 'tendency toward the mysterious and gloomy', as Seyfried puts it, is contrasted with Wölfl's agility and clarity. Second, Beethoven's exclusiveness is compared with Wölfl's accessibility, which Seyfried likens to Hummel's. Conversely, Seyfried refers to Beethoven's pianistic approach as 'the mystical Sanscrit language whose hieroglyphs can be read only by the initiated' and he cites Wölfl as being 'more accessible to the multitude'. Finally Seyfried distinguishes Wölfl from Beethoven by comparing Wölfl with Mozart and, harking back to Wölfl's accessibility, reminding the reader that Wölfl 'trained in the school of Mozart, was always equable; never superficial but always clear and thus more accessible . . .'

Seyfried, therefore, seems to suggest that Wölfl was the more popular of the two musicians, while Beethoven was more appealing to connoisseurs. As Seyfried depicts them, Beethoven and Wölfl represent different and, to a certain extent, distinct, conceptions of music and its audience: on the one hand, the musical experience was one that was accessible to only a few, on the other, music could be viewed as pleasing and openly available to the average listener. Thus, by 1799, I would suggest, we can see the demarcation between popular and serious music being widened and underlined; what is significant is that this distinction is being debated long before the conventional turning point cited by most scholars who describe the bifurcation of serious and light music as occurring some time during the middle of the nineteenth century. The gap between *Kenner* (connoisseurs) and *Liebhaber* (dilettantes) began to widen far earlier than many historians have been willing to recognize; it is clearly visible at this early stage in the public debate over Beethoven's music.

If we turn to the account of the contest offered in a letter to the *Allgemeine musikalische Zeitung*, we find that the comparison between Beethoven and Wölfl is drawn, more or less, according to the same lines.[16]

---

[16] *Allgemeine musikalische Zeitung*, i (1798–9), cols. 524–5. Translation from Forbes, *Thayer's Life*, i, p. 205.

Die Meynungen, über den Vorzug des Einen vor dem Andern, sind hier getheilt: doch scheint es, als ob sich die grössere Parthey auf die Seite des letztern neigte. Ich will mich bemühen, Ihnen das Eigene Beyder ansugeben, ohne an jenem Vorrangsstreite Theil zu nehmen. Beethovens Spiel ist äusserst brillant, doch weniger delikat, und schlägt zuweilen in das Undeutliche über. Er zeigt sich am allervortheilhaftesten in der freyen Phantasie. Und hier ist es wirklich ganz ausserordentlich, mit welcher Leichtigkeit und zugleich Festigkeit in der Ideenfolge B. auf der Stelle jedes ihm gegebene Thema, nicht etwa nur in den Figuren variirt (womit mancher Virtuos Glück und – Wind macht) sondern wirklich ausführt. Seit Mozarts Tode, der mir hier noch immer das *non plus ultra* bleibt, habe ich diese Art des Genusses nirgends in dem Masse gefunden, in welchem sie mir bey B. zu Theil ward. Hiern stehet ihm Wölffl nach. Aber Vorzüge vor ihm hat Wölffl darin, dass er, bey gründlicher musikalischer Gelehrsamkeit und wahrer Würde in der Komposition, Sätze, welche geradehin unmöglich zu exekutiren scheinen, mit einer Leichtigkeit, Präcision und Deutlichkeit vorträgt, die in Erstaunen versetzt; (freylich kommt ihm dabey die grosse Struktur seiner Hande sehr zu statten) und dass sein Vortrag überall so zweckmässig und besonders auch im Adagio so gefällig und einschmeichelnd, gleichfern von Kahlheit und Ueberfüllung – ist, dass man nicht blos bewundern, sondern auch geniessen kann . . . Dass Wölffl durch sein anspruchloses, gefälliges Betragen über Beethovens etwas hohen Ton noch ein besonderes Uebergewicht erhält – ist sehr natürlich.

Opinions are divided here touching the merits of the two [Beethoven and Wölfl]; yet it would seem as if the majority were on the side of the latter [Wölfl]. I shall try to set forth the peculiarities of each without taking part in the controversy. Beethoven's playing is extremely brilliant but has less delicacy and occasionally he is guilty of indistinctness. He shows himself to the greatest advantage in improvisation, and here, indeed, it is most extraordinary with what lightness and yet firmness in the succession of ideas Beethoven not only varies a theme given him on the spur of the moment by figuration (with which many a virtuoso makes his fortune and – wind) but really develops it. Since the death of Mozart, who in this respect is for me still the non plus ultra, I have never enjoyed this kind of pleasure in the degree in which it is provided by Beethoven. In this Wölfl fails to reach him. But Wölfl has advantages in that he, sound in musical learning and dignified in his compositions, plays passages which seem impossible with an ease, precision and clearness which cause amazement (of course he is helped here by the large structure of his hands) and that his interpretation is always, especially in Adagios, so pleasing and insinuating that one can not only admire it but also enjoy . . . That Wölfl likewise enjoys an advantage because of his amiable bearing, contrasted with the somewhat haughty pose of Beethoven, is very natural . . .

Here, the anonymous writer suggests that Beethoven's playing is 'brilliant but has less delicacy and is occasionally guilty of indistinctness', whereas Wölfl is able to play difficult passages with 'ease, precision and clarity'. This description is akin to Seyfried's discussion of Beethoven's 'gloomy' aspect versus Wölfl equability and lightness. Wölfl is further described as providing interpretations, 'so pleasing and insinuating that one can not only admire but also enjoy'. His 'amiable bearing' (as compared to Beethoven's 'haughty pose') is identified as making him the more popular candidate. Thus, in line with Seyfried, the writer suggests that Wölfl is the more accessible of the two and, indeed, that 'it would seem as if the majority were on the side of [Wölfl] because of this'. Where this *AmZ* account differs markedly from Seyfried's, however, is in the way it likens Beethoven's pianism to Mozart's in so far as Beethoven's ability to 'really develop a theme', in the opinion of the reviewer, gives Beethoven the advantage over Wölfl.

One highly interesting feature of these two accounts of Beethoven's and Wölfl's merits is that Mozart is invoked, for different reasons, to describe the playing of *both* Beethoven and Wölfl. In the second account the characteristic feature of Mozart is that he could 'really develop a theme' – something which would have been of real concern to a connoisseur; in the first account, Seyfried's, Wölfl is compared to Mozart because of his Mozartian clarity, equability and accessibility.

By the autumn of 1792 Mozart (who had died the previous December) had become a symbol of Vienna's musical greatness. The concept of Mozart's 'spirit' provided a conceptual mantle under which the greatness of a subsequent composer could be lodged. That Beethoven should become that composer, however, is significant, as to very things for which Beethoven was subsequently hailed (difficulty, complexity, seriousness) were, among Beethoven's contemporaries, usually perceived as antithetical to the nature of Mozart's talent. (Ironically, Mozart's music had sometimes been criticized for these same qualities during the mid to late 1780s when he wrote more self-consciously difficult works.)

How can we characterize the range of issues at stake in the Beethoven–Wölfl duel? In addition to the implications the contest had for the reputations of the two composers, we should consider also that the contest provided a forum where the relationship between connoisseur and dilettante values might have been subject to debate.

Certainly, both musicians represented novel approaches to the piano. Indeed, Wölfl's piano music was not always written with the amateur performer in mind. Wölfl was a showman, and at least some of his pieces were written with virtuosity in mind. But there is a difference between pianistic virtuosity and emotionality, and between pleasingness and obscurity. From the point of view of the contemporary listener, as portrayed in these two accounts, Wölfl's virtuosity was never experienced as 'learned'. Similarly, it was, as far as can be inferred from extant documents, never perceived as over-difficult, disorderly or unpleasant. If we consider contemporary descriptions of responses to Beethoven's works, however, we find that a very different, and far more controversial, picture emerges.

EARLY VIENNESE RECEPTION OF BEETHOVEN

In the same year that Beethoven duelled with Wölfl, a reviewer in the *Allgemeine musikalische Zeitung* wrote that Beethoven's abundance of ideas . . . still leads [him] too often to pile one thought wildly upon another, and, in a rather bizarre manner, to group them in such a way that not infrequently an obscure artificiality or an artifical obscurity is produced' ('seine fülle von Ideen . . . veranlaßt ihn aber noch zu oft, Gedanken wild aufeinander zu häufen und die mitunter vermittelst einer etwas bizarren Manier dergestalt zu gruppiren, daß dadurch nicht selten eine dunkle Künstlichkeit oder eine künstliche Dunkelheit hervorgebracht wird').[17] I think this review can serve as an index of the kind of critical response to Beethoven before 1801, responses shared, it would appear, by at least some of Vienna's musicians.

The pianist Ignaz Moscheles (1794-1870), for example, recalled that sometime around 1804 he heard from his fellow pupils of this person Beethoven 'who wrote the most extraordinary stuff, which no one could either play or understand; a Baroque music in conflict with all the rules' ('welcher das sonderbarste Zeug von der Welt schreibe, so daß es niemand weder spielen noch verstehen könne; eine barocke, mit allen Regeln in Widerspruch stehende Musik'). Moscheles brought a copy of the 'Pathétique' sonata (1798) to his teacher, Friedrich Dionysius Weber, who thought Beethoven's compositions to be 'hare brained'. Weber, he said, 'warned against playing or studying eccentric productions before I had developed a style based on more respectable models' ('warnte mich davor, ekcentrische Productionen zu spielen oder zu studiren, ehe ich meinen Stil auf Grund soliderer Muster ausgebildet hatte').[18] These views were, it seems, shared by others. At a later date, the Abbé Gelinek (who duelled with and subsequently befriended Beethoven early in the latter's career, but who later fell out with him, informing Haydn of Beethoven's secret study with Schenk) said Beethoven's compositions were 'lacking in internal coherency and not infrequently they were overloaded' ('innere Zusammenhang fehle und daß sie nicht selten auch überladen sind').[19] Leopold Kozeluch, who was known during the 1780s and early 1790s as one of the most popular composers in Vienna, reportedly threw a copy of the C minor piano trio (op. 1 no. 3) at Doležalek's feet after the latter (a Beethoven enthusiast) attempted to play it for him. Kozeluch and Haydn apparently agreed that this trio was unusual – 'Of course, we would have done that differently' ('Ja, wir hätten das anders gemacht')[20] is what Doležalek reports he and Haydn said to each other.

---

[17] *Allgemeine musikalische Zeitung*, ii (1799–1800), col. 25. Translation from R. Wallace, *Beethoven's Critics: Aesthetic Dilemmas and Resolutions During the Composer's Lifetime* (Cambridge, 1986), p. 8.
[18] Landon, *Beethoven: sein Leben*, pp. 227–8. Translation from Landon, *Beethoven: A Documentary Study*, p. 100.
[19] See Thayer, *Beethovens Leben*, ii, p. 82. Translation from Forbes, *Thayer's Life*, i, p. 248.
[20] Thayer, *Beethovens Leben*, ii, p. 108.

Doležalek, moreover, reported that Haydn never fully reconciled himself to Beethoven's compositions. There are a number of stories also of hostility to Beethoven's music on the part of musicians called upon to perform it. The string players who first read through op. 59 no.1 were convinced that the repeated note played by the cello at the opening of the second movement was intended as a musical joke at their expense. Indeed, there appears to have been considerable animosity on the part of musicians towards Beethoven and his music.

This controversy took on a more definite shape and became more heated over time. If we follow it very carefully, we can begin to piece together a sense of how various publics responded to his works during these early years in his career. When Beethoven's ballet *Die Geschöpfe des Prometheus* was performed in 1801, the incident was identified by contemporary observers as Vienna's 'Guerre des Bouffons'. Beethoven's supporters hailed the ballet (and the choreography of the junior ballet master – Salvatore Viganò; the senior master was Muzarelli) for its more natural, expressive style, while opponents (and, it seems, defenders of older tastes, and of the more senior ballet master) thought the ballet ungraceful and inharmonious. These latter seem to have been in the majority at the performance attended by Haydn's friend Carl Rosenbaum one month after the opening performance on 28 March; he noted in an entry on Friday, 27 April 1801 that, 'at the end, the ballet was more hissed down than applauded' ('Am Ende wurde der Ballet mehr ausgezischt als beklatscht')[21]. According to the dramatist von Collin (for those play *Coriolan* Beethoven wrote an overture), not even the most important affair of state would have aroused 'more violent divisions of opinion than the battle did at that time over the respective superiority of the two ballet masters. Friends of the theatre divided themselves completely into two parties, who regarded each other with hatred and contumely on account of their differences of opinion' ('Die wichtigste Staatsangelegenheit ist vielleicht nicht im Stande, eine heftigere Entzweiung der Gemüther hervorzubringen, als damals der Streit über den Vorzug der beiden Ballettmeister bewirkte. Die Freunde des Theaters theilten sich sämmtlich in zwei Parteien, die sich wegen der Verschiedenheit ihrer Überzeugungen mit Haß und Verachtung betrachteten').[22]

Needless to say, opinion was further polarized over the issue of the 'Eroica' symphony in 1805. Twice the size of any Haydn or Mozart symphony, the work was criticized on its first performance for 'losing itself in anarchy . . .' ('Regellose zu verlieren') and for being 'shrill and bizarre' ('Grellen und Bizarren').[23] An anonymous critic in the *Allgemeine musikalische Zeitung*, writing of

---

[21] E. Radant, ed., 'Die Tagebücher von Joseph Carl Rosenbaum', *Haydn Jahrbuch*, v (1968), p. 92. Translation from E. Radant, ed., 'The Diaries of Joseph Carl Rosenbaum', *Haydn Yearbook*, v (1968), p. 92.

[22] Landon, *Beethoven: sein Leben*, p. 250. Translation from Landon, *Beethoven: A Documentary Study*, p. 139.

[23] Landon, *Beethoven: sein Leben*, p. 265. Translation from Landon, *Beethoven: A Documentary Study*, p. 155.

the second performance, suggested that the work would 'gain immensely (it lasts a full hour) if Beethoven would decide to shorten it and introduce into the whole more light, clarity and unity . . . But if, as now, its coherence escapes even the most attentive ear after repeated hearings, it must appear peculiar even to the unprejudiced listener. Moreover, there were very few people who liked the symphony' ('aber die Sinfonie würde unendlich gewinnen (sie dauert eine ganze Stunde) wenn sich Beethoven entschließen wollte sie abzukürzen und in das Ganze mehr Licht, Klarheit und Einheit zu bringen . . . wenn nun auch bei öftern Anhören der Zusammenhang selbst der angestrengten Aufmerksamkeit entgeht, so muß dies jedem uneingenommenen Musikkenner sonderbar auffallen. Auch fehlte sehr viel, daß die Sinfonie allgemein gefallen hätte').[24] Meanwhile, Rosenbaum (whom the Viennese historian Else Radant Landon has described as an 'Everyman' of Viennese musical taste) considered that the symphony was not what one would have expected from someone with Beethoven's reputation.

In the responses to the 'Eroica' we see again the issues first identified in the Beethoven–Wölfl controversy: it was difficult, disorderly and startling, rather than accessible, orderly and pleasant; and expressive and self-consciously profound rather than rapid, light, bright and entertaining. In April 1805 a writer – possibly the dramatist Kotzebue who was to collaborate with Beethoven in *The Ruins of Athens* – outlined the ways in which the 'Eroica' was received.[25]

Die einen, Beethovens ganz besondere Freunde, behaupten, gerade diese Sinfonie sei ein Meisterstück, das sei eben der wahre Styl für die höhere Musik, und wenn sie jetzt nicht gefällt, so komme das nur daher, weil das Publicum nicht kunstgebildet genug sei alle diese hohen Schönheiten zu fassen; nach ein paar tausend Jahren aber würde sie ihre Wirkung nicht verfehlen. Der andere Theil spricht dieser Arbeit schlechterdings allen Kunstwerth ab und meint, darin sei ein ganz ungebändigtes Streben nach Auszeichnung und Sonderbarkeit sichtbar, das aber nirgends Schönheit oder wahre Erhabenheit und Kraft bewirkt hätte . . . aber nicht die Hervorbringung der blos Ungewöhnlichen und Phantastischen, sondern des Schönen und Erhabenen sei es, wodurch sich das Genie beurkunde . . . Die dritte sehr kleine Partie steht in der Mitte; sie gesteht der Sinfonie manche Schönheiten zu, bekennt aber, daß der Zusammenhang oft ganz zerrissen scheint, und daß die unendliche Dauer dieser längsten, vielleicht auch schwierigsten aller Symphonieen selbst Kenner ermüde, dem bloßen Liebhaber aber unerträglich werde . . . Sie fürchtet aber, wenn Beethoven auf diesem Wege fort wandelt, so werde er und das Publicum übel dabei fahren. Die Musik könne so bald dahin kommen, daß jeder, der nicht genau mit den Regeln und Schwierigkeiten der Kunst vertraut ist, schlechterdings gar keinen Genuß bei ihr finde . . .

One group, Beethoven's most special friends, contend that this particular symphony is a masterpiece, that it is exactly the true style for music of the highest type and that if it

---

[24] Landon, *Beethoven: sein Leben*, p. 266. Translation from Landon, *Beethoven: A Documentary Study*, p. 155.
[25] Landon, *Beethoven: sein Leben*, p. 264. Translation from Landon, *Beethoven: A Documentary Study*, pp. 153–4.

does not please now it is because the public is not sufficiently cultivated in the arts to comprehend these higher spheres of beauty; but after a couple of thousand years its effect will not be lessened. The other party absolutely denies any artistic merit to this work. They claim that it reveals the symptoms of an evidently unbridled attempt at distinction and peculiarity, but that neither beauty, true sublimity nor power have anywhere been achieved either by means of unusual modulations, by violent transitions or by the juxtaposition of the most heterogeneous elements . . . the creation of something beautiful and sublime, not the production of something merely unusual and fantastic, is the true expression of genius . . . The third, very small party stand in the middle. They concede that there are many beautiful things in the symphony, but admit that the continuity often appears to be completely confused and that the endless duration of this longest and perhaps most difficult of all symphonies is tiring even for the expert; for a mere amateur it is unbearable . . . One fears . . . that if Beethoven continues along this road, he and the public will make a bad journey. Music could easily reach a state where everyone who has not been vouchsafed a thorough knowledge of the rules and difficulties of the art will derive absolutely no pleasure from it . . .

In its discussion of Beethoven as viewed by his supporters, this passage articulates one of the most sociologically and historically interesting themes within Beethoven research: the emergence, through Beethoven's own success, of a discourse of self-consciously 'serious' music and an intellectualized version of a musical canon. Put differently, we can trace, in Beethoven's career, the emergence of a bifurcated taste for music that was, perhaps (as I consider below), socially distributed. These themes, moreover, are not merely relevant to us looking back two centuries later; they were clearly in the minds of at least some contemporary observers during these years and this overlap (between analyst and some lay accounts) provides one way of knowing whether the historical narrative being constructed here would have been meaningful to late eighteenth-century audiences.

In 1799, the writer in the *Allgemeine musikalische Zeitung* suggested (as did Seyfried retrospectively) that the Beethoven–Wölfl contest ended in a draw; Seyfried says that 'it would have been difficult and perhaps impossible to award the palm of victory to either one of the gladiators' and the *AmZ* writer suggests that opinion was divided, but that, probably, the majority was on Wölfl's side. Over the next five years – the period between this report on Beethoven and Wölfl, and the report on Beethoven's 'Eroica' – it would appear that the basic shape of the Beethoven–Wölfl debate was brought into increasing relief.

I have so far written of 'things at stake' in terms of careers and of aesthetics. What I now want to do is to consider the extent to which those aesthetics were specific to particular social groups. Was there any systematic distribution of opinion about Beethoven and Wölfl? If so, who were the advocates of each composer? Asking questions such as these adds a further dimension to the nature of what was at stake in a piano contest: the social identity of the competitors' supporters, and the ways in which their identities were constituted in and through their musical partisanship. The Beethoven–Wölfl piano duel can be conceived, in other words, as a site for conflict or competition between different individuals and social groups.

VIENNESE MUSICAL CONSTITUENCIES IN 1799

With respect to the Beethoven–Wölfl duel, the starting point for this project is clear enough, at least at face value. Seyfried tells us, not surprisingly, that Prince Lichnowsky stood, 'at the head of Beethoven's admirers' while Baron Wetzlar was 'among the most zealous of Wölfl's supporters'.

By 1799, Beethoven's network of supporters included Vienna's major aristocratic patrons. Documentary evidence confirms that he was acquainted with and/or supported by the following aristocrats: Prince and Princess Lichnowsky, the Prince's mother-in-law, Countess Thun, Baron Nicolaus Zmeskall von Domanovecz, Baron van Swieten (who, although a member of the second aristocracy, was at home with members of the first aristocracy because of his connections at court), Prince Nicolaus Esterházy, Count and Countess Moritz Lichnowsky, Countess Keglevics (later Princess Odescalchi) and Baron Gleichenstein. By this time, he was probably also acquainted with: Prince Lobkowitz the younger, Prince Schwarzenberg, Princess Liechtenstein, Countess Guicciardi and Prince Kinsky.

Between 1793 and 1805, Beethoven performed or had his compositions performed at the homes of Prince Lichnowsky, Nicolaus Zmeskall, Baron van Swieten, Prince Esterházy, Prince Lobkowitz the elder, and, later on, Princess Odescalchi, Prince Lobkowitz, and Prince Schwarzenberg. His aristocratic piano pupils included Princess Liechtenstein, Giulietta Guicciardi, the daughters of Therese Brunsvik (with whom he was intimate enough to use the 'Du' form of address) and Countess Josephine de Clary.

These lists are, of course, provisional. They include only those aristocrats who are thought to have had frequent personal contact with Beethoven, those individuals or families, moreover, who helped to support Beethoven materially. But it is also through these individuals that Beethoven would have been introduced and exposed to wider audiences, audiences whose enthusiasm for the composer would, naturally, have varied. Nicolaus Zmeskall, for example, according to Ignaz von Mosel's memoirs (1843), 'gave the most interesting morning concerts to which the élite of the art world thronged' ('wo in höchst interessanten Morgenconzerten, zu denen sich die Elite Kunstfreunde drängte').[26] Through salons such as these Beethoven's works were disseminated. To what extent can we define the social composition of these musical events?

[26] Landon, *Beethoven: sein Leben*, p. 224. Translation from Landon, *Beethoven: A Documentary Study*, p. 97.

Within the Beethoven literature, there have been oblique references to the 'mingling' of all classes who came together under the banner of 'great art' and a common love for Beethoven's music. A similar picture has been most recently offered by Volkmar Braunbehrens in his discussion of Mozart's Vienna. It is, however, not clear that we can extrapolate from the social character of salon life in the 1780s to that of the late 1790s. Mozart's Vienna was not the same as Beethoven's fifteen years later when, according to Count Johann Schönfeld, who published his *Jahrbuch der Tonkunst von Wien und Prag* in 1796, nearly all the *Hauskapellen* had been disbanded. There has been a tradition within Beethoven scholarship, particularly as information about Beethoven is popularized, to presuppose a high degree of unrestricted social movement in salon life, and to confuse the democratic rhetoric employed by the composer (and, in some cases his patrons) with the circumstances of the society within which he actually worked. Moreover, the imagery of Beethoven as a middle-class composer may have been fostered by Beethoven's relations with his supporters later in his career when the social composition of his constituency was indeed broader. Both Beethoven and Schindler, for example, would have been interested in portraying Beethoven's public as occupying a fairly wide base during the middle and latter parts of his career. By that time many of this initial circle of aristocratic patrons had died and Beethoven's need to earn his living by his pen became more pressing. Schindler may have projected back on to Beethoven's early career a social openness of salon life and a taste public that was broader than the one he actually experienced during the 1790s and early 1800s. For these reasons, then, 1790s private concert life, one of the most shadowy eras in the study of Viennese musical life, may have been inappropriately conceived as egalitarian. If this is indeed the case, this misconception may be related to the inappropriate projection forward of circumstances from the 1780s, and from the 1810s and beyond back on to the period of Beethoven's most active salon career.

How can we begin to explore the more concrete circumstances of salon life in the 1790s? One way of exploring this topic is to work on a case-by-case basis, asking whether or not particular members of the merchant, professional and second aristocratic publics would have attended the private salons at which Beethoven performed. Such a project is beyond the resources of this study; it will no doubt be developed by future scholars. Meanwhile, there are ways of beginning the task that draw upon existing materials.

One way of exploring the issue of how restricted the Beethoven salon forums actually were is to consider whether Beethoven had any contact with particular members of these groups. For example, attempting to assess how close Beethoven actually was to Baron Wetzlar is helpful in moving towards a more detailed picture of the kind of contact Wetzlar himself would have had with Beethoven's circle.

It is worth beginning with Wetzlar because it was he, rather than one of Beethoven's closer patrons, who was the host of the Beethoven–Wölfl competition, and because he was singled out by Seyfried as 'one of the most zealous' of Wölfl's supporters. Wetzlar was, moreover, musically active as a patron and dilettante, and he was wealthy.[27] It therefore seems reasonable to suggest that Wetzlar would have been a *likely* person to be found in Vienna's higher aristocratic salon worlds, if these worlds did indeed admit second aristocratic (the newly ennobled upper middle class) and/or professional class participation, and if the tastes for Beethoven and for Wölfl were not socially exclusive. If the salons of Prince Lichnowsky, Nicolaus Zmeskall, Baron van Swieten, Prince Esterházy, Prince Lobkowitz the elder, and, later on, Princess Odescalchi, Prince Lobkowitz, and Prince Schwarzenberg were indeed open to upper-middle-class and second-society audiences, it seems likely that Wetzlar and, probably, members of his family would have come into contact with Beethoven (at least eventually) and would have been present at some of his private performances.

In the 1780s Wetzlar (and other members of the middle class) may have spanned – via support of Mozart – two social worlds, middle class and aristocratic. We know, at least, that Wetzlar attended a private concert held at the Auernhammer household (a middle-class family, the daughter Josepha was an accomplished pianist and a pupil of Mozart) to which Mozart had invited Countess Thun. Baron van Swieten, too, was present on this occasion. Wetzlar also took part in Mozart's private ball in 1783, the guest list of which, according to Deutsch, included a Dr Gilowsky and some of Mozart's musical colleagues: the Adambergers, the Stephanies and the Langes. A decade and a half later (and after Mozart's death), did Wetzlar continue to come into contact with Countess Thun or her son-in-law, Prince Lichnowsky?

Obviously, the limited amount of evidence currently available for exploring this issue requires that all statements must remain speculative. On the basis of secondary sources it would seem that Wetzlar's contact with Beethoven and the circles around him was minimal. If Landon's suggestion that the high aristocratic salons – the ones at which Beethoven and Haydn participated regularly – were 'socially very exclusive affairs' is correct,[28] and this seems to be the most likely hypothesis at present, then Beethoven would probably not have come across the Wetzlar family in the course of private concertizing.

One source of evidence in favour of this claim can be found in a letter Beethoven wrote in May 1803. By this time, Beethoven was reaching a high point in his career: he had emerged as a composer of large-scale symphonic

---

[27] He appears, moreover, to have indicated interest in supporting Beethoven, in that he was a subscriber to the publication by Artaria of the op. 1 piano trios.
[28] See H. C. Robbins Landon, *Haydn: Chronicle and Works. Haydn: the Years of 'The Creation'* (London, 1977), p. 338.

works, he was about to begin an opera, and he had just had his successful academy a month before at the Theater an der Wien. If the Wetzlar family had been attending private salons at which Beethoven played in the preceding years, it seems likely that, by this time, they would have become acquainted with Beethoven.

The letter is to Count Wetzlar's brother, Alexander Wetzlar, also a musical patron. Beethoven writes to recommend George Polgreen Bridgetower, the famous London-based violinist, then on a concert tour of Germany and Austria.[29]

Obschon wir uns niemals sprechen, so nehme ich doch gar keinen Anstand ihnen den Überbringer dieses Hr. Brischdower, einen sehr geschickten und seines instruments ganz mächtigen Virtuosen zu empfehlen – er spielt neben Seinen Concerten auch vortrefflich quartetten, ich wünsche sehr, daß sie ihm noch mehrere bekanntschaften verschaffen – Lobkowitz und Frieß und alle übrigen vornehmen Liebhabern hat er sich schon vortheilhaft bekannt gemacht –

ich glaube, daß er gar nicht übel wäre, wenn sie ihn einen Abend zur therese schönfeld führten, wo so wie ich weiß manche freunde auch hinkommen oder bej ihnen – ich weiß, daß sie mir selbst danken werden ihnen Bekanntschaft gemacht zu haben –

Although we have never spoken to one another, yet I have not the slightest hesitation in introducing to you the bearer of this letter, Herr Brischdower [sic], a very able virtuoso and an absolute master of his instrument – He not only performs his own concertos but is also an excellent quartet player. I earnestly hope that you will obtain for him a wider circle of acquaintances. He has already had a favourable impression on Lobkowitz and Fries and all the other distinguished lovers of music –

It would not be at all a bad thing, I think, if you were to take him some evening to Therese Schönfeld, at whose house, I am told, many friends assemble, or if you even invited him to your house – I know that you too will thank me for having procured you this acquaintance –

The letter raises a number of issues that require further examination and that allow us to speculate on the ways that Wetzlar's and Beethoven's social circles may have been distinct. First, we learn that Beethoven has never spoken to Alexander Wetzlar. The fact that he says this, as opposed to 'we have never met' or 'you don't know me but', suggests that he has little contact with the extended Wetzlar family. Second, Beethoven asks *Wetzlar*, a man to whom he has never spoken, to take Bridgetower along to Therese Schönfeld's. At the very least, this suggests that Beethoven himself was distanced from, or was not acquainted with the Schönfeld salon, and it may suggest also that Beethoven had no other closer acquaintance of whom he could ask this favour. If this was

---

[29] Landon, *Beethoven: sein Leben*, pp. 261–2. Translation from Landon, *Beethoven: A Documentary Study*, pp. 150–1.

the case, it suggests in turn that there was a musical circle to which Alexander Wetzlar belonged that did not overlap (or did not overlap greatly) with those in which Beethoven (and his patrons) moved.

Would the same hold for Alexander's brother Raimund, Wölfl's patron and host of the Beethoven–Wölfl duel? It is not possible to say. *If* Raimund was a regular member of the high aristocratic salons in which Beethoven performed and was present, it seems reasonable that Beethoven would have approached him, if only to ask him to ask Alexander, his brother, to meet Bridgetower. If Beethoven did this, and was told by Raimund to contact Alexander on his own, it seems likely that Beethoven would have mentioned this in his letter: along with 'although we have never spoken to each other . . .' might not Beethoven have added that Alexander's brother Raimund had suggested he write?

The third issue which this letter raises is the fact that Beethoven tells Alexander Wetzlar of how Bridgetower 'has already made an impression' on Lobkowitz, Fries and 'all other distinguished lovers of music'. What seems significant here is that he relates this as if it were 'news', in which case, this would imply that Wetzlar himself was denied access to that group of 'distinguished music lovers' who had heard Bridgetower *first* (and to whom Beethoven has access). The fact, moreover, that this seems to be intended to *impress* Wetzlar is itself interesting as it implies that the names Lobkowitz and Fries were the ones most likely to impress (in which case Wetzlar would have 'looked up' to, but been distanced from them). Assuming, as I think we can, that the reverse of this situation never occurred – that Wetzlar never wrote to Beethoven to suggest that a musician be introduced 'upward' as it were, having already impressed bourgeois families, Beethoven's words point to a 'trickle-down' character of musical taste and its dissemination in Vienna during these years. Those on the periphery of, or outside, circles of aristocratic music consumption may have been receptive to the musicians and music which that 'inner circle' had previously endorsed.

To observe this receptivity is by no means to undercut the argument that these same upper-middle-class and second-society patrons would have tried to 'compete' with aristocrats by proposing a rival pianistic candidate in the shape of Wölfl. Rather it is to suggest that proximity to the exclusive circles around Beethoven was desirable and was pursued through various means according to the resources available, including imitating, patronizing musicians recommended 'from above', and also by cultivating and putting forward challengers. All of these cultural-political practices would have helped to position social 'outsiders' closer to the officially recognized, aristocratically sponsored and therefore, 'legitimate', forms of late eighteenth- and early nineteenth-century musical culture, whether to move closer to what already counted as part of that culture or, conversely, to move that culture closer to where those outsiders currently stood.

The concerts of the Gesellschaft der Associierten Cavaliere, run by Baron van Swieten and a group of aristocrats, and explicitly devoted to 'great' music, were intended to disseminate 'serious' music. Similarly, the circumstances surrounding the presentation of the 'Eroica' symphony would also suggest a 'trickle-down' model of musical taste among aristocrats old and new, and the general public. The piece had three 'premieres' – one for each of the three kinds of high-culture musical public. The first was at a private concert held at the home of Prince Lobkowitz the younger, in 1804. A semi-public premiere was held at Baron Würth's later in the same year, and, finally, the public premiere took place at the Theater an der Wien on 4 July 1805.

It seems likely, then, that Beethoven was not on speaking terms with either of the Wetzlars, that he would have had little or no contact with the Schönfeld salon, and that the Wetzlars – or at least Alexander Wetzlar – attended at least one salon that was socially distant from the circles in which Beethoven ordinarily moved. What can we say about the salon of Therese Schönfeld and, more fundamentally, who *was* Therese Schönfeld?

The issue is complicated by the fact that there were several Schönfeld families in Vienna, and also because – and this point is often overlooked by music historians[30] – there were two Johann von Schönfelds, both of whom were living in Vienna during the 1790s. The first of these we have met before: Johann Ferdinand von Schönfeld, author and publisher of the *Jahrbuch der Tonkunst von Wien und Prag* (1796). As he is described in Wurzbach,[31] this Schönfeld was an industrialist and collector of art objects purchased from churches and monasteries during the years of Joseph II's church reforms. In Vienna, he was a publisher and sold books in his shop in the Kärntnertor. His son Ignaz von Schönfeld was born in 1780. Unfortunately, Johann Ferdinand's wife's Christian name is unknown. Was she the Therese to whom Beethoven referred?

We do know that Therese was not related to the second Johann Schönfeld, the Count Johann Hilmar, Saxon ambassador to Vienna. He was married to Ursula Margareta, née Countess Fries. She is listed in Ritter von Schönfeld's *Jahrbuch* as a piano pupil of Kozeluch. Also, she was most likely the singer to whom Zinzendorf referred in his diary on 4 April 1799.[32]

There are other Schönfelds as well. Next to the entry for Countess Schönfeld, the *Jahrbuch* lists a Fräulein Nanette Schönfeld, 'daughter of . . . Hrn. v. Schönfeld from Trnowa'. There were also some Jewish Schönfelds, three brothers, all officers in the infantry regiment of the Austrian army. One of these, Franz Thomas, born in 1753, was killed during the Reign of Terror in Paris in 1793.[33]

---

[30] Including myself; see T. DeNora, 'Musical Patronage and Social Change in Beethoven's Vienna', *American Journal of Sociology*, xcvii (1991), p. 327.
[31] C. von Wurzbach, *Biographisches Lexikon des Kaiserthums Oesterreich* (Vienna, 1856–86), xvi, pp. 152–6.
[32] Landon, *Haydn: the Years of 'The Creation'*, p. 546.
[33] I am grateful to Else Radant Landon (personal correspondence) for providing the preceding information on the various Schönfeld families living in Vienna at the turn of the century.

To which Schönfeld family was Beethoven referring? Based on the evidence available so far, it seems most likely that the salon to which he asked Wetzlar to bring Bridgetower was not an aristocratic one. First, there were no members of Count von Schönfeld's family with the Christian name Therese. Second, Count von Schönfeld and his family would have moved with ease in the salon worlds in which Beethoven circulated; Ursula was a Fries, and Count Fries was by 1803 a prominent member of Beethoven's world, mixing easily with people like Prince Lobkowitz the younger who, by then, had become one of Beethoven's closest patrons.

Unless we discover that the Christian name of Johann Ferdinand Schönfeld's wife was *not* Therese, I suggest that the salon to which Beethoven referred was hosted by this Schönfeld family. My reason for this is as follows: Beethoven speaks of Therese's as a place where he is given to understand, 'many friends gather'. This implies that Therese is a fairly regular salon hostess. The only regular salons hosted by a Schönfeld that are listed in Schönfeld's *Jahrbuch* are those of Schönfeld's own household ('Hrn. von Schönfeld aus Prag'). This salon is listed in company with second-society ones: Hrn. v. Henikstein, Hrn. Hofrath von Greiner, Fräulein von Martinez.

If this is indeed the case, then there is evidence that Alexander Wetzlar moved in middle-class circles that were distinct from those aristocratic circles in which Beethoven moved. This, in turn, would support the picture other scholars are currently elaborating,[34] of the continuing rigidity of social boundaries in Viennese musical life – of separate but often parallel spheres of musical activity in the late eighteenth and early nineteenth centuries.

Simultaneously, it helps us to piece together a more detailed portrait of the kind of music consumer and patron Schönfeld was, and the ways in which his own support of music was related to aristocratic activities and tastes. Beethoven tells Wetzlar that he hopes Wetzlar 'will obtain for [Bridgetower] a wider circle of acquaintances'. In this case the Schönfeld salon would function as a conduit to broader taste, a gateway for Bridgetower's exposure to the wider (and more middle-class) world of the music-consuming public. In this regard, Schönfeld can be understood as a disseminator of aristocratic taste. This in turn sheds further light on the status and social role of the Schönfeld *Jahrbuch*: we have observed above that it was a kind of 'Who's Who' of the Viennese music world during these years; it may also have functioned as a kind of guide to musical fashion, listing, rather like a social column, the luminaries of Viennese musical society in a way that celebrated society's upper echelons and their musical values. Indeed, we have already seen this in the way that Schönfeld discusses Beethoven and his expected 'greatness' having placed himself in the hands of such excellent teachers (Haydn and Albrechtsberger). Moreover, if Beethoven

---

[34] See J. Moore, 'Beethoven and Musical Economics' (Ph.D. diss., University of Illinois, 1987).

was socially distanced from Schönfeld's salon and vice versa, then we can understand the Schönfeld salon as receptive to, but lagging behind aristocratic taste.

To put Wölfl forward as Beethoven's rival, therefore, both provided a second-society entrée into the high-status activity of musical contests, and helped to substantiate the Wetzlars as partisans of a musical aesthetic distinct from that associated with Beethoven. Wölfl can be understood, in other words, as a representative of a partly separate musical constituency, and the serious music ideology as represented by Beethoven can be further clarified as the property of Vienna's old and highest aristocracy. The Beethoven–Wölfl duel may have served as a vehicle through which two different social networks could be distinguished.

MUSIC AESTHETICS AND THE SOCIAL SEGMENTATION OF VIENNESE MUSICAL LIFE

The Beethoven–Wölfl piano contest does indeed seem to mark a small but important moment in music history. In it we can see the emergence of a subsequently developed ideology of serious music as a *debatable* issue, in contrast to the values of musical accessibility. Simultaneously, we can see in it Beethoven's emerging identity as a highly original, 'specialist's' composer. Moreover, the duel features both of these issues at a time when they were still equivocal, before either the notion of serious music or Beethoven's reputation was fully institutionalized as a dominant part of elite musical culture.

In addition, the duel provides an entrée into the issue of Vienna's taste publics, and it affords tantalizing glimpses into the ways that these publics may have been socially distinct. While these issues require further exploration by other scholars, what seems clear is that study of the circumstances of the Beethoven–Wölfl duel elaborates the ways in which support for Beethoven was linked to the emergence of a serious music aesthetic, and also to the further definition of a serious music public. Through the pursuit of what was recognized as Beethoven's esoteric style, his patrons were able to redefine themselves as princes, not merely of society but also of taste. Thus the duel may have placed at stake the relations, within the high-culture music world, between an upwardly aspiring middle class/second society and some of Vienna's old aristocrats.

Index

Adamberger family, 277
Adler, Guido, 5
Adlgasser, Anton Cajetan, 4, 7
Albrechtsberger, Johann Georg, 9, 198, 201, 204, 281
    Missa in C (Schröder A. II. 2), 92
    Missa pro hebdomada sancta/Missa romana (Schröder A. II. 5), 92
    Missa quatuor vocum/Missa canonica (Schröder A. II. 6), 92
    Missa in G (Schröder A. II. 7), 92
    Offertorium: 'Justus ut palma florebit', 208
    Singgedicht, 198–200, 202
Allanbrook, Wye, 183
Allegri, Gregorio
    Miserere, 90
Allgemeine musikalische Zeitung, 65, 114, 233, 268–72, 274
Alsace-Lorraine, 249, 255
Amalia Wilhelmina (Empress), 16–17, 21
Amsterdam, 3
Angermüller, Rudolph, 222n
Ariosti
    Le profizie d' Eliseo, 20–1
Artaria, 3, 233, 234n, 277n
Asplmayr, Franz, 70n, 83
    Violin Concerto in D, 81
Auernhammer, Barbara Josepha, 264, 277
Aufschnaiter, Benedict, 208n
Augsburg, 252–5, 256n, 258

Babenberg dynasty, 198
Bach, Carl Philipp Emanuel, 111, 252, 256
Bach, Johann Christian, 6, 253
Bach, Johann Sebastian, 241
    Brandenburg Concerto No. 2 (BWV 1047), 43
    Peasant Cantata (BWV 212), 141
Badia
    Napoli ritornata ai romani, 20–1
Badura-Skoda, Eva, 6
Banti, Brigida, 234
Barcelona, 16

Bavaria, 183, 197
Beales, Derek, 9
Beaumarchais, Pierre Augustin Caron de, 217, 222n, 224–5
Beethoven, Ludwig van, 1, 3–6, 89n, 214
    Ballet: *Die Geschöpfe des Prometheus*, 272
    Fidelio, 210, 212, 220
    Missa Solemnis (op. 123), 91n
    'Östreich über Alles' (sketch), 7
    Overture: *The Consecration of the House*, (op. 124), 69
    Overture: *Coriolan* (op. 62), 272
    Piano Concerto No.1 in C (op. 15), 69
    Piano Concerto No. 4 in G (op. 58), 69
    Piano Concerto No. 5 in E♭ (op. 73), 69
    Piano Trios (op. 1), 277n
    Piano Trio in C minor (op. 1 no. 3), 271
    Piano Trios (op. 9), 260
    Quartet in F (op. 59 no. 1), 272
    The Ruins of Athens, (op. 113), 273–4
    Sonata in A (op. 101), 251
    Sonate pathétique (op. 13), 271
    Symphony No.1 in C (op. 21), 13, 65, 69
    Symphony No.3 in E♭ (*Eroica Symphony*) (op. 55), 272–4, 280
    Symphony No.5 in C minor (op. 67), 69
    Trio for clarinet, cello and piano (op. 11), 260
    Variations on 'Ein Mädchen oder Weibchen' (op. 66), 260
    Variations on 'La stessa, la stessissima' (WoO 73), 212
    Variations on 'Mich brennt ein heißes Fieber' (WoO 72), 260
Belgium, 7
Benda, Franz, 71–2, 74, 233n
Benda, Friedrich Ludwig, 74
Benda, Friedrich Wilhelm, 74
Benedict XIV (Pope), 30
Berkovec, Jiří, 141
Berlin, 3, 251–3, 257, 264
Bernasconi, Andrea
    Artarserse, 37, 39

Berne, 253
Bertati, Giovanni, 211
Bethlehem, 143
Biba, Otto, 30, 89n, 115–16, 120, 128, 130, 140
Billington, Mrs, 233
Binder, Johann Michael, 157
Birck, Wenzel Raimund, 257
   Gradual Sonata, 12, 26, 42
   Regina coeli, 64
Bland, John, 233, 244
Bohemia, 7, 114, 118, 126, 128, 132, 183, 256
Böhm & Sohn (Augsburg), 118n
Bonn, Franz, 15
Bonn, Thomas, 14–15
Bonno, Giuseppe, 9, 19, 46–7
   La gara del genio, 20–1, 28, 46–7
   L'eroe cinese, 20–1, 46
Bononcini, Giovanni
   Il natale di Giunone, 20–1
Boog, 116n
Borthwick, E. Kerr, 109n
Boyd, Malcolm, 229n
Braunbehrens, Volkmar, 222, 276
Braunschweig, 252
Breitkopf & Härtel, 265
Bridgetower, George Polgreen, 278–9, 281
Britain, 7
Brixi, František Xaver, 183
   Offertorium: 'Reges de Saba', 188–90
Brno, 118, 205, 264
Brooklyn College, New York, 113n
Brown, A. Peter, 6, 8, 234n, 257n
Bruckner, Anton, 91
Brunati, 222n
Brunsvik, Therese, 275
Bryan, Paul, 51n, 113n
Burney, Charles, 43, 112, 253, 255

Caldara, Antonio, 16, 19, 26–8, 32, 43, 51, 65, 69, 90, 134, 203, 208, 211
   Achille in Sciro, 20–1, 28–9
   Adriano in Siria, 20–1, 27
   Assalone, 20–1
   Caio Fabbrizio, 20–1, 27
   Cajo Marzio Coriolano, 19–1, 24
   Ciro riconosciuto, 20–1, 28
   Enone, 20–1
   Ester, 20–1
   Gianguir, 20–1
   I due dittatori, 39
   Il nome più glorioso, 13, 16, 20–1
   Il trionfo della religione, 20–1
   Il Venceslao, 20–1
   La clemenza di Tito, 65
   La concordia de' pianetti, 19–1, 23, 28
   La forza dell'amicizia, 20–1
   Mitridate, 20–1
   Ormisda, 20–1
   Ornospade, 19–1, 25
Cardiff, 229n, 245n

Carpani, 233
Casti, Giambattista, 214, 216
Charles VI (Emperor) (= Charles III of Spain), 13, 15–18, 21, 28–30, 43, 65, 69, 211
Chew, Geoffrey, 6, 8, 115, 118
Christie's (auction house), 89n
Cimarosa, Domenico
   I due supposti conti, 232n
Clary, Countess Josephine de, 275
Clementi, Muzio, 261–3
Clementia croesi, 207
Collin, Heinrich von, 7, 272
Colloredo (family), 7
Cologne, 256
Constantine (Emperor), 43
Conti, Francesco, 19
   Il trionfo della fama, 20–1, 28
Cooper, Barry, 3n
Corelli, Archangelo, 19, 115, 183
Cristofori, Bartolomeo, 249–50, 256
Croatia, 7, 115
Czech Republic, 7, 112
Czerny, Carl, 262

Danube, 131
Da Ponte, Lorenzo, 6, 211–22, 216
Defranceschi, Carlo Prospero, 229n
Denkmäler der Musik in Salzburg, 4
Denkmäler der Tonkunst in Österreich, 4, 198
DeNora, Tia, 6, 280n
Dent, Edward J., 227
Deutsch, Otto Erich, 277
Diabelli, Anton, 118
Dietmayr, Abbot Berthold, 201
Digl, Roman, 205
Diletto Musicale, 4
Dimpfl, A. A., 118
Dittersdorf, Carl Ditters von, 3, 5, 8n, 70n, 72, 74, 77–8, 83, 156, 262
   Violin Concerto in A, 78
Dlabacž, Gottfried Johann, 113–15, 183
Doležalek, Johann, 271–2
Donberger, Georg Joseph, 116n, 203, 205, 207–8
Draghi, Antonio, 208
   Il sagrificio d'Amore, 20–1
Dresden, 43, 222, 264
Durante, Francesco, 115
Durazzo, Count, 211, 214
Dussek, Franz, 8n

Eberlin, Johann Ernst, 7
   Phoebus sacriatior coelo, 206
Edelmann, Jean-Frédéric
   Ariane dans l'isle de Naxos, 233n
Edge, Dexter, 251n
Ehrenstein, Stepan von, 4
Einstein, Alfred, 257
Eisenstadt, 5, 6, 97, 110, 234n
Eleonore Magdalena, 197
Elisabeth Christine (Empress), 21, 28, 30, 43

Elssler, Johann, 90n
Elssler, Joseph, 56n
Engl, Johann Reinhardt, 14–15
England, 249, 252
Esterházy (court), 3, 5, 51, 71, 91, 97, 109–10, 258
Esterházy, Nicolaus, 110n, 232, 258
Esterházy, Nicolaus (II), 275, 277
Esterházy, Paul
    Harmonia caelestis, 134
Eszterháza, 5–6, 56, 232, 234, 244, 258
Eybler, Joseph, 2, 9

Feder, Georg, 258n
Fellerer, Karl Gustav, 89
Feodorovna, Maria (Princess of Württemberg), 261, 263
Ferdinand I of Sicily, 229
Ferguson, Tepper von, 264
Ferrarese, Adriana, 214
Ferrini, 249
Fiducia in Deum per arma iustitiae virtutis Dei, 203, 205, 208
Fink, Franz Xavier, 205
Fischer, Wilhelm, 5
Fischer von Erlach, J. B., 16
Florence, 211, 250n
Fodor, Joseph, 74
France, 7, 69, 215, 251, 253
Franz I (II) (Emperor), 69
Franz Stephan (Francis of Lorraine, Emperor Franz Stephan I), 30, 31, 37, 201–2
Frankfurt, 16, 201, 253
Frederick the Great, 71, 251, 253
Freeman, Robert, 6, 8
Fries family, 278–81
Fritz, Barthold, 252
Fuchs, Alois, 99n
Fuhrich, Fritz, 207
Fux, Johann Joseph, 4, 17, 19, 26, 30, 43, 51, 69, 90, 97–8, 105, 114n, 134, 140, 208
    Gradus ad Parnassum, 90–1
    Angelica, vincitrice di Alcina (K310), 20–1, 26
    Costanza e Fortezza (K315), 17, 19–22, 26, 28
    Elisa (K312), 20–1, 26
    Enea negli Elisi (K318), 20–1, 26
    Gli ossequi della notte (K305), 16, 19–21, 27
    La corona d'Arianna (K317), 20–1, 26
    Le nozze di Aurora (K314), 19–22, 26
    Missa canonica (K7), 90, 110
    Pulcheria (K303), 19–21, 26–7

Galuppi, B., 210
Garland (publisher), 2, 4, 8
Gasparini, Francesco
    Ambleto, 229
Gassmann, Florian Leopold, 8n, 47, 110, 214
    Il filosofo inamorato, 211
    Il viaggiatore ridicolo, 211
    La contessina, 211
    L'amore artigiano, 211
    La notte critica, 211
    Le pescatrici, 211
Gaviniès, Pierre, 71–2
    Violin Concerto in A, op. 4 no. 5, 80
Gazzaniga, Giuseppe, 222–3
    Don Giovanni, 227
    Il finto cieco, 224–5, 230n
Geib, John, 253
Geiringer, Karl, 235n
Gelinek, Abbé Joseph, 259, 262–3, 271
Genzinger, Marianne von, 232, 234, 242
Germany, 72, 112, 215, 249, 251, 253, 255–6, 278
Germer, Mark, 115–16, 118, 120, 126, 130, 132
Gilowsky, Dr, 277
Giornovichi, Giovanni Mane, 71, 80
    Concerto No. 5 in E, 84
Gleichenstein, Baron, 275
Gluck, Christoph Willibald, 5–6, 9, 47, 50, 210, 215–16
    Alceste, 215
    Il Parnaso confuso, 197, 208
    Orfeo ed Euridice, 235
    Paride ed Elena, 210
    Semiramis, 197
    Telemaco, 197
Goetz, Michelle, 31n
Goldoni, Carlo, 156, 211, 222n
    De gustibus non est disputandum, 156
    I due gemelli veneziani, 211
    La locandieri, 211
    La vedova scaltra, 211
    L'avvocato veneziano, 211
    Le bourru bienfaisant, 211
Gortschek, Georg, 14–15
Göttweig abbey, 142, 176, 203, 205, 206n
Grasl, 116n
Greiner, Franz Sales, 281
Grienauer, Johann Christian, 15
Grosswardein, 6
Grünauer, Johann, 14
Guglielmi, Pietro, 222
    La Quakera spiritosa, 222n
Guicciardi, Countess Giulietta, 275
Gussmann, Abbot Dominik, 205
Györ, 43
Gyrowetz, Adalbert, 8n, 214

Haack, Carl, 74
Häbler, Andreas, 15
Hafeneder, Joseph, 7
Hamburg, 264
Hamilton, Emma, 234
Hammer, Georg Sigmund, 14
Hanisch, Johann, 15
Harding, Rosamond, 249, 252–3
Hauer, Abbot Urban, 201
Haydn, Joseph, 1, 3–6, 8–9, 13, 43, 51, 57, 65, 70n, 71, 74, 78, 112, 114, 127, 131, 133, 141, 156, 183, 201, 215, 256, 258, 264–5, 271–2, 277, 281

Haydn, Joseph (*cont.*)
Entwurf Katalog, 89, 99
Haydn Verzeichnis, 89, 99
'Applausus' cantata (Hob.XXIVa: 6), 110, 206–8
Arianna a Naxos (Hob.XXVIb: 2), 4
Armida, 232
Baryton Trio in C (Hob.XI: 109), 105
Canzonettas, 234, 245n
Capriccio in C (Hob.XVII: 4), 232
The Creation, 5
'Ei, wer hätt ihm das Ding gedenkt' (Hob. XXIIId: G1), 127n, 128, 130
'Grosseorgelsolomesse' (Hob.XXII: 4), 110
Horn Concerto (Hob.VIId: 3), 105
'Infelice sventurata' (Hob. XXIVb: 15), 232n, 245n
La vera costanza, 242n
'Libera me' (Hob.XXIIb: 1*), 89
L'infedeltà delusa, 207
Lo speziale, 110
Miseri noi, misera patria (Hob.XXIVa: 7), 233n
Missa brevis alla capella Rorate coeli desuper (Hob.XXII: 3), 127n
Missa Cellensis (Hob.XXII: 5), 110
Missa Sancti Nicolai (Hob.XXII: 6), 110, 119, 127n
Missa sunt bona mixta malis (Hob.XXII: 2), 6
'Mutter Gottes, mir erlaube' (Hob.XXIIId: 2), 127n
'Non nobis, Domine' (Hob.XXIIIa: 1), 89
Pastorella: 'Der Tag, der ist so freudenreich' (Hob.XXIIId: G2), 191–3
Quartet in F minor (op. 55 no. 2) ('Razor'), 233n
Quartets (opp. 71 and 74), 244
Salve Regina (Hob.XXIIIb: 2), 110
Scena di Berenice (Hob.XXIVa: 10), 233–5, 242–3, 245
The Seasons, 5
Sonata in C (Hob.XVI: 48), 232
Sonata in E♭ (Hob.XVI: 49), 232
Stabat Mater (Hob.XXbis), 110
Symphony No. 20 in C, 13n, 51
Symphony No. 32 in C, 13n, 51, 58–9
Symphony No. 33 in C, 13n, 51, 60–1
Symphony No. 37 in C, 13n, 51
Symphony No. 38 in C, 13n, 51
Symphony No. 41 in C, 13n, 56
Symphony No. 48 in C ('Maria Theresia'), 13n, 56–7, 62–3
Symphony No. 50 in C, 13n, 56
Symphony No. 56 in C, 13n, 57
Symphony No. 60 in C ('Il distratto'), 13n, 56–7
Symphony No. 63 in C, 13n, 51
Symphony No. 69 in C, 13n, 51
Symphony No. 70 in D, 57
Symphony No. 82 in C ('L'ours'/'The Bear'), 13n, 57
Symphony No. 85 in B♭ ('La reine'), 85
Symphony No. 90 in C, 13n, 57
Symphony No. 94 in G ('Surprise'), 57
Symphony No. 96 in D ('Miracle'), 57
Symphony No. 97 in C, 13n, 57
Trumpet Concerto (Hob. VIIe: 1), 57, 64
Violin Concerto in C (Hob.VIIa: 1), 72, 79–81
Violin Concerto in A (Hob.VIIa: 3), 72, 81
Violin Concerto in G (Hob.VIIa: 4), 72
Haydn, Michael, 2, 6–7, 8n, 70n, 74, 83, 90, 110, 114, 156, 206, 264
Missa Sanctae Crucis a 4 Voci in Contra punto (MH56), 92
Rebekka als Braut (MH76) 206n
Sanctificatio Jubilaei (MH300), 203n
Violin Concerto in A (MH207), 82
Heichele, Johann, 257
Hein, Rudolph, 15
Heinisch, Johann, 37, 39
Hellen, Johann Ludwig, 253
Henikstein, Caroline von, 281
Heraeus, G., 16
Herzogenburg abbey, 203, 205, 208
Hiller, Johann Adam, 252–3, 255–6
Hoffmeister, 3, 8n
Hofmann, Leopold, 8n, 70n, 112, 156
Missa alla cappella, 92, 110
Hollandt, Joseph, 14–15, 30n
Holtzl, Ferdinand, 15
Holzbauer, Ignaz, 8n, 156
Hug, R. 203n, 208n
Hummel, Johann Nepomuk, 118, 267–8
Hungary, 7

Ingles, Tim, 231n
Isham Library Conference, 13
Italian Opera 1640–1770, 4
Italian Oratorio 1650–1800, 4
Italy, 215, 253

Jesorka, Nicolaus
Jesuit Order, 134, 206, 208
Johannisberg, 6
Jones, David Wyn, 8, 234n, 245n
Joseph I (Emperor), 14, 16
Joseph II (Emperor), 6–7, 9, 21, 30–1, 47, 197, 199–200, 208, 210–12, 222, 261–2, 280
Josepha of Bavaria, 197, 199, 208

Kapp, Oskar, 198
Kaunitz, Wenzel Anton (Count and Prince), 197
Keglevics, Countess Barbara von, 275
Kelly, Michael, 211
Kempter, 118n
Khämpfl, Marx, 14
Khevenhüller-Metsch, Johann Joseph, 31
Khlepauer, Wolf, 14
Kimmerling, Robert, 8n
Rebekka, die Braut Isaaks, 206n
Kinsky, Ferdinand Johann Nepomuk (Prince), 275
Klemm, Therese, 264

Klima, 116n
Kniže, 118n
Koberer, Rudolph, 15
Koch, Heinrich Christoph, 251
Koch, Matthias, 15
Kohaut, Karl, 200–1
   Securitas Germaniae Josepho II., 204
Kollmann, Abbot Rayner, 206–7
Kotzebue, August von, 273
Koutník, Tomáš Norbert, 143
Kozeluch, Johann Anton, 176, 183
   Offertorium pastorale in G, 176–82
Kozeluch, Leopold, 8n, 271, 280
Kreybich, Franz, 15
Krems, 142, 205
Kremsmünster 37, 206–7
Kreutzer, 118n
Kropf, Father Martin, 201
Krottendorfer, Joseph
   Pastorella in E♭, 158–69, 176
Küffel, Franz Anton, 14–15, 30
Kummer, Edmund, 198
Kurz-Bernardon, 5
Küster, Konrad, 6

Lais, 216
Lambach, 197, 206
Lamotte, Franz, 70n, 83–4
Landon, Else Radant, 273, 280n
Landon, H. C. Robbins, 8, 13, 51, 114, 133, 141,
   245, 258, 277
Lange family, 277
Langthaller, Josef
   Jacob pater optimus, 206n
L'ape musicale, 229–31
Larsen, Jens Peter, 1–2, 4–5, 8, 10
LaRue, Jan, 2
Lavanttal, 206
Leduc, Simon
   Violin Concerto in C, 80
Legnago, 211
Legrenzi, 90
Leipzig, 251–2, 264
Leopold (Archduke), 21
Leopold I (Emperor), 13–14, 21, 197, 211
Leopold II (Emperor), 6, 65
Les fêtes vénitiennes, 211
Les gondoliers de Venise, 211
Les masques de St. Marc à Venise, 211
Lichnowsky, Karl (Prince), 267, 275, 277
Lichnowsky (Princess), 275
Lichnowsky, Moritz, 275, 277
Liechtenstein, Princess, 275
Lindpainter, 118n
Linek, Jiří, 128–9, 132
Linz, 6
Lobkowitz, Prince, 275, 277–9, 281
Lobkowitz, Prince (the elder), 275, 277
Locatelli, Pietro Antonio, 76
Lolli, Antonio, 76–8

London, 3–6, 8, 81, 84, 222, 233, 234n, 244, 249,
   251–3, 264, 278
Louis XVI, 197
Ludi caesarei, 206–7
Lukavec, 5
Lully, Jean-Baptiste
   Armide, 235
Luxembourg, 7

Mannheim, 5, 7, 74
Mantua, 13
Mara, 234
Maria Amalia (Archduchess), 21
Maria Antonia (Archduchess), 13, 21
Maria-Taferl (church), 157
Maria Theresia (Empress), 13, 15, 21, 29–32,
   46–7, 58, 201–3
Marie Antoinette, 197
Marshall Plan, 4
Martin (Slovakia), 56n
Martín y Soler, Vicente, 212, 222–3, 229, 230n
   Il burbero di buon cuore, 211, 223
   L'arbore di Diana, 227–9
   Una cosa rara, 226–8
Martinez, Marianne, 281
Martis und Irene Verbindung, 201–2, 206, 208
Mattheson, Johann, 111
Maximilian Emanuel, 13, 21
Mazzolà, Caterino, 211, 222
Melk abbey, 176, 197–206, 208
Mendelssohn, 89n
Merlin, John Joseph, 252–3
Metastasio, Pietro, 65
Míča, František Antonín,
   L'origine di Jaromeriz in Moravia, 141
Milan, 5–7, 211, 222n
Minato, Nicolò, 208
Mobbs, Kenneth, 257
Mombelli, Domenico, 214
Monn, Matthias Georg, 70n, 83
Monteverdi
   Orfeo, 13
Moravia, 7, 16n
The Morning Chronicle, 253
Morrow, Mary Sue, 262
Morzin (court), 5
Moscheles, Ignaz, 275
Mosel, Ignaz Franz von, 275
Mozart, Leopold, 7, 57, 206, 256n, 264
   Toy Symphony, 184
Mozart, Raimund Leopold, 263
Mozart, Wolfgang Amadeus, 1, 3–7, 9, 57, 65, 70n,
   78, 81, 83, 114, 133, 156, 183, 193, 210,
   215, 217, 220, 222–3, 229, 231–5, 240,
   250–1, 253, 255–6, 258, 261–4, 267–9,
   276–7
   Apollo et Hyacinthus, 207–8
   Così fan tutte, 212, 222, 228–9
   Die Entführung aus dem Serail, 221
   Die Zauberflöte, 184–7, 191, 193, 218, 220

Mozart, Wolfgang Amadeus (*cont.*)
   Don Giovanni, 212, 215, 221, 227–8, 230
   Fantasia in F minor (K608), 265–6
   La clemenza di Tito, 65, 218, 220–1
   La finta giardiniera, 221
   La finta semplice, 211
   Le nozze di Figaro, 183–4, 221–2, 224–6, 228, 230, 242n
   Piano Concerto in C (K415), 65
   Piano Concerto in C (K467), 65
   Piano Concerto in C (K503), 65
   Piano Concerto in D (K537), 65
   Rondo in B♭ for violin and orchestra (K269), 81–2
   Sonata in A ('alla Turca') (K331), 257
   Trumpet Concerto (KE47c, lost), 57
   Violin Concerto in B♭ (K207), 72–4, 81
   Violin Concerto in D (K211), 81–2
   Violin Concerto in G (K216), 75–6, 81–3
   Violin Concerto in D (K218), 81–3
   Violin Concerto in A (K219), 81–3
   Symphony in F (K43), 208
   Symphony in C (K338), 57, 65
   Symphony in D (K385), 65
   Symphony in C ('Linz') (K425), 65
   Symphony in D ('Prague') (K504), 65
   Symphony in E♭ (K543), 65
   Symphony in C ('Jupiter') (K551), 1, 13, 65–8
   Variations on 'Mio caro Adone' (K180, K173c), 212
Munich, 215, 227, 253
Musica Antiqua Bohemica, 4
Muzarelli, 272

Naples, 222n, 250, 255n
Nassoto, Sebastian, 14–15
Neubold, Peter, 59
Neue Mozart-Ausgabe, 184
Nicolai, Friedrich, 112
ninne, 128
Nonnberg, 206n
Novák, Jan František, 128–9, 132
Nové Nechanice, 131

Odescalchi, Princess Barbara, 275, 277
Offenbach, 263
Oginsky, Count, 264
Order of the Golden Fleece, 17–18
Ordonez, Carlo d', 2, 8n, 13, 70n
   Symphony in C (Brown I: C9), 42, 50–1
   Symphony in C (Brown I: C10), 42, 50–6, 64

Pacchierotti, Gasparo, 234
Paganini, Nicolò, 76
Paisiello, Giovanni, 210, 261
   Il re Teodoro in Venezia, 211
Palestrina, G. P., 90–1, 105
Palotta, Matteo, 90
Paradeiser, Carl
   Hirtengedicht: Seladon, 203

Pariati, Pietro, 229
Paris, 3, 5–6, 8, 71–2, 74, 81–4, 216–17, 251, 252n, 257, 264, 280
   Concert Spirituel, 77, 84
   Concert des Amateurs, 77
   Conservatoire des Arts et des Métiers, 153
   Opéra, 222n, 233n
Passau, 197, 208n
Pasterwitz, Georg
   Erchenbertus I, 206n
Paul, Grand Duke, 263
Pernebmer, Tobias Andrea, 14–15
Petrosellini, Giuseppe, 222n
Peyer, Johann Ernst, 15
Pfannhauser, Karl, 134n
Piarist Order, 134
Piazol, Abbot Odilo, 205
Pichl, Wenzel, 6, 8n, 70n, 74, 78, 81, 83
   Symphony in E♭, 83
   Violin Concerto in B♭, 82, 84
Piticchio, Francesco, 222
   Il Bertoldo, 222
Planck, Beda, 37, 39
Plath, Wolfgang, 3
Pleyel, Ignaz, 8n
Pohl, Carl Ferdinand, 98n, 201
Poland, 7, 112, 141
Porro, 234n
Poštolka, Milan, 113, 131n
Prague, 6, 21, 28, 65, 118, 120n, 176, 205, 215, 264–6, 281
Pressburg (Bratislava), 6
Price, Stephen, 245n
Printz, Wolfgang Caspar, 141
   Phrynis Mitilenæus oder Satyrischer Componist, 141–2
Prussia, 257
Pugnani, Gaetano, 71

Quantz, Johann Joachim, 252, 256

Realzeitung der Wissenschaften, Künste und Kommerzien, 47
Rebhindl, Johann Michael, 15
Recent Researches in the Music of the Classical Era, 4
Regensburg, 252
Regnard
   Le distrait, 57
Reichardt, Johann Friedrich, 233n, 235n
Reinhardt, Johann Georg, 19, 90, 134
   La più bella, 20–1
   Pastorella in F, 134–40
Reinhardt, Kilian, 18
Reutter, Georg (the elder), 3
Reutter, Georg (the younger), 3, 19, 30–2, 37, 43, 91, 114
   Il Parnasso accusato e difeso, 33–7, 39
   Intrada, 32, 43
   La forza dell'amicizia, 20–1
   La speranza assicurata, 20–1, 228, 64

'Lateinisches dramatisches Stück', 32, 43
Missa brevis a 4 Voci Capella (Hofer 3),
Messa â 4 da Capella (Hofer 4),
Missa a Capella in C (Hofer 6),
Partitta a due chori, 32, 43
Servizio di Tavola (1757–9), 32, 38–9, 43
Servizio di Tavola (1769–71), 32, 40–1, 43, 64
Sinfonia a due chori, 32, 43
Rice, John A., 6
Richter, Ferdinand
   Le promesse degli dei, 20–1
Ridley, James, 217
Riedel, Friedrich, 19, 31, 90, 205
Ries, Ferdinand, 262
Riepel, Joseph, 70
Righini, Vincenzo, 222–3
   Il Demogorgone, 225, 228
RISM, 2–3, 116
Robinson, 233
Rochlitz, Johann Friedrich, 114
Rohrau, 131
Romania, 7
Rome, 222n, 249
Rosenbaum, Joseph Carl, 272–3
Rosetti, Antonio, 70
Rossini, G., 89
Rotenstein, G. F., 258n
Rushton, Julian, 4
Rushton, Virginia, 245n
Russia, 210

St. Pölten, 205
Sacchetti, Bianca, 234
Sachs, Curt, 249
Saint-Georges, Joseph Boulogne, 78
Salieri, Antonio, 2–3, 4n, 6, 9, 110–11, 222–3, 229
   Axur, re d'Ormus, 212–13, 217–20, 222n, 227–8, 251
   Falstaff, 212, 215, 229n
   Il pastor fido, 222n
   Il ricco d'un giorno, 223, 228
   Il talismano, 211, 222n
   L' Angiolina, 214
   La bella selvaggia, 214
   La calamita de' cuori, 211
   La cifra, 222n
   La fiera di Venezia, 211–2, 215
   La grotta di Trofonio, 216–7
   La locandiera, 211
   Le donne letterate, 214
   Les Danaïdes, 215–7
   Missa Stylo a Cappella, 92, 110
   Prima la musica poi le parole, 214
   Tarare, 217–8, 222n, 227
Salomon, Johann Peter, 233n
Salzburg, 5–7, 57, 255n, 264
   cathedral, 264
   Museum Carolino-Augusteum, 143n
   St Peter, abbey of, 206
   university, 206–7

Sammartini, G., 6
Sarti, Giuseppe, 210
   Giulio Sabino, 214
Sartori, Claudio, 2
Sauer, I., 90n
Saxony, 47, 50, 249
Schantz brothers, 258
Scarlatti, Alessandro, 90, 183
Schachter, Carl, 65
Scheibl, Johann Adam, 205
Schenk, Johann Baptist, 271
Schiedermayr, 118n
Schindler, Anton Felix, 266, 276
Schlöger, Matthias, 70n, 83, 176
Schmid, Johann Baptist, 251
Schmidt, F., 116n
Schmidt, Matthias, 15
Schneider, Franz, 8n
   Pastorella in A, 170–6, 183
Schobert, Johann, 6
Schön, Franz, 15
Schönfeld, Ignaz von, 280
Schönfeld, Johann Ferdinand von, 280–82
   Jahrbuch der Tonkunst von Wien und Prag, 113–14, 258, 264, 276, 280–1
Schönfeld, Franz Thomas, 280
Schönfeld, Count Johann Hilmar, 280
Schönfeld, Nanette, 280
Schönfeld, Countess Ursula Margarete, 280
Schönfeld, Therese, 278, 280–1
'Shoo fly, don't bother me', 130
Schröder, Dorothea, 198
Schubart, Christian Friedrich Daniel
   Ideen zu einer Ästhetik der Tonkunst, 126
Schubert, Franz, 5, 214
   Piano Trio in B♭ (D28), 251
Schumacher, Klaus, 206
Schumann, R., 89n
Schuster, Beda, 198
Schwarzenberg, Prince Joseph Johann, 275, 277
Second Viennese School, 5
Seitenstetten, 199, 205–6
Senigl, J., 206n
Sessler, Ernst, 15
Seuche, 116n
Seven Years War, 257
Seyfried, Ignaz von, 260–1, 266–70, 274–5, 277
Shakespeare
   The Comedy of Errors, 225–6
Silbermann, Gottfried, 251–2, 256
Silbermann, Johann Andreas, 249
Slovakia, 7, 51, 112
Slovenia, 7
Sonnleithner, Christoph, 8n
Sonnleithner, Joseph, 157
Sorau, 141
Späth, Franz Jakob, 252–3, 256
Spielman, 263
Stadler, Maximilian, 203
Stamitz, Anton, 80

Stamitz, Carl, 80
Stamitz, Johann, 71
Starzer, Joseph, 70n, 83
    Violin Concerto in F, 77
Staudt, Johann Bernhard, 206
Steblin, Rita, 126
Steffan, Joseph Anton, 42, 257
Steibelt, Daniel, 262–3
Stein, 205
Stein, Johann Andreas, 252–6, 258
Stein, Matthias, 258
Stein, Nanette, 258
Steiner, S. A., 115, 251
Stephanie family, 277
Stodart, Robert, 253
Storace, Nancy, 214, 233n
Storace, Stephen, 222–3
    Gli equivoci, 225–6
Strasbourg, 253
Süssmayr, Franz Xaver, 9, 264
Svaty Jur, 51
Swanen, Joachim, 253
Swieten, Baron Gottfried van, 275, 277, 280
Switzerland, 7, 253
The Symphony, 2, 4

Tartini, Giuseppe, 71, 76, 82
Taxis, Count, 253
Thayer, A. W., 259–60
Thun, Countess Maria Wilhelmina, 275, 277
Tirol, 142, 143n
Tittel, Ernst, 118, 120
Tomášek, Václav Jan Křtitel, 262, 265
Tomasini, Luigi, 70n, 71, i3
Torricella, 3
Traeg, Johann, 32
Traetta, Tommaso, 210
    Ifigenia in Tauride, 234
Trattner, Johann Thomas von, 263
Trautsohn, Cardinal, 31
Trieste, 230
Tuma, Franz, 9, 43, 46, 114, 201–2, 206, 208
    Overture in C, 42–3, 46
    Sonata in C, 42–6, 64
Turnovsky, Franz, 14–15
Tyson, Alan, 3, 257

Vanhal, Johann Baptist, 2, 8n, 70n, 78, 83, 156
    Mass in C, 114
    Mass in G, 114
    Symphony in B♭ (Bryan B♭1), 131
    Symphony in G minor (Bryan g2), 131
Varaždin, 115
Vélez de Guevara, Luis
    La luna de la sierra, 226–7
Venice, 157, 211–12, 214, 227, 233
Verona, 255n
Vienna, 3, 5–7, 9, 57, 65, 69, 72n, 77, 84, 90, 97, 110, 112, 114, 118, 193, 197–8, 206–8, 210–12, 214–17, 220, 232–3, 244–5, 259–61, 263–5, 269–82
    Burgtheater, 222, 231n, 251, 257, 264
    Gesellschaft der Associierten, 280
    Gesellschaft der Musikfreunde, 31, 157
    Hofburgkapelle, 19, 30
    Hofkapelle, 3, 5, 17–19, 30–1, 84, 90
    Josephstadt Theater, 69
    Karlskirche, 16
    Kärntnertortheater, 264
    Kunsthistorisches Museum, 258
    Piaristenkirche, 30
    St Stephen's 31, 51, 91
    Theater an der Wien, 278, 280
    Theater auf der Wieden, 260, 267
    Tonkünstler-Societät, 264
    Waisenhaus, 57
Viganò, Salvatore, 272
Viotti, Giovanni Battista, 80
Virgil, 109n, 134
Vivaldi, Antonio, 72, 78, 128
Vogler, Abbé, 116, 126, 132

'Wachet auf', 131
Wagenhuber, Andrea, 14
Wagenseil, Georg Christoph, 2, 46–7, 70n, 83, 255, 257
    Armida placata, 20–1, 47
    Gioas, re di Giuda, 20–21
    Il roveto di Mosè, 20–1
    L'olimpiade, 20–1, 47, 51
    Missa à 4^{tro} dà Capella, 92
    Prometeo assoluto, 20–1
    Symphony in C (Kucaba C7), 42, 47–51
    Symphony in C (Kucaba C10), 42
    Symphony in C (Kucaba C12), 42
    Vincislao, 20–1
Walter, Anton, 256, 258
Walter, Horst, 201, 258n
War of Polish Succession, 202
Warren, Joseph, 233
Warsaw, 264
Weber, Friedrich Dionysius, 271
Weidinger, Anton, 57
Weidlich, Ferdinand, 15
Weigl, Joseph, 214, 222–3
    La caffettiera bizzarra, 229
Weinmann, Alexander, 112–13, 114n
Weiss, Joseph, 201–2, 206
Weltmann, 252
Werner, Gregor, 3, 91, 97–8, 109–10
    Missa alla Zoppa, 109
    Missa contrapunctata a 4 voci alla Capella, 92, 97–105
    Missa hic labor hoc opus est, 109
    Missa in contrapuncto, 92
    Missa Lydia, 92
    Missa quasi vero, 109
    Missa pro Quadragesima alla Capella, 92
    Missa Quadrages, 92
    Missa sunt bona mixta malis, 109
Wetzlar, Alexander, 278–81

Wetzlar, Baron Raimund, 259, 263, 267, 275–82
Wetzlar, Karl Abraham, 263
White, Chappell, 8
Wien, H., 207n
Wiennerisches Diarium, 28n, 43, 249, 250
Wilhering, 140
Wlach, Thomas Augustin, 15
Wölfl, Joseph, 6
    Das schöne Milchmädchen, 264
    Der Höllenberg, 264
    Der Kopf ohne Mann, 264
    Grand concerto militaire, 264
    Liebe macht kurzen Prozess, 264
Wollenberg, S., 90n
Wood, Father, 249
The World, 234n

Würth, Baron, 280
Wurzbach, C. von, 280

Zechart, Andreas, 15
Zechner, Johann Georg, 142, 156, 205
    Pastorella in C, 142–53
Zedler, 251
Zeno, Apostolo, 211, 229
Ziani, Marc'Antonio, 90, 211
Ziegler, Joseph Paul, 42
Zimmermann, Anton, 8n
Zinzendorf, Count Carl, 280
Zmeskall von Domanovecz, Baron Nicolaus, 275, 277
Znaim (Znojmo), 28
Zwettl abbey, 206